PUBLISHER'S NOTE

The Audio-Tutorial system was begun in 1961 by the senior author of this text. It soon became clear that the system would have wide application and be adopted extensively so it seemed worthwhile to provide in writing appropriate guidelines for others to use. The first attempt at this was an edition entitled, *The Integrated Experience Approach to Teaching Botany,* which was published in 1965. Since then, Dr. Postlethwait has had an opportunity to discuss the merits of various components of the system with a great many leading educators and has had a great deal of practical experience with the system under classroom conditions. Several basic ideas have come into focus more sharply, and some new features have been added to the system. Therefore it seems practical and highly desirable to totally revise the original book so the benefits of these experiences can be shared. Thus, this book, with the new title, *The Audio-Tutorial Approach to Learning,* reflects the current thinking of the authors and new insights into the learning process. The reader will find some changes in administrative techniques and procedures but the same basic philosophy of "desire to help students learn" still permeates each paragraph.

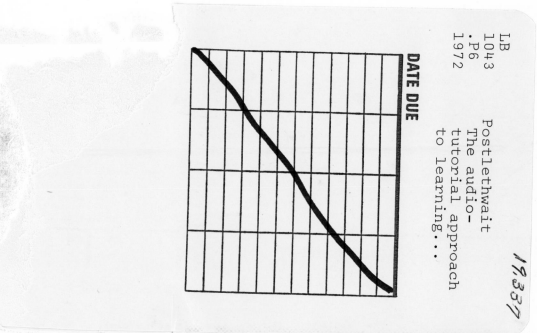

The Audio-Tutorial Approach to Learning

Through Independent Study and Integrated Experiences

THIRD EDITION

S. N. POSTLETHWAIT
Purdue University

J. NOVAK
Cornell University

H. T. MURRAY, JR.
Southern Colorado State College

BURGESS PUBLISHING COMPANY • Minneapolis, Minnesota 55415

PREFACE

Dr. S. N. Postlethwait introduced audio-taped presentations to augment the instruction in his freshman botany course at Purdue University in 1961. His purpose—then as now—was to offer maximum educational opportunity to students of every background and level of aptitude or skill, even within the framework of a large, multi-section class.

From its inception the Audio-Tutorial concept proved its worth by allowing slow and average students to absorb the course material through as many senses as possible while freeing the rapid learner, the well-grounded student, and the good reader to proceed as quickly and in as much depth as desired.

Dr. Postlethwait accelerated the development of the Audio-Tutorial program in 1962, when he converted the entire course to the multi-faceted methods approach he had devised, centering on a supervised self-instructional laboratory. Emphasis was shifted from the instructor's pedantry to the student's learning. The tapes freed the senior instructor to devote his dedicated time to the real business of teaching—inspiration, motivation, orientation, and meaningful personal contact.

A study guide designed to accompany the tapes was prepared and made available to other schools, and by 1963 a complete course on tapes and in manuscript form was available. Introduction of these materials occasioned widespread interest among educators and triggered a flood of visits, correspondence, questions, and requests for further information. This book represents an attempt to answer such questions and to present a history of the birth, growth, and development of the Audio-Tutorial system of instruction. During the decade which has passed since its inception there have been many variations and modifications tried, some successful, others less so. The Audio-Tutorial approach has spread to many different subject areas and is no longer regarded as being restricted to the life sciences. Study guides, audio-scripts, films, slides, and other accessory materials have been and are being developed to supply the growing demand.

In 1969 Dr. Postlethwait had an opportunity to explore two further innovations involving the Audio-Tutorial system. The new concepts were *mastery* and *mini-courses*. Dr. Robert N. Hurst joined the Purdue staff to place the zoology course on the Audio-Tutorial approach and John Welser of the Veterinary Science Department also began an experiment with these two concepts in a course in Veterinary School. The strategies developed and the successes and problems related to the implementation of these two concepts seemed sufficiently important to be recorded for the information of other teachers who might have similar interests, and this Third Edition therefore includes a chapter (VI) on this subject.

In addition, Dr. Novak's research on the use of Audio-Tutorial methods in elementary education has been expanded and this new information has been added especially for the encouragement of elementary school teachers. Only minor modifications and corrections were made in Chapters I through V since most of the information contained therein was still valid and many teachers beginning the Audio-Tutorial system may wish to follow the model presented in those chapters instead of the variations described in Chapter VI.

It is hoped that the book in this new edition will continue to serve as both invitation and blueprint for your participation in the continuing growth of a program that represents an unusual opportunity for improved teaching.

S.N.P.

J.N.

H.T.M.

January, 1972

CONTENTS

Page

CHAPTER I: NEW WINE IN OLD SKINS 1

CHAPTER II: THE AUDIO-TUTORIAL SYSTEM 7

   History and Development 9

   The Restructured Course 10

    1. Independent Study Session (ISS) 10

    2. General Assembly Session (GAS) 13

    3. Small Assembly Session (SAS): 14

      A. Integrated Quiz Session (IQS) 14

      B. Other Small Assembly Sessions (SAS) 15

    4. Other Activities 15

   Rationale for Course Structuring 16

    1. Independent Study Session (ISS) 16

    2. General Assembly Session (GAS) 18

    3. Integrated Quiz Session (IQS, formerly Small Assembly Session—SAS) 18

    4. Other Activities 20

   Personal Contact 20

   Inquiry 22

CHAPTER III: AN EXAMPLE OF A WEEK'S UNIT OF STUDY 24

   Independent Study Session (ISS) 24

   General Assembly Session (GAS) 45

   Integrated Quiz Session (IQS) 46

   Other Activities 48

CHAPTER IV: PHYSICAL FACILITIES 51

   The Learning Center 51

    1. The Check-in Check-out Area and Bulletin Board 52

    2. Booths 53

      A. Student Electronics 55

      B. Projectors 55

    3. Central Tables 57

    4. Study Table and Reference Library 57

    5. Other Features 59

   Workroom and Prep Room 59

    1. Preparation and Storage Facilities 60

    2. Refreshments and Special Projects 61

   The General Assembly Hall 61

   The Small Assembly Session (Integrated Quiz Session) 62

Other Facilities 63

Costs 64

Summary 64

CHAPTER V: OPERATIONAL ASPECTS 66

Personnel 66

Planning an Audio-Tutorial Lesson 71

Preparation of Tapes 72

Use of Films 73

Preparation of Printed Materials 76

Other Materials 78

Study Sessions 78

1. Scheduling 78

2. The Operation of the Independent Study Session 80

3. The Operation of the General Assembly Session 83

4. The Operation of the Integrated Quiz Session
   (Small Assembly Session) 84

5. Other Activities 86

Test and Grades 87

CHAPTER VI: MINICOURSES—A FURTHER POSSIBILITY 90

The Minicourse Concept 90

1. Application 92

2. Advantages 92

3. Disadvantages 94

Pilot Study I—Botany and Zoology 96

Identification of Minicourse Categories and Topics 96

Facilities, Scheduling, and Quiz Format 97

Record Keeping and Personnel 98

Study Sessions 99

Grading Procedures 99

Results 101

Pilot Study II—Comparative Veterinary Anatomy 103

Results 105

Cognitive 105

Affective 107

**CHAPTER VII: THE USE OF AUDIO-TUTORIAL METHODS IN
                ELEMENTARY SCHOOL INSTRUCTION** 110

Genesis of the Program 110

Program Development 111

Lesson Evaluation 116

Patterns of A-T Utilization 121

How Children Learn 125

References 129

CHAPTER VIII: IN CONCLUSION 131

APPENDIX A: SAMPLE ORIENTATION MATERIAL FOR DISTRIBUTION
              DURING THE FIRST WEEK OF SCHOOL 133
APPENDIX B: RECORDS 140
APPENDIX C: INSTRUCTIONS FOR NEW STAFF 144
APPENDIX D: STUDENT RESEARCH PROJECTS 149
APPENDIX E: PROBLEMS AND PITFALLS IN AUDIO-TUTORIAL METHODS 162
APPENDIX F: IDEALIZED LEARNING CENTER ARRANGEMENT 167
APPENDIX G: SAMPLE ORIENTATION MATERIAL FOR MINICOURSES 168
APPENDIX H: SAMPLE BEHAVIORAL CHECKLIST 180

Chapter I

NEW WINE IN OLD SKINS

This is the Golden Age of man. Never in man's history has it been possible for a single lifetime to span so many exciting events. If one were to list graphically the "breakthrough" events having an important impact on man's "way of living," the points initially would be far apart and would become progressively more frequent as one approaches the present. Such a graph might look comparable to a growth curve with a long lag phase changing relatively quickly during the last century to a steeply ascending slope. For example, it was a major advance when man learned to record his thoughts through writing only a few thousand years ago. Perhaps the next major advance was the invention of the printing press in the 1600s. Later came the telegraph (1820-32), then the telephone (1876), and the radio (1895). Many of us can remember when we had no television (1946), or transistorized devices. Now—satellites have provided us with "round-the-world" television. Many companies use electronic information retrieval systems; and tape recorders and radios can be purchased so cheaply they are used as inexpensive gift items. So many communication devices and innovations exist that it would be folly and wasteful of time to try to list them. If these are available now, what will communication be like in the next hundred years?

Those of us who are recipients of the many long years of painstaking development find ourselves somewhat overwhelmed by the new potential which is available to us. It is especially difficult in this "age of transition." We find ourselves enveloped in patterns adjusted to the earlier communication devices. Now it is necessary to refocus on the basic problems and resist the strong temptation to use the new communication tools as we have "always done in the past." How easy it is to use the television as a means of extending to a greater audience a lecturer performing in the traditional fashion. Some interesting studies done by Paul Cameron at Wayne State University reveal that at any given moment of time lecturing commands the attention of only 12 per cent of the audience. It is clear that if one uses TV to expand the audience to a greater number of students this 12 per cent will represent a greater number of people becoming informed. However, is it necessary to operate so inefficiently, or is it possible to use television and other devices in a more effective and functional way?

Would it be possible to reexamine the activity called education and start at zero to redefine the problem? Could one discard traditional structure as a starting point and look for a solution based on a definition of objectives? A fundamental guideline which must be given prime consideration is that "learning is an activity done *by* an individual and not something done *to* an individual." The structuring of an educational system should be done on the basis that the program must involve the learner. The teacher at best can only create a situation conducive to learning by providing the direction, facilities, and motivation to the individual learner. Immediately, it becomes apparent that the program must allow for individual differences in interests, capacity, and background.

Obviously, guidance is one of the most important roles of a teacher. Yet, frequently the meetings of students and teachers are occasions of a "cat and mouse" game where the teacher tries to camouflage the topics which are likely to make good exam questions and the student tries to discover the subtle connotations or mannerisms by which the teacher discloses them. The careful writing of behavioral objectives is a revealing experience to most of us. It helps in the writing of test questions related to what has been taught, and it helps in determining study activities which will enable the student to achieve the objectives. It is a depressing fact that most of us have never even thought of objectives, and certainly have never taken the trouble to write them in behavioral terms. Somehow, students are supposed to move forward purposefully and vigorously through an "ocean of words" inventing the compass, drawing the map, and constructing the ship. Vague goals such as "to provide an understanding of..." or "to develop an appreciation of..." provide no constructive basis for structuring study activities or guidelines for the student. A typical reaction to behavioral objectives is illustrated by the remarks of a professor who discovered the mimeographed handouts of objectives in an Audio-Tutorial learning center. "What's this?" she said in a shocked voice. "Objectives." "You don't let the students see these, do you?" "Yes." "My goodness, they will learn it all!"

It is an amazing paradox that a crisis in education exists at a time when communication facilities are almost unlimited. Never in the history of man have so many communication devices been available. Actually, the problem is simple and basically related to the aforementioned principle that "learning must be done by the learner." Practically all information known to man is written as soon as it is discovered. Supposedly, anyone who can read potentially can learn whatever he wishes. If this were true, the only effort necessary would be writing and distributing text books. No one accepts this as the solution because the nature of human beings is such that this would result only in limited success. It is necessary to create a learning environment in which the learner is motivated to become involved. Important components in the environment are sometimes rather nonintellectual and seemingly insignificant—e.g., the proximity of related materials can be a key factor in successful achievement. It is not enough to build a complex of laboratories, classrooms, and libraries, and to establish a routine of schedules. This structuring frequently is a deterrent to learning and may frustrate the process it is supposed to facilitate.

Perhaps the most important factor in motivation is success. In a good learning program, students must have successful experiences at frequent intervals. Such a program must be flexible enough that the student can pace the progress to his capacity to achieve. To some teachers this implies a pattern geared to the rate of the slowest student, whereas in actual fact it suggests that one should provide a pattern which enables the fast student to make adjustments in the program. In other words, the student must participate in the decisions as to how he can best achieve the objectives and he must be permitted to select those parts of the program which are most helpful to him. This flexibility is impossible where there are no defined objectives and the teacher is merely exposing the students to that which he, the teacher, knows. A high percentage of students could learn more and in less time if they just had a list of behavioral objectives and the freedom to pursue their study independently.

It is obvious that much learning takes place outside the confines of an educational system. People, of necessity, must learn many things not taught in schools if they are to survive. People learn many complicated concepts outside of classrooms. Even in a small city, a delivery boy must be able to determine a reasonable route for a series of deliveries and traverse the route while maneuvering complicated equipment. The mental exercises and skills involved are not unlike the tracing of biochemical pathways and the manipulation of certain research equipment.

If one asks "What are the kinds of situations or activities that result in learning in an informal situation?" perhaps one can learn some ingredients which serve as guidelines for development of an educational program. A few of these are listed below:

1. Repetition

Repetition is an important factor in the learning of many skills and information. However, repetition ought to be according to the individual needs. A student who has already learned a topic or skill should not be required to listen or participate in learning activities designed to achieve these ends, whereas a student who has not learned them might require repetition many times for successful learning. To the first student, repetition becomes a frustration and makes the subject matter distasteful. To the second, repetition is necessary. Therefore, a good educational vehicle would permit the learner to adjust the amount of repetition to his individual needs.

2. Concentration

It is clear that learning requires the attention of the learner. The best lecture that was ever given is totally ineffective to a student who is sleeping. Both students and lecturers are sometimes misled by the presence of a student whose mind is elsewhere. The student salves his conscience through attendance and the lecturer justifies himself by saying "Well, I told them." A realistic approach would provide a situation in which worthwhile information is presented only when the student is alert and receptive.

3. Association

Only a relatively few people have the talent to memorize dissociated numbers and facts and other unrelated material. A well-structured education system would take this point into consideration and provide materials with important points associated with appropriately related items. Live materials, photographs, diagrams, and charts should be used to focus attention on the real specimen or situation and abstractions should be minimized.

4. Unit Steps

Programmers have demonstrated the effectiveness of small unit steps in a sequential program. However, the program should have the added feature of allowing the student to adjust the size of the unit to his intellectual capacity. Some students can move forward in large steps whereas others must proceed in smaller increments. A good educational vehicle will permit either. This is in contrast to the prevailing situation in which subject matter is commonly presented in an assembly line fashion. The students are faced with a continuous flow of words, and those who miss some particular point have no opportunity to stop the rate of presentation and go back over important points. They are exposed to new subject matter with a poor foundation and the result is frustration and unsuccessful effort. The effect is cumulative as the educational program proceeds. The lack of success becomes humiliating and the student develops a defense mechanism. This usually takes the form of a pretence that he doesn't care. With time, this creates mental barriers that are difficult to overcome. On the other hand, "success begets success." If students can enjoy some success in learning, they will not only be better prepared for learning subsequent material but will be more highly motivated. The desire to learn is universal and is an attribute which can be enhanced or thwarted depending upon the educational programs we develop.

5. Use of the Communication Vehicle Appropriate to the Objective

Many subjects (botany, for example) are complex and demand a great variety of learning activities. One cannot use a single communication vehicle to provide students a full range of experiences. To lecture to a group of students concerning the development of a skill may be a waste of time. Skills can be developed only when the student is involved in a manipulative procedure. Clearly defined objectives give important guidance to the nature of study activity required. The common practice in many sciences "to involve students with experimental procedures and collection of data" with the idea that this teaches them how to think critically is a mistake. Developing skills in manipulation of equipment is a worthy objective and should be included in a course of science. However, if this manipulation were a requirement for critical analysis, teachers in their own research labs would not be able to employ technicians and mechanical equipment to do much of the labor and time-consuming tasks of collecting data for them. Each researcher would have to do all this detailed work himself. An argument sometimes put forward in favor of having students perform experiments is that they should experience some of the frustrations of scientific investigation and participate in every aspect of an experiment to provide the substance of association. However, if critical thinking is the major objective, it is likely that students will gain more experience with analysis and critical thinking if they can obtain the data quickly.

6. Use of a Multiplicity of Approaches

People differ in receptivity to different approaches to a subject. There is a tendency in this age of technology in education to become a faddist and attempt to use one device to the exclusion of all others. This is unfortunate, for some people may learn and respond best through an audio approach, others through a video approach, and yet others through examination and handling real objects. It would seem logical that one would permit students to pursue any appropriate avenue to accomplish the objective.

7. Use of an Integrated Experience Approach

The logic of sequencing or programming learning activities appropriate to the objectives hardly needs to be presented. In nearly every field of experience an appropriate blend of components is recognized as a necessary approach. Musical instruments sounded in random fashion result in cacophony, but the same sounds if sequenced and appropriately timed produce a melody or arrangement which is meaningful and pleasant to hear. Seldom does one eat any foods which are not a blend of several components, and it is a natural approach at mealtime to have a sequence of foods and in a specific order. The physical growth of an organism is a sequence of highly ordered events with hormones acting in specific succession and in appropriate balance one to another. Undoubtedly, the same pattern exists in intellectual growth. Several study activities when appropriately sequenced and related to each other will cause the student to experience greater achievement and understanding than if these same events are randomly sequenced and disassociated. Basic ideas upon which subsequent information is dependent must be given first. The viewing of a film on germination at the time that live seedlings and seeds are available for dissection will make both the dissection and the film meaningful experiences. Each activity supplements the other and results in greater total achievement. This point is so significant that a total restructuring of an educational program administratively and materially will be worth the investment. (See pages 162-165).

In these days of exploding population and knowledge it has become obvious that traditional methods are too inefficient and ineffective to keep pace with current educational demands. The percentage of the population demanding more education is increasing and, as more educated people contribute to the enlarging volume of knowledge, the problem increases in geometric proportions. The problem is to provide a learning situation with enough flexibility to allow each student to make adjustments according to his interest, background, and capacities. It is unnecessary to present evidence here concerning this growth. We are constantly bombarded with such facts and figures from many sources.

This book asks whether the educational community is leading in the adoption and utilization of new technology or if we are playing the role of the reluctant farmer. Not many years ago many farmers resisted the change from the use of the horse to the tractor as a vehicle for farming. It is easy to visualize the first attempts to use a motorized vehicle to plow a field. No doubt bystanders predicted that it would run out of gas and bog down in the wet field, that it would have flat tires, and would wear out. Indeed, all of these problems were experienced. However, had the kibitzers prevailed, we could not enjoy the abundance of food which now prevails. Costs in manpower and money to produce this food would be much greater. Some of the sentimentalists explained that one cannot love a tractor but one could love a horse. This is no doubt true, but it is a minor factor in the overall significance of the utilization of tractors.

As communication technology has improved, the teacher is in a comparable situation. The technology is now available but its utilization is severely limited by sentimentalists and those who would like to maintain a status quo. In many cases, these are selfish interests related to a reluctance to learn new methods and the desire to hang on to past traditions, vested interests, and small empires which would have to be discarded. Many of us would need to acquire new skills. The prospect of this is frightening and, when coupled with a loss of certain ego-inflating exercises, it is easy to rationalize away our responsibilities. We want desperately to "put new wine in the old skins" even though it will result in disaster. A good case in point is the early attempts to give traditional lectures and hold recitations over television. It was a waste of a good communication tool and it gave educational television a setback which will take years to overcome.

It is a paradox that those of us who are educators, and, by implication, leaders of the population, are literally a limiting factor in the educational process. It is time for a soul-searching inquiry in which we reassess our objectives and ask whether our program is realistic in enabling students to achieve these objectives. Kipling's poem "If" pretty well describes the situation in which many of us find ourselves. We are geared to a procedure which has become obsolete and restrictive, but to discard it would be to waste years of investment and effort. Many of us would have to start all over again learning new techniques and subject matter. "If you can bear to see the things you've given your life to, broken, and stoop to build them up again with worn-out tools..., and—which is more—you'll be a man, my son."

Chapter II

THE AUDIO-TUTORIAL SYSTEM

Emphasis on student learning rather than on the mechanisms of teaching is the basis of the Audio-Tutorial approach. The teacher should identify as clearly as possible those responses, attitudes, concepts, ideas, and manipulatory skills to be achieved by the student and then design a multi-faceted, multi-sensory approach which will enable the student to direct his own activity to attain these objectives. The program of learning should be organized in such a way that students can proceed at their own pace, filling in gaps in their background information and omitting the portions of the program which they have covered at some previous time. It should make use of every educational device available and attempt to align the exposure to these learning experiences in a sequence which will be most effective and efficient. The kind, number, and nature of the devices involved will be dependent on the nature of the subject matter under consideration.

The term "integrated experience" used in connection with the Audio-Tutorial system is derived from the fact that a wide variety of teaching-learning experiences are integrated, with provision for individual student differences, and each experience planned to present efficiently some important aspect of the subject. In the Audio-Tutorial booth, the taped presentation of the program is designed to direct the activity of one student at a time; the senior instructor, in a sense, becomes the student's private tutor. It is important to emphasize at this point that the tape represents only a programming device and that the student is involved in many kinds of learning activities. Further, it should be noted that those activities which by their nature cannot be programmed by the audio-tape are retained and presented in other ways. For example, guest lecturers and long films are shown in a general assembly session, and small discussion groups are held on a regular basis to provide for those activities which can best be done in a small assembly. Flexibility and independence, accompanied by helpful guidance when necessary, are the key concepts of the approach.

In the Audio-Tutorial system the instructor's voice is available to the student to direct and supplement his study effort (Fig. 2.1). This does not mean that a taped lecture is given!! It refers to an audio programming of learning experiences logically sequenced to produce the most effective student response. Each study activity has been designed to provide information or skill leading to the proper performance of the next activity or else it builds on the foundation of knowledge previously laid. The overall set of integrated experiences includes lectures, reading of text or other appropriate material, making observations on demonstration setups, doing experiments (Fig. 2.2), watching movies, and/or any other appropriate activities helpful in understanding the subject matter. This system differs from the written programmed instruction and the conventional lecture-laboratory approach in at least two important ways:

1. Many subjects require student involvement in a variety of learning experiences. The conventional teaching system makes this adjustment through the scheduling of

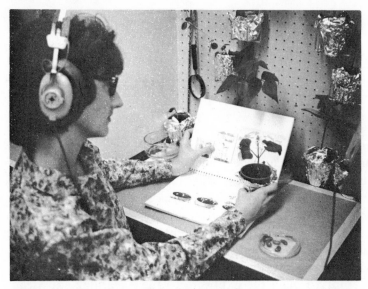

FIGURE 2.1–A student listening to the senior instructor discuss various aspects of germination while she examines a live specimen and associated photographs in the study guide.

FIGURE 2.2–A student setting up an experiment as a part of the study sequence. Experiments can be included in the study program at the time when the data are most meaningful.

lectures, laboratories, recitations, etc. In the Audio-Tutorial system, these activities can be organized in a stepwise fashion with reduced disassociation in time and space encountered in the conventional approach, while at the same time, the logical learning progression characteristic of written programmed instruction is retained. Further, the learning events need not be limited to the vicarious participation of the student through his reading only, as in written programs. Hour-long lectures of necessity cover several units of information. Some of these topics are covered more meaningfully when student involvement is associated with them through experimentation, observation, textbook reading, and other appropriate activities. The limitations of time and physical facilities make this kind of integration unfeasible under the conventional system but it is clearly practical under the Audio-Tutorial system utilizing audio-tape programming.

2. In the Audio-Tutorial booth the voice of the instructor provides timely information, definitions, and parenthetical expressions with minimal effort for the learner. These helpful asides are often omitted from a student's study because of the inconvenience involved in looking up words, and because such thoughts seldom fit well as part of a written text. The tone of voice places emphasis on important points and expresses authority not sensed through reading the written word.

HISTORY AND DEVELOPMENT

The inception of the Audio-Tutorial system as currently employed at Purdue University was in 1961. The senior author by making supplementary lectures on audio-tape attempted to provide an opportunity for students with poor backgrounds to keep up with the class. The student could listen to these lectures from 7:30 A.M. to 11:30 P.M. on weekdays and from 12:00 P.M. to 11:30 P.M. on Sundays through the facilities of the Audio-Visual Department. The first tapes were purely supplemental lectures. During the progress of the semester, the nature of the tape lectures progressively changed toward an audio programming of a variety of learning experiences. At first, only diagrams and photographs were made available with the tape. The student's attention was directed to various items in these diagrams and photographs while he listened to a discussion about them. Later the student was asked to open his textbook and follow the text explanation while listening to the instructor's discussion of the information. Thus, the author's point of view and the instructor's point of view were considered at the same time. Soon living plants were added to the other materials, and ultimately the student was asked to do experiments from the laboratory manual in context with the study of the text and tape discussion. By the end of the semester, a weekly "learning kit" was prepared and students could do the full range of study for the week without attending any of the formal sessions of the course. The students' reactions to this supplemental material were so favorable that it was decided to set up an experimental section of 36 students who would receive all instruction programmed by audio-tape. During the second semester of 1961-62 this was done. The experimental section met with an instructor only once each week to take quizzes and for a discussion session. They were required to take the same exams that were given to the conventionally-taught group, and at the end of the semester, although they had not done better than the conventional group, they had done just as well. The 36 students were consulted as to how one could best set up a study program for plant science which would incorporate the flexibility desired, yet retain the quality of instruction necessary to prepare them for their advanced courses. As a result of these discussions, the course in freshman botany at Purdue has been completely restructured to give the student maximum freedom for independent study and an opportunity to make adjustments for his interests, background, and capacity.

THE RESTRUCTURED COURSE

The terms "lecture," "recitation," and "laboratory" are not used in connection with the Audio-Tutorial program. This is to emphasize the role of the student in the learning process. The connotation one receives from the term "lecture" is activity on the part of the individual who is doing the lecturing while students are passive, if involved at all. The formality of a laboratory and recitation as conventionally conducted also implies a degree of regimentation of the students. Therefore, the term "study session" has been adopted to place emphasis on learning rather than teaching. Three basic study sessions plus other specially assigned activities are involved:

1. *Independent study session (ISS)*
2. *General assembly session (GAS)*
3. *Small assembly session (SAS)*
    a. Integrated quiz session (IQS)
    b. Other small assembly sessions
4. *Other activities*

1. Independent Study Session (ISS)

This study is at the student's convenience in a learning center (Fig. 2.3). The center is open over an extended period of time which permits the student to adjust study activities

FIGURE 2.3—The learning center is open from 7:30 A.M. to 10:30 P.M. Monday through Friday. The student comes in at her convenience.

to his campus responsibilities. The center is equipped with booths (Fig. 2.4) for individual study and a central table (Fig. 2.5) for bulky materials. The basic equipment for each booth is a tape recorder, an 8 mm movie projector, and the other materials appropriate for the week's work. The student assigns himself to a specific booth by the use of a

FIGURE 2.4—There are 32 booths to serve up to 600 students. All booths are set up alike for the week's study.

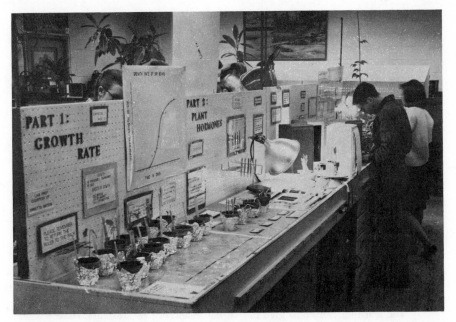

FIGURE 2.5—Bulky materials and expensive items are placed at a central location for use by all students.

record card. He places the card in a numbered slot to indicate the booth is occupied. Each booth in the learning center is equipped identically so the student can study independently of the progress of the other students. The taped program covers a week of study material or subject matter. The student begins his study by picking up a mimeographed list of the behavioral objectives for the week's work. He also arranges his textbook and study guide for convenient reference and places the headphones in position. When he activates the tape player the voice of the senior professor tutors him through a great variety of learning activities. These activities may include performing an experiment, collecting data from the demonstration materials, reading short segments from his text or appropriate journal article, making observations through the microscope, filling in diagrams, charts, or appropriate blanks in his study guide or laboratory manual, viewing sections of films, and other kinds of learning activity suitable to the topic under consideration. The voice of the instructor on tape is not a substitute for a laboratory manual or a study guide, but rather is a programming device and provides the additional potential of incorporating special sounds into the study program. As the student proceeds with his study, he has the option of working independently or with other students and can request assistance from the instructor on duty if he experiences any difficulty (Fig. 2.6).

The study can be interrupted at the convenience of the student for adjustment to other scheduled responsibilities or simply to take a rest break to improve his receptivity. No student is a captive of any of the activities included within the learning center and may omit any of these for which he can demonstrate his ability to accomplish the objectives. Casual encounters during rest breaks or during excursions from the booth often result in discussions between students or between instructors and students. These discussions can clarify specific problems or result in the investigation of a topic to a

FIGURE 2.6–An instructor is on duty during the open hours of the learning center to give individual assistance to students. Here an instructor is manipulating magnets as chromosome symbols to illustrate critical steps in a plant life cycle.

FIGURE 2.7–Students setting up an experiment which will involve collecting data over a period of two or three weeks.

greater depth. Thus, it is not necessary for a student to proceed poorly prepared from one unit of information into a successive unit.

It has been the experience of the authors that no learning activity commonly used in conventional education procedures needs to be omitted from this program. Actually, in many cases some activities which were not possible under the conventional organization may be included. Obviously, one can include experiments commonly used in the conventional laboratory which require two to three hours for completion. However, since students are unscheduled and are not required to spend a specified amount of time in the laboratory, one can also include experiments which require collection of data at time intervals not correlated to the routine of conventional scheduling (Fig. 2.7). Experiments requiring the use of specialized equipment making costs prohibitive under the conventional approach can be included since the use is distributed over a greater time range and fewer such items are required for a greater number of students. Field trips are conducted by use of portable tape recorders and have proven to be highly successful, especially in the amount of learning that occurs. When the student has completed his independent study he is free to leave. He restores the booth to its original condition ready for the next student, removes his record card from the booth assignment slot, records his departure time and files the card for the next occasion of study.

2. General Assembly Session (GAS)

The general assembly is scheduled near the end of a week's work and is correlated with the IQS session. The senior instructor is in charge of this session. It is designed to cover several kinds of activities which can best be done in a large group. These include the presentation of a guest lecturer, showing of long films, help sessions, giving major exams, or any other appropriate activity. Students are only required to attend those sessions covering specific materials not covered elsewhere in the course.

3. Small Assembly Session (SAS)

A. Integrated Quiz Session (IQS)—The small assembly session has been modified during the past few years to a specialized session and renamed the Integrated Quiz Session. This session terminates the week's work and involves eight students scheduled to meet with an instructor for approximately 45 minutes. The first half hour includes a 10-point oral quiz and the remaining time involves a 20-point written quiz. The eight students are assembled around a table on which have been placed the various items included in the independent study session for the preceding week's study (Fig. 2.8). These items include such things as charts, photographs, diagrams, specimens, movies, experimental equipment, or any other material which has been used to enable the student to achieve the objectives listed on the objective sheet. The instructor presents the items in a programmed fashion to one of the eight students selected at random. All students will have at least one or more opportunities to discuss an item during the half hour. The student's discussion follows a rather specific format which is as follows: First, the student identifies the item; secondly, he relates it to a specific objective on the objective sheet; and thirdly, he fulfills that objective through either discussion or demonstration as the case may require.

The purpose of this session is to structure the student's approach to study. A common cliche is that "you really learn a subject when you have to teach it." If this statement is true, a good technique for helping a student learn would be to have him prepare to teach the subject. His preparation would take the form of "investigating the items." Since the oral quiz is a short lecture about some item which was included in the

FIGURE 2.8—An instructor and eight students meet for an oral quiz in the IQS.

independent study session, to some degree it places each student in the role of a teacher. All students must prepare for all items since they are randomly selected to respond. At first, students were not awarded grades, but experience has suggested that the session is more effective when each student receives a score. As each student completes his presentation, the instructor assigns grades by placing him in one of three categories. If the instructor is much impressed, the student is placed in the category of excellent and given nine points; if the instructor is not much impressed, the student is placed in the category of average and given seven points; and if the instructor is disappointed with the student, he is placed in the category of poor and given five points or less. The student is told his grade immediately and the seven other students are requested to make additional corrections or comments as they may desire. These contributions by students are kept in mind by the instructor and at the end of the session a student's grade might be raised from nine to ten or from seven to eight points. On the completion of the oral quiz all students take a 20-point written quiz.

B. Other Small Assembly Sessions (SAS)—Other sessions may be desirable, depending on the nature of the subject matter. No attempt is made here to identify all possible small assembly sessions. They may even be specially called ones not scheduled over an entire semester. The concept is not rigid—it is limited only by the imagination.

4. Other Activities

Some important learning activities either cannot be accomplished within the sessions already mentioned or may need to be supplemented by additional assignments. Among these are experiences gained by doing a relatively major research project. In the plant science course being described, all students are required to do one miniature research project and all the students who anticipate a grade of "A" must do an additional project.

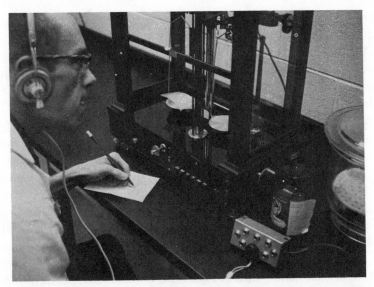

FIGURE 2.9—A student setting up a small research project. All students must do one project and "A" students must do an additional one.

The first project is initiated at the very first meeting of the small assembly session. The 32 students assemble with the instructor and go through the procedure of defining a problem, designing an experiment to give relevant data, and setting up the first phases of the experiment. The students are expected to follow through by collecting the appropriate data and, after the experiment has been terminated, the class data are compiled. In a general assembly session a statistician may be invited to give assistance in analyzing the data. All students are then required to make the analysis of their own data as well as that of the entire class and to write up the project in the format of a scientific paper. These papers are either accepted or rejected based on how nearly they fulfill the requirements of a scientific paper.

The second project is required of all students who anticipate an "A" grade and must be started immediately following the completion of project I (Fig. 2.9). In this project the student is expected to use his own initiative to do each step in the procedure from the definition of the problem to the final write-up. The only restrictions imposed are those of time and available materials. The student must decide whether he is in the category of an "A" student. His grade ultimately is dependent on the accumulation of 90% or above on test scores plus the completion of an acceptable second project.

RATIONALE FOR COURSE STRUCTURING

This portion of the chapter is devoted to an explanation of some of the reasoning behind each of the study sessions and to suggestions of some possible alternatives for extensions of these sessions.

1. Independent Study Session (ISS)

The independent study session is based on the premise that learning must be done by the learner himself and that all study activities should involve the learner as actively as possible. The entire approach to this study session is one of permitting the student maximum freedom and yet providing additional help at any time he requests it. For this reason the session is on an unscheduled basis. The total emphasis is placed on learning rather than the length of time involved in the actual study itself. The flexibility of scheduling permits the student to make adjustments to his individual requirements. If he is ill or other studies are pressing, he is not forced to give divided attention to his botany and other concerns. While this freedom sometimes leads to problems of crowding at favored times (the end of the week), some steps can be taken to avoid these problems, as will be shown in a later chapter. About 98% of the students favor retaining the unscheduled approach despite the occasional crowding.

In the independent study session the student can make knowledgeable and positive progress with the only limitation being his own skill in achieving the objectives listed. All sensory inputs can be brought to bear on any given topic and these organized in a logical sequential pattern by the senior instructor in the course. Any portion of any program can be repeated and achievement can be verified with the instructor on duty before the student is forced to proceed to the next study unit. If the senior instructor does well in programming the learning events in a logical sequence, the student can proceed stepwise with each step becoming a firm foundation on which to build successive steps. Should the student wish to pause during the program to go into greater depth on any topic of special interest, the opportunity is available and supplementary materials are provided in the learning center. A small library plus colleagues and instructors give him access to additional points of view. Occasionally an "in depth" treatment of some special topic is made available for independent viewing using a slide projector. Photographs, diagrams, charts, *Scientific American* articles, and 2 × 2 slides are liberally distributed around the learning center to facilitate study in greater depth.

Subject matter for which motion picture viewing is most appropriate can be placed on 8 mm film and through the use of a movie projector the student can be programmed through a series of technical steps of a procedure. He can imitate the scenes from the film using the real materials which are at hand. Thus he can turn on the projector, see the first step of the procedure, turn off the projector, do that step, turn on the projector, see the second step, turn off the projector, do that step, etc. A student who is especially skilled in the procedure can move quickly through the exercise and can see specifically how the procedure is to be accomplished. He is not looking over the heads of other students as commonly is the case during a demonstration under the conventional system. Frequently, the events are photographed from close-up angles so that he can view critically the more obscure stages of how a procedure is done.

In addition, the 8 mm film can be used to view time-lapse sequences at a time when this information is important to the material under consideration. For example, a student who is making a study of germination can have available: plants at various stages of development; information from his textbook concerning germination; the voice of the senior instructor on tape with his discussion and programming; and, in addition, a filmed time-lapse sequence which will permit him to view the sequence of events during germination.

Movies also provide an opportunity for a time saving in certain studies. Sequential microscope sections of a specimen which have been photographed on movie film can be projected and viewed quickly without time being lost in manipulation of several hundred microscope slides. If it is desirable, the student may be asked to synchronize the tape and film so that the normally soundless 8 mm film can be narrated. Sometimes it is useful to have the student view the film while listening to a taped introduction and then have him watch it again without sound.

The most important feature of the independent study session is the opportunity to bring many different approaches to bear on a single topic in a coordinated series of learning events. The student, having been forewarned of the level of achievement he is expected to obtain through the use of the objective sheets, can now in a purposeful and positive way prepare himself for the exam sessions.

In summary, one may ask the question "What procedure would I use to teach a friend botany?" It is unlikely the answer would be "two lectures, a recitation, and a three hour laboratory each week for a semester." It is more likely that one would meet with this friend at a mutually convenient time with the materials available which are useful in helping him learn botany, and would then tutor him through a series of learning events. There would be a one-to-one relationship and the student would be involved in the program at all times. While it is not feasible to use this approach for 1,000 students, under the Audio-Tutorial system it is possible to simulate this relationship for an unlimited number. The appropriate materials can be collected and the instructor can sit among them talking into a tape recorder as if he were instructing one individual. The arrangement of materials and the resultant tape can be duplicated as many times as required for the number of students involved. In this way hundreds can have the benefit of personalized instruction by a competent and knowledgeable instructor. The program can be tested and revised until it produces consistent and satisfactory results. In addition, the student can participate in adjusting the program to his background, interest, and capacity.

Perhaps most important of all, this system places the responsibility of learning on the shoulders of the student. All students who make the decision to enter the learning center are using their own time and naturally will use their time effectively. Since the best learning is done through concentration, the student now will be a captive of his own decision and consequently will put forth his most effective efforts. All students are free to ignore the taped program or any other segment of the sequence. He may use the objective sheet as a guide and structure his own study program in the way that he pleases. Flexibility and diversity are the key components of the independent study sessions.

2. General Assembly Session (GAS)

Basically, the rationale for including a general assembly session in the course is to ensure that all students will have had an occasion to see the personality whose voice is on tape. While there are many occasions for closer contact with the senior instructor than are afforded in the general assembly session, many students do not avail themselves of this opportunity. This is no different from the conventional course structuring and perhaps the GAS is not a necessary component of a learning system, but if it does have any motivation value for some students, at least the potential has been retained in the Audio-Tutorial system. Aside from this, a general assembly session is useful for orientation activities at the beginning of the course and provides possibilities for including guest lecturers and long films as important components in the learning program. Perhaps the inclusion of this session needs less rationalization than the other sessions since it is a normal feature of a conventionally structured course. It is important to emphasize however, that the general assembly session is not used in the Audio-Tutorial system as a straightforward lecture except on very special occasions, two or three times in a semester at most.

3. Integrated Quiz Session (IQS, formerly Small Assembly Session—SAS)

It was mentioned earlier that the small assembly session has been altered considerably. As it is currently used, this session makes several important contributions to the success of the Audio-Tutorial program. Perhaps its most important function is to structure the student's method of study. When one prepares to teach a topic, the depth and nature of preparation appear to be significantly different from that of the level of preparation for responding to written questions. Since the nature of preparation is dictated by the method of quizzing, the integrated quiz session is an attempt to exploit the principle that "one really learns a subject when one prepares to teach it." Every student is required to investigate all items in a manner which will enable him to present a brief lecture about these items. The student's lecture is somewhat structured by the behavioral objectives, but still represents his point of view. Each student can go well beyond the objectives to emphasize his interests and flavor his presentation with his own background of experiences. Thus students tend to expand their investigations beyond that which they think might be included in a conventional written quiz. They have confidence that they will receive credit for any information that is relevant and demonstrates their comprehension of the topic involved. This aspect of the session is a strong motivating factor from the standpoint of developing interest in the subject.

Each student has an opportunity to compare his level of understanding of the topics under consideration with that of the students who are making the presentations. During the discussion of an item by one student, the other seven students are vicariously involved. They have prepared for a presentation on the same item themselves and they know they will have an opportunity to make additions or corrections at the close of the presentation. This approach leads to some abuses by vociferous students but the value achieved is worth the compromise. The session becomes one of review, reinforcement, and correction and frequently causes students to get together with friends for a practice session preceding the IQS. When the items for discussion are distributed in a programmed fashion the integrated aspect of the study sequence is emphasized and points which were previously obscure are clarified.

The instructor's attitude during the session can exert considerable influence in further structuring the student's approach to preparation. Students who need encouragement can be given recognition for that which they do well and made to feel pleased with their success. On the other hand, students who are making poor progress can be identified at an early date and appropriate action can be taken to adjust for their problems. The intimacy of a session with eight students results in each student becoming well known by at least one instructor in the course and all students in the course know at least one instructor well. No student is just a number even in a course with a large enrollment.

A very significant feature of the integrated quiz session is the feedback to the instructor on the success of the instructional program. In many cases the response patterns can be analyzed and valuable clues can be obtained for the alteration of the program of study activities. Unsuccessful programs are clearly evident and the senior instructor now has some basis on which to intelligently approach the restructuring of the sequence of learning events. A bonus feature of the integrated quiz session is the opportunity for each student to express himself orally. While this is not a basic objective for a botany course, it is valuable experience for the student. Many students show considerable improvement in oral expression during the semester interval.

While measurement of student achievement is not the primary purpose of the oral quiz, it is a necessary evil. Students who are highly selected may not need this kind of motivation. However, at a freshman level this system, or some modification of it, is necessary. In the initial use of oral quizzes students were merely scored on a pass-fail basis. However, this approach appeared to be unsatisfactory to both student and staff. As a consequence, a system of subjective grading was established.

Many administrative details can be cared for in this session such as the assignment of the final grade in the course and evaluation of the special research projects.

In summary, the integrated quiz session has been a very effective device for establishing rapport with the students and making adjustments for individual students in a direct and positive way.

4. Other Activities

The rationale for inclusion of other activities naturally will depend on the nature of the activities involved. In a course in plant science it seems logical that a student should experience some of the very basic activities that contribute to the concepts of science—namely, a research project. Clearly, in a comprehensive course it is not feasible for students to do many of the basic experiments which led to the current understanding of the subject matter. It is important to expose them to a reasonable balance between discovery-type experiments requiring manipulation of experimental procedures and a more straightforward inquiry which can be assimilated quickly. Short experiments which must be completed in two to three hours and are merely demonstrating known information do not give the student the same perspective of inquiry that is achieved when a student does a genuine research project. It is true that some degree of the reasoning of a great scientist can be experienced vicariously by imitating bits of his experiments but a two or three hour experiment (or even an experiment which may involve two or three weeks) which is "supposed to come out in a specific way" does not fool the student and is often done halfheartedly. The research projects suggested in the course described in this book, even though limited in scope, are genuine. They may not be a success from the point of view of making a new discovery or answering an original problem, but this possibility has been accepted as one of the hazards of the effort. At least all students are forced to use the library and involve themselves with the various procedures of a research project. (See p. 149.)

Perhaps it is not necessary to discuss the rationale of such activities as field trips and special reading assignments. Under the Audio-Tutorial system the nature of subject matter and objectives can be the guidelines for structuring additional study activities. On occasions where the size required for a study group may differ from the general assembly session or the small assembly session, one can easily arrange for it by sign-up procedures (Chap. V). It is important that certain learning experiences which demand specific arrangements and only occur occasionally during a semester do not become the basis for the total structuring of course organization. Such activities frequently can be included as a simple modification of the general assembly session or small assembly session or by special arrangements with the students directly.

PERSONAL CONTACT

During recent years much concern has been expressed about depersonalization of education. The idea is that with increased enrollments the senior staff is having less

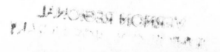

contact with students and much of the instructional procedure has been turned over to graduate students or personnel who have had limited teaching experience. The implication is that contact with the professor is important because professors are filled with enthusiasm for teaching and, because of their understanding of their specialty and long history of communication, they will be a great inspiration to the younger generation. This point could become one of considerable debate; however, one can easily accept the idea that the combination of intelligence plus experience is more likely to produce effective educational programs than intelligence minus experience. The ideal situation would be to provide all students the benefits of intelligence plus experience.

Two important components of a good educational system are: (1) a well-structured sequence of learning events and (2) a pleasant personal relationship between instructors and students. The ability to create a situation which includes both of these is not always present in the same individual. Some instructors have a great capacity for presenting information logically and effectively but have little or no rapport with students, and others are just the opposite. In other words, personal contact with the senior instructor in the course may or may not make an important contribution to the success of the course.

If one can assume that personal contact with the senior instructor in the course will enhance the motivation of students, the opportunity for making this contact direct and frequent is greater under the Audio-Tutorial system than under the conventional system.

The personal contact of a senior instructor in the conventional structuring of a course in botany involving two lectures per week, a one-hour recitation, and three-hour laboratory for 600 students might be somewhat as follows: Assuming that such a person had eight contact hours per week in the course, this instructor would probably use four hours of the time for the two lectures per week (2 lectures × 2 sections of 300 students each equals 4 hours), and the remaining four hours might be spent with one one-hour recitation involving 30 students and one three-hour laboratory contact with 30 students.

The instructor spending the same amount of time under the Audio-Tutorial system would spend two of the eight hours in general assembly session (1 hour GAS per week × 2 sections of 300 students each equals 2 hours) and the remaining six hours might be spent with three hours of half-hour integrated quiz sessions in which the contact would be with 48 students, and three hours in the independent study session which should place him in contact with 32 students as a minimum, but a potential contact of 60 or more students.

In the conventional laboratory the senior instructor would visit with only 30 students. The Audio-Tutorial system also provides simulated personal contact through the tape-recorded voice of the senior instructor.

Further personal contact can be achieved under both systems through a weekly coffee hour to which all students are invited, special office hours, casual and frequent visits to the learning center. (At Purdue an open house in the home of the senior instructor once each semester has become a tradition.)

Personal contact is not reduced by the use of the Audio-Tutorial system, but is increased. In many instances personal contact is more direct, less formal, and takes place in a more pleasant environment. In the final analysis, personal contact under either system is dependent on the level of interest of both the students and the instructor.

INQUIRY

The word "inquiry" is open to a great variety of interpretation and usually refers to "the way I teach." It is fashionable to say, "My course is inquiry-orientated," and the connotation is that the speaker is a modern educator. It is the opinion of the authors that this word has been much abused; many who suggest that they employ an inquiry approach often merely mean that they use laboratory experiments in their course.

To inquire means to seek information, to question, and to investigate. It implies curiosity on the part of the inquirer, and a desire to accumulate information which may have a bearing on the problem from as many sources as possible. Inquiry suggests that one has an open mind and will exercise some selectivity and judgment in arriving at one's conclusions from the information at hand. Equating the manipulation of laboratory equipment with an inquiry approach is an unfortunate practice. Experimentation is only one mechanism whereby data can be collected. Simple observations, data collected by others, or any source of information which will enable the inquirer to make a sounder judgment on the question under investigation should be included under the heading of inquiry. Inquiry is an attitude and a way of thinking.

On this basis one might propose a hierarchy of levels of inquiry. Perhaps the first order of magnitude would include the entire sequence of events and thinking related to a research project. It would involve participation in the definition of the problem, development of the criteria for an experiment which would give relevant data, physical manipulation of the procedure of the experiment, collection of data, analysis of the data, and the preparation of a paper to communicate the results and conclusions of the study.

On a second level of inquiry the student might have the problem defined and the experimental procedure outlined for him. The student's participation begins at the point where he performs the experiment, collects the data, and makes an analysis of the data. This is a common approach in most conventional laboratory courses where the teacher wishes to illustrate some known scientific principle for which an experimental design has been established that is likely to give reproducible results. Inquiry at this level is usually written up as a part of a laboratory manual or study guide and the materials are made available during the interval of a two- to four-hour laboratory period.

A third level of inquiry is one which is commonly used for experiments requiring materials too sophisticated or which demand undue time and space to be practical for involvement of a large number of students. The experimental procedure is carried out by the instructional staff and the students are merely involved in collecting and analyzing data. A case in point is an experiment in photoperiodism. It is not practical in a course with an enrollment of 600 students to have all 600 students set up plants under photoperiod and temperature regimes in controlled climate facilities. The students can inquire into the effects of photoperiod satisfactorily when the instructional staff provides the definition of the problem, does the experimental procedure, and provides the students with plants which have been exposed to the specified photoperiods. From these plants the students can collect the appropriate data and make their own interpretations.

A fourth level of inquiry might be a logical extension of the preceding categories where the student, already having been exposed to some aspects of the experimental design, might be provided with raw data for his analysis. This would enable him to participate vicariously in experiments similar to those he had done in the past and, with a minimum of time investment, he would have the additional experience of interpretation and exposure to the scientific principles involved. In the Audio-Tutorial system as employed by the authors this has been accomplished in two ways: (1) raw data presented and discussed in the general assembly session, and (2) assignment of problems in a specially prepared manual.

A fifth level of inquiry may not involve experiments in any sense but a satisfaction of curiosity through straightforward observation and investigation of that which is already known through the use of textbooks, journal articles, and discussion with colleagues and instructors.

In summary, it should be emphasized that inquiry is an attitude and approach to learning rather than the mere performance of an experimental activity. The curiosity of individuals is often stimulated through the posing of pertinent questions and through learning activities which will enable the student to make associations and draw conclusions on some logical basis. Experimental manipulation within a laboratory is only one method of obtaining data, and the successful performance of an experiment does not necessarily mean that the student understands the reason for the experimental design or is capable of applying the principles to which he was exposed. However, if the objective is to enable the student to deal critically with raw data, the procedures for obtaining these data may be of limited value and may interfere with the rate of the student's progress.

Neither the structuring of the Audio-Tutorial system nor that of the conventional system assures the use of the inquiry approach to teaching. The extent to which inquiry is employed under either system is dependent on the way the content is organized by the instructor in charge. It is sufficient to state here that the Audio-Tutorial system in no way limits the opportunity for the inquiry approach, but for the higher levels of inquiry the possibilities are greatly enhanced.

Chapter III

AN EXAMPLE OF A WEEK'S UNIT OF STUDY

This chapter is an attempt to provide the reader an example of an integrated lesson as it might be experienced by the students. The tape has been transcribed, manual pages have been reproduced, and the plant materials have been photographed, but obviously, printed materials cannot possibly substitute for the elements of sound, movies, etc., available under the Audio-Tutorial setup. The unit of information to be treated is entitled "Plant Growth and Development" and involves two weeks' work. Only the second week's study is included here. The independent study session, the general assembly session, and the integrated quiz session will be discussed in appropriate sequential relationship.

INDEPENDENT STUDY SESSION (ISS)

The study of growth and development is initiated in the independent study session. The reader should visualize himself arriving at the learning center, and as he reads the transcription of the tape which is reproduced below he should recognize that the student will be hearing this information presented through the earphones of a tape player and in the voice of the senior instructor. The objectives, taped lesson, and appropriate section of the student's study guide are reproduced on the pages that follow. The transcribed words

FIGURE 3.1–Student picking up a list of objectives for the week's work.

FIGURE 3.2–Student beginning study by checking objectives and listening to introductory remarks of the senior instructor.

of the audio taped information are in the small print to separate it from the text of this book.

The student enters the learning center, puts down his books, locates his record card, checks the clock, enters the date and time in the appropriate box on the record card, places the card in a numbered slot, picks up books, obtains an objective sheet from the rack (Fig. 3.1) and goes to the assigned booth (Fig. 3.2). He sits down at the booth, arranges his text and study guide for convenient reference, makes a quick survey of the objectives (Fig. 3.3), notes carefully the first objective, positions the headphones for listening, turns on the tape player, moves the control to "play," and hears the following:

> **Music**–Hello there! This is Bio. 108–week 11. This week's study is a continuation of study begun last week. The subject is "Plant Growth and Development." Speaking of plant growth and development, have you ever seen the cherry blossoms in Washington, D. C.? If I told you I was in Washington last year at cherry blossom time what season would you think of? If you thought springtime that would be right–but why not fall? How do plants know the time of the year? I guess many people would be satisfied with the simple explanation that plants bloom at specific times of the year, but a university student might want to know why, and see how much explanation one could give to account for plant response to the environment–that's you, right?
>
> Flowering is just one event in the development of a plant, and perhaps it would be helpful if we would remind ourselves of some of the important points that we examined last week concerning this topic of growth and development. Please turn to page 1 in your study guide and let us look at this page for a few minutes.

The student pauses the tape and opens the study guide to page 1 (Fig. 3.4). The tape is started again.

> Notice in paragraph 1, line 5, that we pointed out that the initial cell of a plant body is a zygote

WEEK'S SUBJECT MATTER   BIOLOGY 108   WEEK II

Numbers in parentheses indicate related problems in Murray's Manual. The student should be able to apply information obtained from his study to solve the assigned problems in Murray's Manual.

MAJOR OBJECTIVES: PLANT GROWTH AND DEVELOPMENT (continued)

3. Light and Growth
   a. Be able to describe the effects of light on lettuce seed germination describing specifically how the experiment was set up, a statement of the hypothesis it was attempting to clarify, and state two justifiable conclusions.
   b. Be able to discuss the results of the experiment in Exercise 2 page 9 in the study guide and relate them to the hypothesis in Exercise 1.
   c. Be able to describe the experiment demonstrating the relationship between inhibiting wavelengths and promoting wavelengths on lettuce seed germination.
   d. Be able to describe the interactions between light and gibberellic acid and between light and coumarin with respect to the effects on lettuce seed germination. (3-2)
   e. Be able to describe the effects of etiolation on plants in terms of gross morphology. Suggest four physiological factors such as changes in photosynthesis, growth hormone distribution, etc. which account for these effects.
   f. Be able to associate particular light quality specifically involved in changes which occur during plant growth and development such as chlorophyll production, lignin formation, hypocotyl unhooking, hypocotyl elongation, anthocyanin production, and leaf expansion. (21-1)
   g. Be able to state which wavelengths of light are involved in producing the effects of etiolation.
   h. Be able to explain (in terms of the changes in phytochrome) the red, far-red pigment system.
   i. Be able to explain (in terms of the changes in phytochrome) the effects of red and far-red light in the following processes: seed germination, leaf expansion, opening of the hypocotyl hook, normal internode length, anthocyanin formation, lignin formation, coleoptile elongation, and flowering. (21-2, 3)

4. Photoperiod and Temperature
   j. Be able to define the terms long-day, short-day, and day neutral in terms of the critical period.
   k. Using data such as those on page 13 of the Study Guide, be able to state whether a given plant is long-day, short-day, or day neutral.
   l. Be able to identify the plants on display as to whether they are all long-day, short-day, or day neutral, and point out the relative critical period. (Note: Can all the plants be classified into one of the three categories? Can any of the plants "fit" into more than one category?)
   m. Be able to describe how one could determine whether a plant is a long-day, a short day plant, or a day neutral plant and how the critical point can be determined. (22-1, 2)
   n. Describe the interacting effects of light and temperature on the growth and flowering of Guar plants.
   o. Using the graph on demonstration, be able to explain thermoperiodism as applied to growth of the tomato plant.

FIGURE 3.3—A mimeographed handout listing the objectives for the week.

AUDIO TUTORIAL BIOLOGY SERIES

Plant Growth and Development

STUDENT STUDY GUIDE

by SAMUEL N. POSTLETHWAIT
HARVEY D. TELINDE
DAVID D. HUSBAND

Department of Biological Sciences
Purdue University
Lafayette, Indiana

The importance of the faithful transmission of genetic information from cell to cell during the development of a multicellular plant body has been emphasized. The mechanism of mitosis is such that each cell of an organism receives a complement of genetic material equivalent to the initial cell from which it was derived. If the initial cell was a zygote it contained two complete sets of chromosomes - one set from the sperm and one set from the egg. The number of chromosomes per set varies in different species from as low as 2 per set in *Haplopappus* to over 100 per set in certain ferns. If the initial cell was a spore it contained only one set of chromosomes. In the first case there would be at least two genes present in each cell affecting a specific trait and in the latter case there might be only one gene present affecting a specific trait.

The DNA carried in chromosomes appears to exercise its control through a series of sequential steps. It serves as a code for the synthesis of RNA which migrates to the surface of a ribosome. Here proteins are assembled from amino acids according to the RNA pattern. Some proteins are enzymes and, as such, control the synthesis and digestion of the thousands of cellular components. In as much as a differentiated cell is but a reflection of its components, DNA controls the destiny of a cell.

Considering the fact that all cells of an organism receive DNA equivalent to the initial cell from which they were derived, one would expect that differentiation of all the cells would lead inevitably in the same direction. The most casual observation would show that this is not true, for even adjacent cells in an organism may be strikingly different.

How do variations in cell types occur? This is one of the foremost problems in biology. The myriad of factors involved and the role they play are just beginning to be identified. Our study during the next two weeks will help to introduce you to the nature and magnitude of the problem.

No two adjacent cells can be exactly identical and have identical environments. Within the cells there are gradients of substances and each cell has a measure of polarity. As a large number of cells become involved in growth, the availability of certain critical materials may be unevenly distributed. Synthesis would then differ in different cells. Substances diffusing from adjacent cells would create still greater differences. It has been suggested that certain of these diffusing substances may act as suppressors or evocators of DNA functioning so that a portion of a cell's complement of DNA may be inactive at certain stages of development and active at others. Certainly the mechanisms are complicated and the organism as a whole must be considered in the elucidation of this challenging problem.

Plant Growth and Development

FIGURE 3.4—Page 1 of the unit on Growth and Development in the Study Guide.

which has a couple of sets of chromosomes, one from the sperm and one from the egg. Now there are a great many events that take place between this one cell and the multicellular plant body that ultimately produces flowers. We know what the basic steps of growth are—that is, cell division, cell enlargement, cell differentiation, and as indicated in the paragraphs on this page we know several of the activities that take place in an individual cell. I'd like you to stop the tape, and read these paragraphs on page 1 just to remind you of some of the cellular events as a background for this week's study. Pause the tape now and read these paragraphs, please. **Music.**

The student pauses the tape at this point and reads as directed from the study guide already open. He starts the tape again.

Did you notice the last sentence in the last paragraph? "Certainly the mechanisms are complicated, and the organism as a whole must be considered in the elucidation of this challenging problem." Well, this is what we're trying to do this week—to unravel, insofar as we are able, some of these mechanisms. So for this week's work we are going to begin on page 9 and consider the effect of light on growth. Will you turn to page 9 please. **Music.**

The student pauses the tape and turns to page 9 (Fig. 3.5). He starts the tape again.

Aside from light's important role in the production of food (photosynthesis), light has several other effects on growth. As you know, light has three basic attributes, or aspects, which are important. They are, No. 1, quality, No. 2, intensity, and No. 3, duration, or periodicity. I'm sure that you remember that the electro-magnetic radiation spectrum includes radio waves, infrared waves, the visible radiation, ultraviolet, X-rays, gamma rays, and cosmic rays. The visible rays, or the white light, is composed of wavelengths of light from about 400 to 750 microns. When white light is passed through a prism, a spectrum of wavelengths is displayed. It is composed of violet, blue, green, yellow, orange, and red. From our study on photosynthesis, you remember that chlorophyll absorbs the blue and red wavelengths, so that a curve indicating the rate of photosynthesis superimposes pretty well on a curve which indicates the percent of absorption of wavelengths—not quite, but close. You will recall also, that absorption is done by a pigment, chlorophyll. One might say then that chlorophyll is a photoreceptor pigment. Knowing the nature of a pigment and that there are many other compounds in a plant, one might ask if there are some other compounds which behave as pigments and absorb light, and if they affect other physiological reactions in plants other than photosynthesis. In other words, one might hypothesize that light is a factor in the control of some growth events and that pigments other than chlorophyll are involved in absorption of the light. A series of experiments have been set up to enable you to collect some data and make some analysis of these data in relation to the hypothesis just proposed. The first experiment is Exercise 1, and since we are more interested in the data than the manipulation of the experiment, the materials have been set up for you and are available on the central table. Will you turn off the tape player and do Exercise 1 and then return to the tape for further discussion.—**Music.**

The student turns off the tape and collects data (Fig. 3.6) showing a high percentage germination in the light and low in the dark. He fills in the study guide, writes out an analysis, and returns to the tape.

From the data you collected it is obvious that light does affect germination. Something about light impinging on the seeds activated the events of growth, cell division, cell enlargement, and cell differentiation within the young embryo. So our original hypothesis that some events other than photosynthesis are affected by light is reasonable. However, it is possible that the light through photosynthetic activity produced the events of germination. What were your conclusions concerning the first part of our hypothesis—that some pigment other than chlorophyll might be involved in a growth event? You might like to look at the seeds again.—**Music.**

The student might look again or if he is thinking ahead he will have already noted that

PART 3. LIGHT AND GROWTH

Light has three aspects which affect growth - intensity, quality, and periodicity. Some of the effects are subtle and the experimental design to demonstrate them is rather involved and time consuming so you will be asked to make observations on materials previously setup.

Exercise 1   What is the effect of light on germination?
Fifty seeds of Grand Rapids lettuce were placed in each of 2 petri dishes and germinated for 24 hours in the dark. After 24 hours one petri dish (A) was placed in the light and one (B) kept in darkness. Now, approximately 72 hours later, record germination data.

	Petri dish A	Petri dish B
Total seeds		
No. germinated		
% germinated		

Conclusions:

Exercise 2   Do all wave lengths of light affect germination in the same way?
Four petri dishes were set up at the same time and in the same way as in Exercise 1 except all were kept in the light and were covered with colored cellophane as follows: blue cellophane (C); green cellophane (D); red cellophane (E); and blue and red cellophane (F). A was exposed to fluorescent and incandescent light; C, D, and E were exposed to fluorescent light; and F was exposed to incandescent light.

Results:

Petri dish	A	B	C	D	E	F
Total no. of seeds						
No. Germinated						
% germinated						

Conclusions:

FIGURE 3.5—Page 9 of the unit on Growth and Development in the Study Guide.

FIGURE 3.6—Student collecting data from experimental setup.

the seeds did not appear to be green. Most likely he will continue the tape without stopping.

Since the seeds did not appear green until after germination, one might conclude that if chlorophyll is involved, the amount of chlorophyll necessary for activating the germination process is so small that its presence is not detectable with such superficial observations, or that the alternative is true that a pigment other than chlorophyll is involved. Exercise 2 is another experiment designed to give some further information on the hypothesis. Remember the action spectrum of chlorophyll? If chlorophyll is the pigment involved, germination should occur with the exposure to red and blue wavelenths of light. Now, turn off the tape player and do Exercise 2, please.—**Music.**

The student turns off the tape player and collects data from the experiment set up for Exercise 2. He finds a high percentage seed germination in red light but a low percentage in all other test situations. He completes Exercise 2 in the study guide and returns to the tape.

From the data you have collected, one can see that the seeds germinated in red light but not nearly as well in blue light, and the number of seeds germinating in blue light is approximately equal to the number of seeds germinating in darkness. Therefore, the evidence is strongly in favor of a pigment other than chlorophyll being involved. If there is another such pigment, one might ask what are some characteristics of this pigment? Do certain wavelengths of light deactivate or nullify the effect of the red wavelengths of light? Exercise 3, page 10 is designed to provide some information in this regard. Turn off the tape and do Exercise 3.—**Music.**

The student turns off the tape and collects data as directed in Exercise 3 (Fig. 3.7). He finds far-red wavelengths prevented germination even though the seeds were previously exposed to red light. He returns to the tape.

Exercise 3   What is the relationship between the response of inhibiting light wave lengths to the promoting light wave lengths in the germination of lettuce seed?
Four petri dishes were prepared in the same manner as in Exercise 2 and placed in the dark for 24 hours. After 24 hours each was exposed 10 minutes to conditions indicated below and then returned to darkness an additional 48 hours.
Conditions were:
    A - red cellophane followed by red and blue cellophane;
    B - red and blue cellophane followed by red cellophane;
    C - red cellophane;
    D - red and blue cellophane.
Use the results from Exercise 1 as the control.

Results:

Petri dishes	A	B	C	D	Control
Total no. of seeds					
No. germinated					
% germinated					

Conclusions:

Exercise 4   Can certain chemicals overcome the light effect? Study an experiment in which lettuce seeds were placed in the dark and treated with gibberellic acid. Compare these results with results obtained when lettuce seeds were placed in the dark without gibberellic acid in Exercise 1.

Conclusions:

Study an experiment in which lettuce seeds were placed in the light and treated with coumarin. Compare these results with results obtained when lettuce seeds were placed in the light without coumarin in Exercise 1.

Conclusions:

FIGURE 3.7–Page 10 of the unit on Growth and Development in the Study Guide.

From the data obtained with this experiment, it appears that the far-red wavelengths of light which transmitted through the red and blue cellophane can nullify the effects of the red light. In other words, the pigment is affected by both, red, and far-red wavelengths of light. There is indeed another pigment other than chlorophyll that is a receptor of light and influences the event of germination. This pigment is present in plants in such small quantities that it doesn't impart any color to the plant, despite the fact that it is there. Evidence of its existence is the effect that it has on plant activity or growth. This pigment is called phytochrome (phyto, p-h-y-t-o. referring to plant, and chrome, c-h-r-o-m-e, referring to color) has two forms, one form which absorbs red wavelengths of light, that is, wavelengths about 660 mμ, and a second form which absorbs the far-red wavelengths between 710 and 730 mμ. Red light converts the phytochrome to its far-red absorbing form and far-red light converts the phytochrome to its red absorbing form. The presence and action of the far-red absorbing form, in some manner not clearly elucidated yet, sets in motion physiological events which culminate in control of certain growth processes. There are some compounds which are known to affect growth and development, two of which are gibberellic acid and coumarin. The effect of these two compounds on Grand Rapids lettuce seed germination is illustrated by the experiment set up for Exercise 4. Will you turn off the tape player, collect the data, and make your conclusions for Exercise 4, please.—**Music.**

The student turns off the tape player and does Exercise 4 (Fig. 3.8). The data he collects shows gibberellic acid stimulated germination and coumarin inhibited it. He completes the exercise and returns to the tape.

From these data it is clear that the gibberellic acid can in some way substitute for the action induced by red light. It is also clear that certain substances such as coumarin can block this action. Now will you turn to page 165 and 166 in your textbook and study figs. 11-44, 11-45, and 11-46. Pause the tape now please, and read your text.—**Music.**

The student pauses the tape and studies the text to reinforce and elaborate what he has learned from the previous study. He then returns to the tape.

Now will you turn please to pages 8 and 9 in the *Scientific American* article "Light and Development."—**Music.**

FIGURE 3.8—Student collecting data from experimental setup.

The student pauses the tape and finds the appropriate article. He returns to the tape.

In the *Scientific American* article on pages 8 and 9 you will notice that germination was high in those petri dishes receiving a final exposure to red light and low in those petri dishes receiving a final exposure to far-red light. In other words, those seeds exposed to red light will germinate but if the exposure to red light is followed by exposure to far-red, these seeds will not germinate. These exposures may be alternated back and forth and in each case the seeds will respond to the last exposure whether it be red or far-red wavelengths. It is important to note that in some instances certain growth substances such as gibberellins may be substituted and eliminate this light requirement, while coumarin may act as an inhibitor.

Now let us look again at our hypothesis. "There are pigments in plants which affect physiological phenomena in addition to the chlorophyll pigment." The phenomenon affected may be some phenomenon other than photosynthesis. Our answer thus far is "yes, there is another pigment called phytochrome, and a phenomenon germination which is affected by red wavelengths of light and far-red wavelengths of light. One might then hypothesize still further that there are other pigments and other phenomena affected by light."

Earlier in the semester you viewed two films on germination, one on the germination and development of the bean seedling and one on the germination and development of the corn seedling. I'd like you to view these films again and see if you can identify a growth phenomenon affected by light that we have not discussed yet. Will you turn off the tape now please, and view the film.—**Music.**

The student turns off the tape and views the films (Fig. 3.9), then returns to the tape.

To confirm, or modify, the conclusions you made while observing the films concerning growth responses, turn to page 11 in the study guide and do Exercise 5 (Fig. 3.10). Once again we have grown the plants under the conditions required to facilitate and expedite your collection of data. Will you go to the center table and collect data for Exercise 5. Turn off the tape and do this.—**Music.**

FIGURE 3.9—Student viewing a movie at a central location in the learning center. All students view this movie.

The student turns off the tape and collects data from the materials set up for Exercise 5. On completion of the study he returns to the tape.

Now, let us see how keen you were in making observations. Let us consider the bean plant first. The bean plant grown in the dark was taller than the one grown in the light. The bean leaves on the plant grown in the dark were smaller than the leaves on the bean plant grown in the light. The bean plant grown in the dark was yellowish to white, whereas the bean plant grown in the light was green. The top of the bean plant grown in the dark was curved toward the ground, whereas the bean plant grown in the light was erect. Now, consider the corn seedlings grown in the dark versus the corn seedlings grown in the light. Again the plant grown in the dark was yellowish, whereas the one grown in the light was green. The plant grown in the dark had long leaves, whereas the plant grown in the light had shorter leaves.

Which of these phenomena can we account for from our previous study? The formation of chlorophyll is dependent on light—so the green in light and the non-green in dark is likely correlated with the chlorophyll pigment system. Last week we concluded that the tropisms were related to a carotenoid system. We have just learned about the phytochrome system—could it account for any of the other phenomena? The experiment set up for Exercise 6 may give some assistance in identifying which of the phenomena is related to the phytochrome system. Turn off the tape player, please, and make your observations for Exercise 6, answering the questions at the bottom of page 11.–**Music.**

The student turns off the tape player and does Exercise 6. He then returns to the tape.

Now, let's summarize. Plants in light differ from those in darkness in several aspects: (1) formation of chlorophyll in light and little or none in darkness; (2) internodes are short in light, longer in darkness; (3) stems are stiff in light, relatively weak in darkness, suggesting a smaller amount of lignification in darkness; (4) the epicotyl hook unfolds in light, remains curved in darkness; (5) leaves enlarge in light, remain small in darkness; and perhaps there were other differences also but this is sufficient for now. From Exercise 5 it can be seen that seedlings grown in the dark will not produce chlorophyll, and from Exercise 6, one sees that apparently development of chlorophyll in young seedlings occurs either in red light, blue light, or white light. The opening of the epicotyl hook and the expansion of leaves are controlled by red light. If the seedling is grown in blue light or darkness, the leaves do not expand, and the epycotyl hook does not elongate or straighten out, so these aspects of the growth of the seedling are controlled by the red or far-red reaction (the phytochrome system). Now, if you have understood the study so far, you should be able to do problems 21-1, 21-2, 21-3 in Murray's Problem Manual. Will you pause the tape now and do those problems, please.–**Music.**

The student pauses the tape player and does the problems indicated (Fig. 3.11). He requests assistance if necessary from the instructor or another student. (If he wishes, he can repeat any of the preceding study.) He then returns to the tape.

Now turn to page 13 in your study guide. (Fig. 3.12)

The student might do this without stopping the tape player.

For the next few minutes I would like to talk to you about another growth process which is under the control of light. You may wish to take some notes on this discussion. This growth process is one which involves the change of the apical meristem from the production of vegetative parts (leaves and stems) to the production of floral organs. This change is under the control of quality and duration of light (periodicity). The phenomenon has been referred to as photoperiodism and it too involves the pigment phytochrome.

Photoperiodism was first discovered by Garner and Allard of the U. S. Department of Agriculture back about 1918 or 1919. These two gentlemen were studying various kinds of tobacco

How many pigment systems can you identify which are involved in plant responses?

Exercise 5   One group of seedlings has been grown in light and one group grown in darkness during the past 20 days.   List the differences you can observe between the two groups.

Light	Dark

Exercise 6   Are all wave lengths of light effective in preventing etiolation? Three groups of seedlings were grown as in Exercise 5 except they were exposed to: A - red light, B - blue light, and C - far-red (this quality of light is obtained by using blue and red cellophane in combination).   Use the plants from Exercise 5 as controls.   What was the effect of the different light quality?

Seedlings A	Seedlings B	Seedlings C

Which wave lengths allowed expansion of leaves? _____;
straightening of the hypocotyl hook?_____;
and elongation of the hypocotyl?_____ .

What pigments were involved in hypocotyl elongation?_____;
straightening of the hypocotyl hook?_____;
expanding of leaves?_____; and food synthesis?
_____.

FIGURE 3.10–Page 11 of the unit on Growth and Development in the Study Guide.

21-1. The descriptions of 3 seedlings are given below. Determine what color of light each plant was grown under. Consider only the following 3 colors: red, blue, and green.

_____ (A) Green, elongated hypocotyl, unopened epicotyl or hypocotyl hook, unexpanded leaves, abnormal internode growth, no anthocyanin.

_____ (B) Green, short (normal) hypocotyl, opened epicotyl or hypocotyl hook, expanded leaves, normal internode growth, anthocyanin present.

_____ (C) Yellow, elongated hypocotyl, unopened epicotyl or hypocotyl hook, unexpanded leaves, abnormal internode growth, no anthocyanin.

_____ (D) Which of the above descriptions also describes a plant grown in the dark or in far-red light?

21-2. In each of the comparisons below, check (√) the item (1 or 2) that is greater.

(A) ____(1) The amount of red absorbing phytochrome in a bean plant at sunrise.
    ____(2) The amount of red absorbing phytochrome in a bean plant at sunset.

(B) ____(1) The amount of far-red absorbing phytochrome in an etiolated pea plant.
    ____(2) The amount of far-red absorbing phytochrome in a pea plant grown under continuous red light.

(C) ____(1) The amount of far-red absorbing phytochrome in a lettuce seed after 30 minutes exposure to red light.
    ____(2) The amount of far-red absorbing phytochrome in a lettuce seed after 30 minutes exposure to far-red light.

21-3. (A) Plot the absorption spectrum for phytochrome. Plot the action spectrum for the promotion of hypocotyl unhooking and the action spectrum for the inhibition of hypocotyl unhooking.

(B) What color is phytochrome?_____ The phytochrome molecule has 2 parts - a pigment and a protein.

(C) What function might the protein part serve? _____

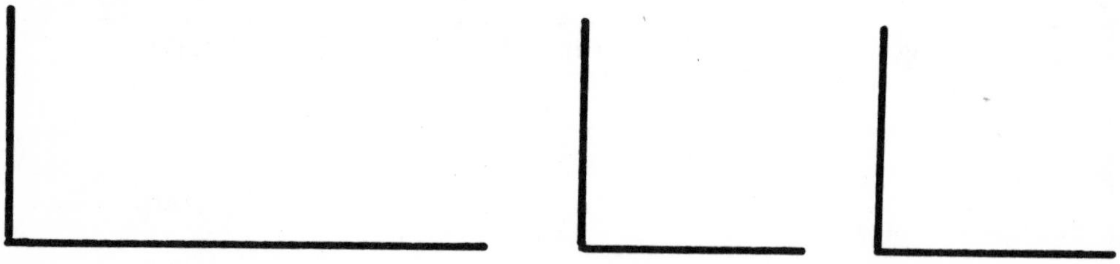

FIGURE 3.11–Problems from Murray's Problem Manual. These problems are used by the students to check their progress.

PART 4. **PHOTOPERIOD AND TEMPERATURE**

The change in the product of a meristem from leaves to flowers is influenced by age, exposure to dark and light periods, and temperature.

Species react differently to the same condition. Plants have been categorized as *long day, short day,* or *day neutral,* depending on their response to certain *critical periods* of light and darkness. The names applied to the categories are somewhat misleading for the length of dark period may be more critical than the light period and the critical period is not always less or greater than 12 hours as implied by the term short day and long day. Study the plant responses in the diagrams below:

V - vegetative
F - flowering
↓ - critical period

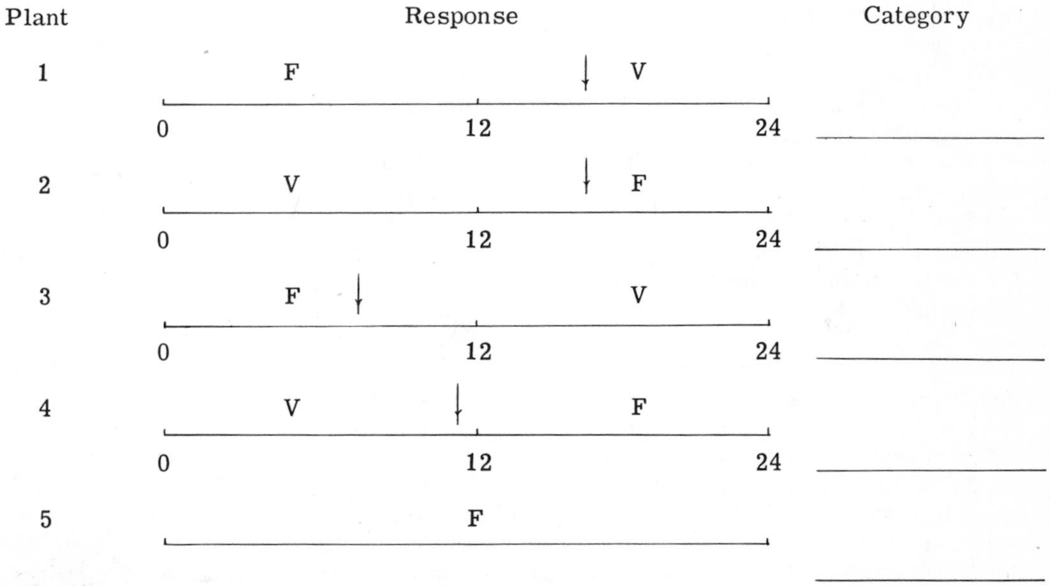

Plant	Response	Category

Plant 1

F   ↓   V

0   12   24   _____

Plant 2

V   ↓   F

0   12   24   _____

Plant 3

F   ↓   V

0   12   24   _____

Plant 4

V   ↓   F

0   12   24   _____

Plant 5

F

    _____

Exercise 1   What is the photoperiod of Guar?
This plant is a legume which is sensitive to temperature and photoperiod. On the next page is a photograph of Guar plants grown under several combinations of photoperiod and temperature. Study the table and the pictures.
What conclusions can you make concerning the response of Guar to photoperiod and temperature?

FIGURE 3.12—Page 13 of the unit on Growth and Development in the Study Guide.

and were attempting to cross two particular varieties. One came into bloom in the summertime and the other came into bloom in the wintertime. In order to determine what factors were affecting or controlling the flowering of these two plants, they extended the light period on the one and found that if they gave it a long day-length it would flower, whereas the other tobacco variety required a short day-length to flower. They were intrigued by this aspect of growth and did an extensive investigation of several plants. They found that plants fall into certain categories based on their response to photoperiod, or day-length. They found three major categories: (1) plants which flower when exposed to a series of short days and long nights; (2) those which flower when exposed to a series of long days and short nights; (3) those which flower whether the day and night lengths are long or short.

Immediately after they reported their discovery many people began to check plants and investigate this phenomena. Even today we are not really clear on exactly what happens. Apparently a growth substance and the pigment phytochrome are involved. It appears that the length of night may be more important than the length of day. In any event, a 24-hour rhythm is involved and flowering is dependent on some threshold or critical length of exposure to darkness under which or over which plants will respond in a specific way. The amount of exposure, once the critical period has been reached, does not have much effect on the response. Bryophyllum requires a 12-hour day or less (at least 12 hours of night), chrysanthemum and cocklebur require a 15-hour day or less (at least 9 hours of night), yet all are listed as short-day plants. Most plants classified as long-day will flower with a very short night but some long-day plants will flower over a wide range of dark periods from 0 to over 12 hours (the dill for example, and Italian rye grass). The number of hours involved in the day is not the critical aspect of photoperiod. In order for us to understand this better, consider the diagrams on page 13.

The symbols to be used are V for vegetative (plants which are not producing flowers), F for flowering (plants which are producing flowers), and an arrow for a critical period.

Consider the symbols of plant 1. The black line represents a time range from 0-24 hours. The critical period arrow is placed at 15 hours. Now notice—if the plant were exposed to a day length of any duration from 0-15 hours the plant would flower. For example, if the plant 1 was exposed to a photoperiod of 4 hours light and 20 hours dark, it flowered; 6 hours light and 18 hours dark, it flowered, 10 hours light and 14 hours dark, it flowered, 15 hours light and 9 hours dark, it flowered—but at 16 or more hours light and 8 or less hours dark it remained vegetative. To say it another way, this plant flowered with any dark period greater than 9 hours (on the scale of a 24-hour day this would be any light period less than 15 hours, the critical period). Since the plant flowers at any day length shorter than the critical period it is considered a short-day plant.

Notice for plant 2, the critical period is the same as for plant 1 but it flowers only if the day is longer than 15 hours. Plant 2 produces flowers when exposed to day lengths longer than the critical period, i.e., night lengths of nine hours or less. Therefore, it is classified as a long-day plant. Plant 3 flowers when the day length is shorter than the critical period, therefore it is a short-day plant. Plant 4 is a long-day plant, and plant 5 is a day-neutral plant.

In summary, long-day plants require a day length greater than some critical period for flowering, whereas the plant which we consider to be short-day (or which fits into the category of short days) is one which requires a day length less than some critical period to initiate flowering. Day-neutral plants do not require any particular day length but flower in any day length. Actually, the length of the dark period is the important factor and day length is just a necessary corollary within the 24-hour period. In many cases a short flash of light will accommodate the light requirement. Read your text, pages 159-165, and the *Scientific American* article "Light and Plant Development," pages 2-5.—**Music.**

The student turns off the tape player and does these readings. On completion he returns to the tape.

A limiting factor in the flowering of all plants, of course, is the age of the plant, and many plants need to grow to a point where they are beyond some juvenile stage before flowering may occur. Apparently the photoperiod has much to do with this juvenility.

Cocklebur is a short-day plant. If it receives a day length greater than some critical period (the critical period being 15 hours) it will not flower but remains vegetative. If the cocklebur plant is placed under short-day conditions but the long night is interrupted very briefly with light, this interruption will result in vegetative development, so that really the cocklebur responds to the length of night rather than the length of day. Even a low intensity of light causes the cocklebur to remain vegetative so long as this is extended past the critical period. If a cocklebur plant is placed under short-day conditions for only one day and one night and then is removed to long-day conditions, it will flower. Only one leaf needs to be exposed to the day length inducing conditions of short days for the entire plant to flower. If a plant has been induced to flower under short-day conditions and this plant is grafted to another cocklebur plant which has been under long-day conditions, both plants will flower. This strongly suggests then that there must be some substance produced under the daylight or under the dark conditions which is dependent on these conditions for development, and this substance is transmissible from one plant to another or from the leaf to the apex. A substance which functions in this way we call a hormone. This hormone must be a flowering hormone (florigen). Do problem 22-1 in Murray's manual, please.—**Music.**

The student pauses the tape player and does the problem (Fig. 3.13). Again he obtains assistance if necessary. He then returns to the tape.

If you are still uncertain about photoperiod, study your text, Figs. 11-38. Guar plants have been grown under certain photoperiod and temperature regimes for your study. Do exercises 1 and 2, pages 13, 14, and 15. (Fig. 3.14 and 3.15)

The student turns off the tape and applies the information just learned to a group of plants exposed to a series of photoperiods and temperatures (Fig. 3.16). On completion he returns to the tape.

These plants were grown in controlled climate facilities. In a controlled climate chamber there are various compartments which are separated based on temperature control and photoperiod control. There are a series of compartments in which the temperature is maintained at 60 degrees F, 70 degrees F, and 80 degrees F. These compartments of controlled temperature are further subdivided for control of photoperiods of 8 hours, 12 hours, 16 hours, 20 hours day lengths. The response of plants to temperature and photoperiod regimes is tested by growing plants of a given species under all of these conditions. The photograph on page 15 in the study guide is of guar plants grown under these conditions. Data collected on these plants are shown in the table on page 14. Guar flowered under 8 hour and 12 hour photoperiods, but not at 16 and 20 hour photoperiods, therefore it is a short-day plant. No flowers were produced under 60 degree temperature—the plant scarcely grew at all. Flowering was earlier in the 80 degree temperature by three weeks than in the 70 degree temperature, but flowering eventually occurred in both of these temperatures. There is little or no correlation of flowering to the size of the plants except in the extreme cold. Apparently then these two factors, light and temperature, may affect the production of flowers and some other morphological developments as well.

A low temperature preconditioning of soaked seeds has an interesting effect on growth of certain plants. This has been used especially in connection with the growth of winter wheat. This process has been called vernalization. It hasn't been used much with the growth of wheat in the United States, but it has been useful in Russia where the temperature of certain wheat-growing areas in the winter is so low that it would freeze out winter wheat. By subjecting the soaked seed to low temperature for certain periods of time, then taking the seeds, drying them and planting them in the early spring, the winter wheat will grow very much comparable to spring wheat. Spring wheat, as you know, will complete its life cycle during a single spring and summer season, producing a crop of wheat. But winter wheat planted in the springtime is not exposed to cold (nonvernalized) and will not produce a good crop of wheat during the one season. Winter wheat is planted in the fall. Having been planted in the fall, the young seedlings growing in the wintertime are exposed to low temperatures which affect the growing point. When the winter wheat is planted in the spring (not

22-1. The following facts have been experimentally established with regard to the flowering of cocklebur plants:

(A) Plants kept on 16-hour days (i.e., 16 hours light, 8 hours dark) will grow indefinitely without flowering.

(B) If an intact plant, previously grown on 16-hour days, is placed in the dark for one 12-hour period, it will flower, regardless of the day-length to which it is subsequently exposed.

(C) If the 12-hour dark period (in B above) is interrupted for 10 minutes by light from a 25-watt bulb in the middle of the dark period, the plant will not flower.

(D) If all the leaves but one are removed from a plant, and it is given a 12-hour dark period, the plant will flower.

(E) If the blade of a single leaf is covered with dark paper for 12 hours, while the rest of the plant is exposed to light, the plant will flower.

(F) If a plant which has had at least one 12-hour dark period is grafted to a plant which has had 16-hour days, and the two plants are thereafter kept on 16-hour days, both plants will flower.

(G) A short-day plant growing under its optimum photoperiod can induce a long-day plant growing under short days to flower, if the two plants are grafted together.

(H) Young plants cannot usually be induced to flower.

Explain the above facts.

FIGURE 3.13—Problem 22-1 in Murray's Problem Manual.

Table of Data on Guar Response to Photoperiod and Temperature

	Plant Height After				Plants Flowering After				Pods Set After	
	3 wks.	6 wks.	9 wks.	12 wks.	3 wks.	6 wks.	9 wks.	12 wks.	6 wks.	12 wks.
8 hr. photoperiod 60°F	1.2cm	-	-	-	-	-	-	-	-	-
8 hr. " 70°F	2.9cm	3.9cm	4.7cm	5.6cm	-	+	+	+	-	-
8 hr. " 80°F	7.0cm	9.1cm	12.2cm	15.2cm	+	+	+	+	-	+
12 hr. " 60°F	1.2cm	-	-	-	-	-	-	-	-	-
12 hr. " 70°F	2.6cm	3.5cm	5.0cm	8.0cm	-	+	+	+	-	-
12 hr. " 80°F	6.4cm	12.2cm	25.4cm	39.1cm	+	+	+	+	-	+
16 hr. " 60°F	1.1cm	-	-	-	-	-	-	-	-	-
16 hr. " 70°F	2.3cm	3.0cm	5.4cm	11.3cm	-	-	-	-	-	-
16 hr. " 80°F	4.5cm	10.9cm	30.9cm	51.0cm	-	-	-	-	-	-
20 hr. " 60°F	1.4cm	-	-	-	-	-	-	-	-	-
20 hr. " 70°F	2.6cm	3.1cm	6.5cm	13.2cm	-	-	-	-	-	-
20 hr. " 80°F	4.4cm	10.1cm	24.0cm	55.6cm	-	-	-	-	-	-

Exercise 2   Study demonstrations of photoperiod and temperature effects on other plants.   Write a brief summary of these effects.

FIGURE 3.14–Page 14 of the unit on Growth and Development in the Study Guide.

FIGURE 3.15—Page 15 of the unit on Growth and Development in the Study Guide.

FIGURE 3.16—Student studies plants which have been exposed to a series of photoperiod and temperature regimes.

having received this low temperature) the growing point does not receive the vernalizing effect, few or no flowers are initiated, and a poor crop is produced. This low temperature received normally by seedlings growing in the winter is substituted for by the low temperature treatment to the seeds.

Read your text pages 161-162 and do problems in Murray's Study Problems, 22-5, 22-6, and 23-1. (Fig. 3.17)—**Music**

The student pauses the tape and studies as indicated. He then returns to the tape.

The last phenomenon to which I would like to call your attention is endogenous rhythms in plants. Apparently some of the actions of a plant are set in motion by the rhythm of its environment, that is, the diurnal cycles of the day, a lunar cycle of 29½ days, or the yearly cycles or seasons. Once these rhythms are established within the plant they continue without the influence of the external environment. These reactions are called endogenous rhythms. An example of this is in Dictodia, a brown alga which produces eggs and sperms once a month in phase with the lunar tidal period. Another example is the ordinary bean plant which opens and folds its leaves daily. Apparently once this action has been initiated by light, the rhythm is established and it does this without regard to the stimulus of light, at least for a time. Study the time lapse film which illustrates this phenomenon and read your text, pages 163-164.—**Music.**

The student views a film (Fig. 3.18) which shows several examples of nastic movements and reads his text. He then returns to the tape.

Perhaps much more could be said concerning the effects of light and temperature on plant growth and development; however, the study you have just completed will suffice as an introduction to this exciting area of plant science. I hope that you have found this study interesting and will be able to use your knowledge to understand some of the everyday phenomena you observe in plant growth. This is all for this tape.—**Music.**

The student then restores the booth to its original condition ready for the next student, removes his card from the booth assignment file, writes the time in the

22-5. Day length data for 3 latitudes in the northern hemisphere:

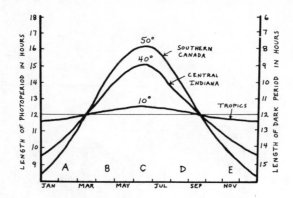

(A) Match the following with the zones shown above for a plant growing in Indiana.

_____(1) dormancy   ZONE
_____(2) dormancy induced   A
_____(3) seed germination   B
_____(4) short-day plants flower   C
_____(5) long-day plants flower   D
_____(6) beginning of vegetative growth   E

(B) Assume that plants X and Y will grow in the tropics. Plant X is a long-day plant from central Indiana with a critical period of 14 hours. Plant Y is a short-day plant from central Indiana with a critical period of 14 hours. Will the plants flower (+) or not (-)?

_____(1) Plant X is transplanted to the tropics.
_____(2) Plant Y is transplanted to the tropics.

(C) Criticize or defend the following statement: The critical day length for a short-day plant may be <u>longer</u> than the critical day length for a long-day plant.

22-6. Annual henbane flowers in the same season in which it is sown, while biennial henbane produces only vegetative growth during the first year and flowers the second year. Look at the data below. V = vegetative. F = flowers produced. The results were obtained at the end of the first year of growth. Explain the data in the table.

Growing Conditions→	Not subjected to cold		Subjected to cold		Not subjected to cold. Treated with gibberellin.	
	Short Days	Long Days	Short Days	Long Days	Short Days	Long Days
Annual	V	F	V	F	F	F
Biennial	V	V	V	F	F	F

23-1.

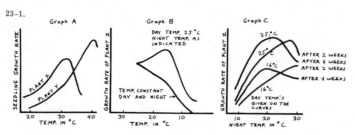

GRAPH   QUESTIONS

A   Why does the growth rate first increase and then decrease with increasing temperature? What are the minimum, maximum, and optimum temperatures for the growth of plant X? _____ _____ _____

B   Under what temperatures would you raise plant Z for best growth? _____

   Formulate a general rule for plant growth using graph B.

C   Formulate a general rule for plant growth using graph C. When trying to determine whether a plant will grow well in a certain geographical area, what aspects of temperature and plant growth should you consider?

FIGURE 3.17—Problems 22-5, 22-6, and 23-1 from Murray's Problem Manual.

FIGURE 3.18—Student viewing film.

appropriate space, files his learning center card, and leaves the learning center. Naturally, he is free to discuss any of his study further with fellow students or instructors before leaving and he can come back at any time to review, do a simulated oral quiz, or study in any way he sees fit. His study may be broken into time blocks to suit his personal schedule, talents, and state of mind. He can take brief breaks for coffee or visiting at his discretion. His home study also is at his own volition and to the extent of his own interest. The only limitation is the student's desire and capacity.

GENERAL ASSEMBLY SESSION (GAS)

Contrary to the usual practice of optional attendance, it is expected that all students will be present for the general assembly session accompanying this unit of study. A guest lecturer discusses his research on naturally occurring root-inducing compounds and shows a documentary film of his work. This detailed account is meant to reinforce the pattern of thinking which served as a basis for the presentation of many of the laboratory experiments in the independent study session and to expose the students to some new techniques which are not feasible for inclusion in a general course. Several students can identify with the project because of the similarity of some aspects of the research to the research they are doing for their own problem 2 project. One or two questions covering the content of this general assembly session are usually included in the quiz.

INTEGRATED QUIZ SESSION (IQS)

The student is scheduled for an IQS on the Thursday or Monday following the study activities previously described in the ISS. The eight students in the IQS meet around a seminar table and take part in an oral discussion-quiz, moderated by the IQS instructor (Fig. 3.19). Following the oral quiz, the students move to another table in the room and take a written quiz.

The oral quiz might proceed as follows: (Assume an instructor and eight students seated around a table. On the table are the various items that have been included in the independent study the preceding week).

Instructor: Will someone correlate the week's study within the total semester's study, please? Ron.

Student: We are currently studying Calvin's second attribute of life, namely reproduction at a cellular level. We are specifically concerned with how a single cell develops into a mature plant body and how external factors such as light and temperature influence the destiny of the cell within the plant body.

Instructor: Do any of the rest of you have additional comments?

Student: We are specifically concerned with light quality, periodicity, and with temperature influences on growth.

Instructor: Thank you. Now let us begin our oral quizzes. John, will you take the first two petri dishes?

Student: Yes. These two petri dishes contain lettuce seed germinated under two different conditions. They relate to objective No. 1 which states "Be able to discuss the effect of light on germination of Grand Rapid lettuce seed describing specifically how the experiment was set up, a statement of the hypothesis it was attempting to clarify, and state justifiable conclusions." This experiment was set up to test the hypothesis that

FIGURE 3.19—Students taking oral quiz in IQS.

pigments other than chlorophyll may serve as photoreceptors and that a phenomenon other than photosynthesis may be influenced by light. The experiment involved 100 dry Grand Rapid lettuce seeds which were divided into two lots; 50 were placed in a petri dish and exposed to light, and the other 50 seeds were placed in the dark, all under comparable temperatures. Of the 50 seeds placed in the light there was 90% germination and of the seeds placed in the dark there was 8% germination. It is reasonable to assume that the difference in germination was due to the one factor, light. Therefore one may conclude that light is necessary for the germination of Grand Rapid lettuce seeds, which supports the hypothesis that a phenomenon other than photosynthesis might be affected by light.

Instructor: John, your grade is 9 for that discussion. Are there other comments? Yes, Betty?

Student: The experiment is not conclusive. It could be that the seeds contained a small amount of chlorophyll, but enough so that the light induced a small measure of photosynthesis, the end product of which was necessary to induce germination.

Instructor: Right, Betty. Any other comments? Joe?

Student: The pigment, chlorophyll, could be operating in controlling two phenomena, photosynthesis and germination, but by separate mechanisms.

Instructor: Possible, Joe, but our experiment doesn't help with this, does it? Perhaps the next experiment will help. Now, shall we move to the next item? Karen, will you take these items, please?

Student: These are four petri dishes in which Grand Rapid lettuce seed germination has been tested in a little more refined way. These relate to objective No. 2 which states "Be able to discuss the results of the experiment in Exercise 2 page 9 in the study guide and relate them to the hypothesis in Exercise 1." This experiment was set up comparable to the one we just discussed except the petri dishs were covered with colored cellophane and kept in the light for the duration of the experiment. One petri dish was covered with blue cellophane and one with green cellophane, one with red cellophane, and one with blue and red cellophane. Germination in the petri dish with blue cellophane was around 20 percent, with the green nearly 30 percent, with the red 80 some percent, and with the blue and red cellophane less than 10 percent. I don't remember that figure. Those seeds receiving red light germinated nearly as well as those in plain light so it could be concluded that it is the red wavelengths of light which are affecting germination.

Instructor: What about the blue light?

Student: Seeds did not germinate well in blue light. I'm not sure what that means.

Instructor: All right, Karen, that was a fair answer, your grade is 7. Do any of the rest of you have any additional information or comments? Yes, Dick?

Student: We learned earlier that chlorophyll absorbs red and blue light and since there was relatively little germination in blue light, but high percentage in red light, it seems reasonable to conclude that the germination phenomenon is not related to photosynthesis and absorption by chlorophyll, for if it were, there should have been germination in blue light also. Therefore one could reason that the original hypothesis is correct—that there are certain phenomena that are affected by light other than photosynthesis and that some other pigment than chlorophyll is involved.

Instructor: Thank you, Dick. That is fine. Now, Joe, will you take these four petri dishes, please?

The integrated quiz session would continue in this fashion until all students had had an opportunity to discuss one or more items and until the half hour was nearly exhausted. Just before the end of the period the instructor would interrupt as follows:

Instructor: Sorry, we cannot continue, our time is gone. John, I'll bring your grade up to a 10 for your additional contribution. Karen, your grade remains 7, Betty, your grade . . . etc.

After the grades have all been corrected, the students would then be handed their written quiz and would be asked to go to a different table to write the exam. Since there are multiple sections, there would be various versions of the quiz. One version is included below to indicate something of its content (Fig. 3.20). A specific question concerning the *Scientific American* article is written on the board or given orally to the group for those who read the article and who wish to demonstrate this by answering the question for two bonus points. When the student has completed his written quiz, he turns it in, and is free to leave, thus completing the week's work. The student will be examined over this subject matter again on the final examination.

OTHER ACTIVITIES

Running concurrently with the student's study in the independent study session, the general assembly session, and the integrated quiz session, the student may have under way one or two special research projects. In the early part of the semester this project will be problem No. 1, and usually involves an investigation of some aspect of growth. The nature of one such problem is indicated by the mimeograph handout which is included as Appendix D. Later in the semester the students who anticipate making an "A" grade in the course will be doing a second research project. These projects range from relatively simple experiments to fairly complex ones depending on the capabilities and interests of the individual student. The mimeographed handouts which are given the students planning to do problem 2 are included as Appendix D and an example of a student's problem has been included to give some idea of the nature of this project.

In summary, in this chapter an attempt has been made to provide the reader an opportunity to see some of the details of the student study program. Obviously, it is impossible to expose the reader to those activities which cannot be written or simulated through photographs, and since one particular week of study was selected, some of the kinds of activities that might be included in other subject matter, such as field trips, setting up of experiments, microscope study, etc., necessarily were omitted. The reader should not be misled by this but should realize that all activities normally included in a conventional course can be programmed under the Audio-Tutorial system. It should be noted further that the subject matter content of a course changes from semester to semester and the entire program is constantly revised both in content and method.

BIOLOGY 108   IQS WRITTEN QUIZ WEEK 11   FORM 1

NAME _____
              Last   First   Middle

IQS: Mon.   Tues.   Sec. A   Sec. B   (Circle 2)

TIME: _____   INSTRUCTOR: _____

In each of the questions pick the correct answer.

_____ 1. The pigment phytochrome absorbs mostly in the region of:
          a. 450 mP.
          b. 660 mP.
          c. 730 mP.
          d. Two of the above.
          e. All of the above.

_____ 2. Diurnal rhythms occur in:
          a. Bean plant leaves.
          b. Cocklebur flowering.
          c. Dictodia production of eggs.
          d. Two of the above.
          e. None of the above.

_____ 3. A Mung bean seedling is green, has a short hypocotyl, opened hypocotyl hook, expanded
          leaves, short internodes, and has anthocyanin in its hypocotyl. This plant must have been
          grown under:
          a. Green light.   d. Two of the above are correct.
          b. Blue light.   e. All of the above are correct.
          c. Red light.

_____ 4. Lettuce seeds were given the following treatments, then placed in the dark. Which treat-
          ments will yield a high % of germination?
          a. Red light - 24 hours in the dark - far-red light.
          b. Red light - far-red light - white light - blue light.
          c. Red light - far-red light - gibberellin.
          d. Two of the above are correct.
          e. All of the above are correct.

_____ 5.

Seed X		unwashed	washed	washed + gibberell'n	washed + coumarin
	dark	-	-	+	-
	light	-	+	+	-

          Look at the seed germination data in the table.
          a. Seed X is not light sensitive.
          b. Seed X probably contains a water-soluble germination inhibitor.
          c. Coumarin inhibits the germination of seed X.
          d. Seed X is sensitive to gibberellin.
          e. Two of the above are correct.

FIGURE 3.20—One version of a 20-point written quiz given in the IQS.

_____ 6. Tomato seeds removed from fresh fruits and placed on moist filter paper will germinate in the light or dark, however far-red light will inhibit their germination. This far-red inhibition is reversed by red lihgt. From this information one may tentatively conclude that:
  a. Tomato seeds contain phytochrome.
  b. Light sensitivity in tomato seeds may be induced by treatment with red light.
  c. Tomato seeds are probably treated with far-red light before seed companies package them.
  d. Most of the phytochrome in a seed taken from a fresh tomato fruit is in the P660 form.

_____ 7. Plant X is a short day plant with a critical light period of 12 hours. Plant X is old enough to flower, if treated properly. Three samples of plant X are treated. Which ones will flower?
  a. Those put on a daylength regime of 14 hours of light and 10 hours of darkness.
  b. Those put on a daylength regime of 10 hours of light and 14 hours of darkness.
  c. Those put on a daylength regime of 8 hours of light and 16 hours of darkness, however, the dark period is interrupted in the middle by a bright 10 minute flash of light.
  d. Two of the above will flower.
  e. All of the above will flower.

plants flowering after	8 hours light			12 hours light			16 hours light		
	60°F	70°F	80°F	60°F	70°F	80°F	60°F	70°F	80°F
3 weeks	-	-	+	-	-	+	-	-	-
6 weeks	-	+	+	-	+	+	-	-	-

_____ 8. Look at the above data for plant X.
  a. Plant X is a long-day plant.
  b. Plant X flowers sooner at 80° than at 70°F.
  c. The critical light period for flowering in plant X is 12 hours.
  d. Two of the above are correct.
  e. All of the above are correct.

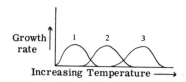

_____ 9. Look at the above graph.
  a. Plant 1 would not grow naturaliy in a geographic area which is optimum for the growth of plant 3.
  b. Plants 1 and 2 might grow together naturally in certain geographic areas.
  c. Plants 1, 2, 3 might conceivably represent plants which grow in Canada, Indiana, and Alabama, respectively.
  d. Two of the above are correct.
  e. None of the above are correct.

_____ 10. A certain midwest crop plant is a long-day biennial with a critical light period of 15 hours. A biennial produces only vegetative growth the first year, and flowers the second (after having gone through a cold winter). Assume that the plant can be grown in the tropics. Some of its seed is taken to the tropics and planted outdoors.
  a. The plants will produce vegetative growth the first year and flowers the second year.
  b. If the seeds are pretreated with cold before planting, the plants will produce flowers.
  c. The plants will flower only if grown in a special controlled climate room under the proper conditions.
  d. Two of the above are correct.
  e. None of the above are correct.

_____ Oral Quiz Score (10 pts.)
_____ Written Quiz Score (20 pts.)
_____ Scientific American Bonus "Light and Plant Development" (2 pts.)
_____ Total Score for Week 11 (30 pts. or 32 pts. with the bonus)

FIGURE 3.20—One version of a 20-point written quiz given in the IQS.

Chapter IV

PHYSICAL FACILITIES

This chapter is a description of the physical facilities used in a botany course at Purdue University, taught by the Audio-Tutorial system. It includes some suggestions for possible alternatives and a presentation of some of the rationale for the materials used. In view of the rapidly changing technology it is important to maintain utmost flexibility in the design of any educational facility. The number of fixed and permanent installations should be minimized and the maximum potential should be retained for alteration and rearrangement of furniture and equipment. The basic requirements for the Audio-Tutorial system are: the *learning center; a prep room; a small assembly room; a general assembly hall;* and *other facilities* used on special occasions.

THE LEARNING CENTER

The learning center currently used for the botany course was converted from an ordinary laboratory. Originally, the laboratory was designed to serve up to 36 students. It had the typical arrangement of three rows of tables running parallel to the length of the room. At the front of the room was a demonstration table behind which was a blackboard. All tables were equipped in the conventional fashion with four gas outlets and four electrical outlets per table. The demonstration table was equipped with a sink at either end and with the usual storage cabinets underneath. This original arrangement of demonstration tables created needless traffic problems and restricted the kinds of activities which could be accomplished in the independent study session. These tables were detached from the floor and from each other to permit a total rearrangement of the room. The front demonstration table was permanently removed except for one section containing a sink and a source of water.

This room, now rearranged with 32 booths, serves 600 or more students effectively. Currently, booths are distributed around the periphery of the room and a table for experiments and demonstrations is located in the center of the room (Fig. 4.1). The advantages of this arrangement are: (1) the easy access of the center table to and from any of the booths; (2) the opportunity for the independent study instructor to keep the entire room under surveillance and to respond quickly to the students' needs; (3) effective utilization of both sides of the center table; and (4) the possibility of setting up materials in a sequential series around these tables.

Perhaps other room arrangements might be more effective for other types of subject matter. Various booth configurations are now available. In any event one should consider the efficiency of traffic flow as well as the accomplishment of defined objectives in the organization of the room. This is facilitated when booths and other equipment are detached and can be rearranged as the occasion demands.

FIGURE 4.1–Current arrangement of booths and central table in the learning center.

Rooms without windows are especially good because wall space can be used for the location of booths and storage cabinets and for hanging pictures and murals to improve the decor of the learning center. The entry to the room should be confined to one door primarily to control the flow of traffic in and out of the room. Rooms should be air conditioned and structured so that the general noise level is low. Where feasible, carpeted floors would assist in helping reduce sound reverberations.

1. The Check-in Check-out Area and Bulletin Board

The check-in, check-out facilities are made as attractive as possible but are designed to expedite the flow of traffic in and out of the learning center (Fig. 4.2). Each student has his own 5 X 7 time card filed with others in his section of the general assembly session. His card is filed alphabetically only to the extent that it is placed with the group of cards behind a divider marked with the letter corresponding with the first letter of his last name. A clock is clearly visible from the check-in area. The time card has spaces for entering the date, booth number, time in and time out. Four spaces for each of these categories per week are enough to accommodate most students (Appendix B). A 35 mm photograph of the student is taped to the card to assist the instructor in recognizing the student by name. The booth assignment device is a series of slots in a specially structured box with each slot numbered to correspond to a booth (Fig. 4.2). The file is so constructed that the numbers and cards are clearly visible and this facilitates the quick location of an available booth. Table space is available at the check-in center for the student to temporarily deposit books while making entries on the card.

Since all students pass through the check-in area, it is an excellent location for critical announcements and messages. A bulletin board is provided for this purpose with appropriate signs to encourage examination of the announcements carefully. Among

FIGURE 4.2—The check-in area located at the entrance to the learning center. Moving from left to right, the following items can be seen on the table: booth assignment file, alphabetical card file, calendar, card file for outside visitors to our learning center, suggestion box, and note paper.

these signs are the perennial type reminders such as "Refile your card, please," or "Can't find your card? Solution—(1) Look under the letter before or after your letter section; (2) Look in the back of the box; (3) Look through all the cards; (4) If none of these work, see your ISS instructor who will help you fill out a new card." A Suggestion Box labeled "The Student's Voice" and note paper are made available in this area for student comment. Near the check-in area is a good location for special handout sheets such as objectives, and other material which may need to be distributed to the students. Messages for specific students often are attached to the student's record card in the file. In general, an attempt is made to keep this area attractive by the addition of decorative items. An aquarium and terrarium are appropriate for this purpose.

2. Booths

The booths in use at Purdue were specially designed and constructed for use in Audio-Tutorial centers by Burgess Publishing Company, Minneapolis, Minnesota. Each student station provides table space 42 inches wide by 20 inches deep. The height of the partitions is 24 inches (Fig. 4.3). The booth provides the student with some degree of privacy during the study interval. In addition, it is easily moved for regrouping to serve different kinds of subject matter.

There are several features which are helpful in the booth design. Pegboard areas

FIGURE 4.3–Students studying in a typical A-T learning center.

within the booth permit the flexibility of display of materials to accommodate the nature of the week's work. The student electronics (Audio-Tutorial System Model SC-1) are recessed into a panel at the rear of the student station so that the table area remains clear. This will provide writing space and a place for books, equipment, and other materials to be used in connection with the lesson. Shelf space is provided for the storage of the student's extra books and to provide space for the occasional items needed for a specific study. Two electrical outlets are supplied at each station for equipment other than the tape recorder. Individual projectors and supplemental lighting may be added if desired. A comfortable chair should be provided and it is helpful if it is on castors comparable to a secretary's chair.

The number of booths required for a course depends on several factors. Currently 32 booths in a learning center which is open from 7:30 in the morning to 10:30 at night Monday through Friday are adequate to serve 600 students for 4 hours of conventional study equivalent. Obviously, if one were to reduce the number of hours that the learning center was open the number of booths would need to be increased if the subject matter content and the number of students remained constant. Perhaps a beginning point for estimating the number of booths required is a careful consideration of the conventional equivalent. Based on the Purdue experience, a course which is taught conventionally with two hours of lecture, one hour recitation, and three hours of laboratory might be expected to require at least one hour more per week per student than when taught by the Audio-Tutorial system. Therefore, disregarding the one-hour small assembly session (in our case an IQS), a theoretical calculation could be made for 600 students as follows: (This calculation is on the basis that each student spends 4 hours per week in a 32 booth learning center which is open for 15 hours per day, 5 days per week.) 600 students × 4 booth hours per week = 2,400 booth hours per week. Fifteen hours a day × 5 days a week × 32 booths is equal to 2,400 booth hours per week. Thus, there would be provided sufficient facilities for 600 students 4 hours per week if this facility were used 100 percent. In actual practice this ratio of booth number : time open : student number has been satisfactory despite some inefficiency of booth utilization and a considerable increase in subject matter content. The average booth time per week for all students is about 2.8 hours instead of the 4 hrs/wk used in the above calculation. The provision of booth space should not be made on the basis of 100 per cent utilization. Obviously, some extra booth time must be made available if students are to use the learning center on an unscheduled basis.

A. Student Electronics—Recessed in the back wall of each student station is an ATS Model SC reel-to-reel student recorder. The built-in electronics occupies no table top space while providing maximum student access to the controls. A basic condition is that each tape player operates independently of other tape players so that each student can progress at his own pace.

A time and money saving feature of this equipment is the provision for simultaneous recording of student tapes from the instructor's master recorder. When the instructor wishes to duplicate his narration on the student decks, he takes his master recorder to the learning center where a centrally located System Control Panel has been installed. This key-operated switch will allow the instructor complete control of the record and start-stop functions during tape duplication. There are several advantages to this duplicating system: The instructor is free to make last-minute revisions without causing an inconvenience to others; preparation of the master tape can be done at the most opportune time for the instructor and does not have to relate to a set schedule; tapes played back on the same recorder used for recording do not distort the voice because of a variation in playback speed; close surveillance of tape quality can be exercised by the instructor; and this ability to prepare readily a set of tapes from one master tape eliminates the need to keep a library of sets of each lesson for each student station and thus the total number of tapes required under these conditions is considerably reduced.

Although the authors have made no study of the advantages and disadvantages of various kinds of tape recorders we have found the Model SC-1 produced by Audio-Tutorial Systems to be convenient for both our staff and students to operate. After thousands of hours' use they are still functioning in a convenient and reliable manner with a minimum of routine maintenance.

Since we began our program new cassette recorders have been developed. Depending upon the nature of your program you may wish to consider cassettes. If you do select cassette equipment make sure it has been designed to withstand the heavy use encountered under the Audio-Tutorial method of instruction. It is not unusual for a machine to be used ten to fourteen hours per day. Remember equipment failure can be costly—it is not always the original purchase price which counts. Equipment failure can prevent a viable educational concept from functioning properly.

B. Projectors—(1) Movie Projectors—The addition of 8mm movies permits the inclusion of instruction which is best done by the use of motion and color. During the first few semesters of the Audio-Tutorial system no 8mm projectors were available. However, as the loop film projector became known, its use was incorporated and a new and important dimension to the presentation of information was made available. Super 8 cartridge loaded projectors have now replaced the standard 8mm.

The senior author has very strong feelings as to the nature of the projection device and the features it must possess to provide a useful aid to learning. A good projection device permits the student to repeat the viewing of specific segments of a film without the delay encountered by the continuous loop, cartridge-loaded type. The argument that cartridge-loaded films are only two or three minutes in length and thus require only a short amount of time until the film segment in question is repeated is not valid. In practice, most cartridge-loaded films are about four minutes in length and are composed of several concepts. A student involved in a lesson using four or five loops could have a major time investment viewing unrelated subjects just to repeat one segment of film in each cartridge. Students will not spend this extra time voluntarily, and even if they did, the extraneous film they would be forced to view would be a distraction and a minus factor in the learning process. In addition, the difficulty of editing film loaded within the cartridge is restrictive. A reel-to-reel feature enables the instructor to easily edit film to suit the specific lesson. The instructor can splice together segments of film derived from many sources.

Some super 8 projectors incorporate several features which facilitate some of these important study practices. These projectors are compact and durable units featuring forward, backward, hold, automatic load, zoom lens, and a simple conversion device for projection of either regular 8 or super 8 film. This range of features provides a flexible projection facility.

Under the Audio-Tutorial system it has been practical to ask the students to synchronize the film and the tape for simultaneous projection and playing. This permits the instructor to narrate the film in his own words and adjust the narration to the specific use of the film.

Films which do not demand critical study but are included for enrichment can be viewed at a central location using a loop film projector. These films are of two types—four-minute loops and up-to-20-minute loops. Some loop film projectors provide for the incorporation of longer films into the study program. Usually it is best to place the projector and film for the short loops on the central table and longer loops in a spare booth to be used by those students who wish to investigate some particular subject in greater depth.

Currently some projectors are featuring the addition of optical or magnetic sound. It is the opinion of the senior author that this addition is unnecessary and in some cases wasteful except for the longer loops.

(2) Other Projectors—Depending upon the nature of your program, other types of projectors may offer distinct advantages. As an example, the 35mm projector offers an opportunity to use color where appropriate. Many commercially prepared slides are now available which may be combined with your own to meet the needs of your individual students. Sequencing of these individual slides may be easily changed from term to term or new ones may be added without having to rearrange your entire program. Review and test slides can be easily prepared locally to meet individual needs. Various other types of

projectors are available. The authors have made no in-depth study of the entire selection available. If you have other types, it would seem logical that you attempt to integrate them into your Audio-Tutorial program.

3. Central Tables

Two central tables (Fig. 4.4) are used in the Purdue learning center for those materials which are too bulky or for some other reason are not to be included in the booth. The tables are 4 feet wide by 8 feet long and equipped with strips of electrical outlets around the edge. The tables are placed end to end and partitioned longitudinally by a pegboard divider which serves as a backdrop for the mounting of charts, diagrams, and other explanatory materials, as well as distribution of plant materials. A wire strung between metal rods extending above the divider is used for hanging posters and decorative materials. These tables have been adequate for experiments, demonstrations, and the storage of materials for experiments to be done elsewhere or in the booth. The tables are placed in a location readily accessible to all students from the booths. A more elaborate table including such facilities as vacuum, gas, distilled water, and sinks might be needed for some subjects. Growth chambers, refrigerator, incubators, and an oven could be included as added features.

4. Study Table and Reference Library

One section of the learning center is set aside as a general study area (Fig. 4.5). A

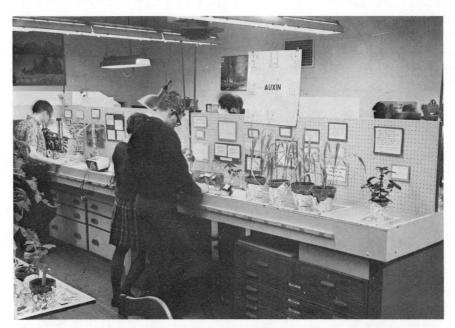

FIGURE 4.4—Central tables used for locating experimental materials, demonstrations, equipment, and other items which are used by all students. The student turns off the tape and comes to this location at the appropriate stage in the sequence of learning events. The area beneath the tables is used for storage.

FIGURE 4.5—Study area for students who are reviewing the previous week's work or are waiting for a booth.

long table seating approximately ten students, a pegboard display area, and a reference library serve this purpose. The study table provides space for students to read (reference books, *Scientific American* articles, or text assignments), to do study problems, or to wait for a booth. Sometimes this table is used for special ISS setups, for stereo microscope work, general movie viewing area, and for special displays. The reference library consists of bookshelves containing several books belonging to the course, some books on special loan from the school library, and several current journals (Fig. 4.6). Students are allowed to check out these materials for overnight. Handy references are a general dictionary, a dictionary of biological or botanical terms, general botany or plant physiology texts, *Life*

FIGURE 4.6—A small library of books, journals, etc., available for supplementary study on the week's subject.

FIGURE 4.7—A blackboard at one end of the room is used for individual instruction.

Nature Library volumes, Merck Index, Chemistry-Physics handbook, taxonomic keys, scientific journals, and paperbacks. The pegboard display area is used to display certain scientific journals such as the *American Journal of Botany, Science, Scientific American, American Scientist, BioScience,* and *Plant Physiology* and to make available copies of the. currently assigned *Scientific American* reprints.

5. Other Features

A blackboard located at one end of the room obviously is a necessary item for use by both students and instructors (Fig. 4.7). Adjacent to the blackboard area, a pegboard and bulletin board are made available for special displays. In one end of the room a large metal growth rack equipped with fluorescent lights is available for displaying and growing plants over a long period of time (Fig. 4.8). This is especially helpful for experiments requiring students to collect data and make observations on long-range projects. Cabinets placed strategically around the room provide storage for microfilms, movie projectors, cartridges, tapes, extra headsets, and other items of this nature. Much effort is made to create a pleasant atmosphere in the learning center and abundant use is made of potted plants, wall murals, and other decorative items which on many occasions are functional as well as decorative. A 2 × 2 slide projector is available at one location in the room to permit students to review and to quiz one another (Fig. 4.9). It may also be used for an occasional reference to a colored slide as an integral part of the study sequence.

WORKROOM AND PREP ROOM

It is highly desirable to have a workroom and prep room adjacent to the learning center. This facility can function well for use by both staff and students.

FIGURE 4.8—A plant growth rack located at one end of the room and used for long-term experiments.

FIGURE 4.9—A 2 x 2 slide projector placed at a central location for use by all students. Duplicate photographs in black and white are usually included in the study guide so the 2 x 2 projector is used mainly for review and spontaneous discussions.

1. Preparation and Storage Facilities

One of the obvious uses of such a room is to provide space for the preparation and storage of materials to be used in the independent study session. The prep room is equipped with shelving and drawer space in which materials have been cataloged for

FIGURE 4.10–Student setting up an experiment in the prep room area.

future use (Fig. 4.10). These materials may include charts, diagrams, experimental equipment, preserved specimens, and any other especially designed materials for a given week's subject matter content. One area is reserved for storage, one for future preparation, one for common stock items such as dixie cups, aluminum foil, paper towels, and other general prep materials, and one for students' experiments.

2. Refreshments and Special Projects

The prep room serves an additional function as a place for students to take a break and have refreshments. One end of the room is equipped with a sink and water. The associated shelf area has a water heater and other appropriate items for making coffee and tea (Fig. 4.11). Certain materials are available to students for doing special research projects. These include a refrigerator, an incubator, an oven, a centrifuge, a colorimeter, manometers, and other equipment. A table in the center of the workroom provides an extra study facility and doubles as worktable for setting up materials. A blackboard is available at one side of the room to encourage discussions by students and staff.

THE GENERAL ASSEMBLY HALL

The general assembly hall has a capacity for 420 students. It is well-equipped with a great variety of projection devices. A permanent screen is located above the blackboard and serves for projection of 2 × 2 slides, 3¼ × 4¼ slides, overhead projection, and movies. A projection booth in the back of the general assembly hall is equipped with a 3¼ × 4¼ projector, a 2 × 2 projector, and a carbon arc movie projector. A special attendant is

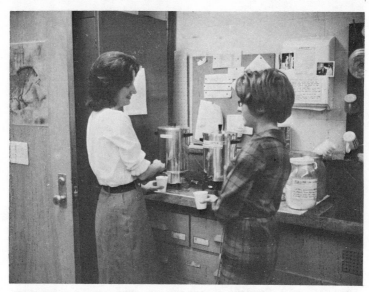

FIGURE 4.11—Students taking a brief break in the prep room. Coffee and tea are provided to assist students to relax and enter into discussions with other students.

available to give assistance in the use of these facilities or the instructor can exercise remote control through use of the front desk control panel.

The front lecture table is equipped with an exhaust fan, distilled water, and a variety of electrical facilities. It has a public address system with a remote microphone pickup which can be connected directly to a tape recorder. The control panel permits a great variation of lighting conditions within the hall. Two portable demonstration tables are detachable from the central lecture table and can be set up in an adjacent preparation room prior to their use.

The general assembly hall is equipped with a closed-circuit television facility. The camera can be mounted either on a tripod or on a special cart for vertical orientation to use with a microscope or table-top viewing. This facility is designed for control of the operation by the instructor.

In addition to the above items, there is a large blackboard made of metal which permits the magnetic attachment of materials to the board along with conventional chalk presentation.

THE SMALL ASSEMBLY SESSION (Integrated Quiz Session)

The physical facilities necessary in the small assembly room are those typically found in a recitation room. The integrated quiz session as described in Chapter II of this book is best accomplished in a relatively small room with a table just large enough for an instructor and eight students to sit around conveniently and a space nearby for eight students to do a written quiz. The table should be relatively low in height to permit easy viewing of the materials on display by all students. A small cart is often useful for transporting relatively heavy materials or for display items of special interest used in the preceding week's work. Occasionally some projection facilities are useful during the quiz session, but with a little ingenuity these can be made available in almost any small room. It is helpful if this room is large enough for the eight students who are taking their written quiz to be somewhat detached, yet near enough for close surveillance by the instructor in charge. The authors have used cloakrooms, ordinary laboratory facilities, and recitation rooms for the integrated quiz session.

OTHER FACILITIES

One of the obvious needs for a course in botany is a greenhouse. In the course described in this book the greenhouse is used for three major purposes: as a conservatory, for growing classroom materials, and for student research projects. The conservatory is small and located in one section of the greenhouse. A few plants are grown here and some attempt is made to simulate certain ecological situations. Some of these plants are transferred to the learning center for study and others are studied on location. The major portion of the greenhouse is used for producing expendable classroom materials. These include seedlings at various stages of development, plants for tropism experiments, and other comparable items. The section devoted to student research projects consists of a ground bed at one end, three greenhouse benches in the center, and a workbench facility along one edge (Fig. 4.12). No section of the greenhouse is devoted exclusively to one course and many of the materials are shared with several other courses.

A display case is located in the hallway adjacent to the learning center and serves several useful purposes. It is commonly used to display the answers for the weekly tests

FIGURE 4.12—Student collecting data for problem 2. One section of a greenhouse is used primarily for this purpose.

and sometimes used to display pertinent information to which the students might need access during the hours when the learning center is closed. Occasionally a long-term display of supplemental information is placed here.

COSTS

It is difficult to compare accurately the cost of the Audio-Tutorial system and the conventional system. It is necessary to know specifically all the associated materials involved and the situation under which the system has developed. A switchover from the conventional system to the Audio-Tutorial system involving the use of existing materials compounds the difficulty of cost estimation. Despite this lack of accuracy, certain definite savings are obviously accrued as evidenced by the very nature of the number and kinds of items involved. For example, since only one or two students are at a given point in their study at a given time, one or two items of equipment can be used by a large number of students. This is in contrast to the conventional system where it is necessary to supply enough of that particular item for several students proceeding simultaneously. Thus, expensive materials such as delicate instruments or special microscope slides can be placed at a central location, and one or two such items will be adequate for a large number of students.

Some savings on staff time result when the system is used in large courses. High quality instruction can be given with the Audio-Tutorial system with a low number of staff, but as with conventional systems, the more staff available the more quickly and directly one can care for specific needs of the students. In other words, the use of the system does not replace the need for teaching assistants but only provides the possibility of doing a better job of teaching when the total staff available is limited. Also, since much of the study program is structured by the senior instructor, it now becomes feasible to use undergraduate teaching assistants who, though not capable of structuring classroom programs, are able to handle questions which arise in the learning center on an individual basis.

Space savings result from more efficient usage of laboratories. Odd times such as meal times and evening hours which are not routinely scheduled may be convenient for some students and these times will be used on a volunteer basis. Perhaps most important is the time saved by not having space occupied by students who are not actually participating in the class. This includes students who already know the subject matter and those who do not care to learn it. Students in both categories are often captive audiences under the conventional system and occupy space unproductively. The following tables indicate some items on which savings may result. Actual savings would have to be calculated on an individual course basis (see table below).

SUMMARY

The physical facilities, however elegant and elaborate, in no way assure successful learning experiences for students. Let us emphasize that communication vehicles such as tape recorders and movie projectors are merely a means to an end. A tape recorder and a movie projector have tremendous potential for extending the capacity of good teachers to a greater number of students. The most important feature of the Audio-Tutorial system is the programming of a sequence of meaningful learning experiences. The proper use of these tools permits the teacher to devote much of his time to the kinds of student-teacher contacts which are not possible under the conventional system. While it is possible to show cost saving through reduced space and staff, this feature is a happy coincidence and a bonus item. Practices which improve the rate and amount of learning should be incorporated into the educational system even if they are more expensive.

Comparison of Conventional and Audio-Tutorial Requirements

	Conventional			Audio-Tutorial		
Student number		**600**			**600**	
Study sessions	Lab.	Lect.	Rec.	ISS	GAS	IQS
Student time required:	3 hrs	2 hrs	1 hr	2.8 hrs (avg.)	1 hr	½ hr
*Staff time required: Senior instructor Instructor Teaching Assts.	2/30/20 3 hrs 6 hrs 111 hrs	1/300/4 4 hrs	1/30/20 1 hr 6 hrs 13 hrs	1/32/80 3 hrs 7 hrs 69 hrs	1/300/2 2 hrs	1/8/75 3 hrs 5 hrs 31 hrs
Total	120 hrs	4 hrs	20 hrs	80 hrs	2 hrs	38 hrs
Space required:	2 labs	Hall (300) 4 hrs/wk	Room (30) 20 hrs/wk	1 lab	Hall (300) 2 hrs/wk	Room (16) 38 hrs/wk
Materials and equipment required: Microscopes, microscope slides, and similar equipment requiring individual study	72			32		
Spectrophotometer, hot plates, and similar equipment	18			1		
Experimental and demonstration materials	18			1		
Tape recorders				32		
Movie projectors				16		

*Based on the ratio indicated (no. of staff/no. of students/no. of sections)

Chapter V

OPERATIONAL ASPECTS

The operation of any course of necessity reflects the specific ideas and attitudes of the individuals who present the course. The information in this chapter represents the opinions of the senior author as they have been modified by the experience of teaching a freshman botany course over a period of 19 years. Many of the ideas and procedures have been suggested by teaching assistants, students, and other personnel associated with the course.

The following items are not meant to be restrictive. Rather, it is hoped that the experience of the authors may serve as a basis for others to further innovate and experiment with helping students learn. Many of the details are merely for the reader's information and do not constitute a rigid pattern of procedure. The course on which this information is based is a freshman botany course at Purdue University. The enrollment over the past 19 years has varied from 150 to as many as 600 students. It is a four-hour credit course required for agriculture students and may be taken as an elective by liberal art students. Conventionally, the course was taught by two one-hour lectures, one one-hour recitation, and one three-hour laboratory per week.

PERSONNEL

The senior instructor in charge of the course is the only instructor of professorial rank. Other personnel required to serve 600 students include a full-time instructor, ten half-time teaching assistant equivalents (some teaching assistants work quarter, half, three-quarters, or full-time, and some undergraduate assistants are used if graduates are not available), extra labor, and half-time secretarial help.

The senior instructor has the overall responsibility for the course. The general organization and planning of course content, procedures, timing of tests, and items of this

Table of Distribution of Staff Time

	(1) Senior Instructor	(1) Instructor	*(10) Teaching Assistants	Total
ISS	2 hrs.	8 hrs.	70 (7/TA) hrs.	80 hrs.
GAS	2 hrs.			2 hrs.
IQS	4 hrs.	4 hrs.	30 (3 /TA) hrs.	38 hrs.
Total	8 hrs.	12 hrs.	100 hrs.	120 hrs.

*Teaching assistants serve 10 hours contact time and 10 hours preparation time per week.

nature are decided by the senior instructor. His contact time includes being in charge of all of the general assembly sessions, meeting with all the students in one of the first small group sessions to introduce them to the course and to become acquainted (20 sections), two or four hours of integrated quiz sessions on a scheduled basis, two or three hours of contact time in the independent study session in the learning center, and he attends all briefing sessions for the personnel. The total contact time of the senior instructor is six or more hours per week. The senior instructor prepares all of the audio tapes and instructional materials used in the general assembly session.

The full-time instructor in the course supervises the preparation of all other materials in the course. He is responsible for the writing of test questions, planning and providing materials for student research problems, supervising the preparation of independent study materials, and scheduling of work assignments. His student contact includes four to six hours of regularly scheduled integrated quiz sessions, four to eight hours in the independent study session, and occasionally he substitutes for the senior instructor in the general assembly session.

Most of the teaching assistants are working either on M.S. or Ph.D. degrees. Their student contact will include one or more integrated quiz sessions (after one semester's experience in the independent study session) and sixteen hours in the independent study session. The total contact time will be ten hours per week. It is anticipated that each teaching assistant will spend approximately ten hours per week in preparation, or a total work load of about twenty hours per week. At the beginning of each semester each teaching assistant is assigned one or two weeks for which he is responsible for preparation of materials for the independent study session. He is expected to listen to the tapes over the units assigned to him and to become completely familiar with the necessary materials for demonstration and experimentation for that particular unit. He supervises the growing of any live specimens necessary, makes sure that appropriate materials are available, places purchase orders for needed items, and develops other materials as necessary. Under the direction of the full-time instructor he plans the arrangement and distribution of materials on the center tables and within the booths. He can develop new ideas or variations of the original experiments within the limitations imposed by the basic tape and budget. He is responsible for setting up one booth as a guide for duplication by undergraduate help and is responsible for the maintenance of all materials on display during the time it is in use (Fig. 5.1). He is further responsible for the disassembling and storing of these materials at the end of the presentation of his unit. New teaching assistants are required to attend and assist the senior instructor in the general assembly session. Naturally, during the week he is responsible for materials in the independent study sessions his hours of work will exceed the ten hours per week preparation but a lighter work load for other weeks compensates for the extra time. His grading responsibilities involve the evaluation of his IQS students on oral quizzes, grading the written quizzes and research projects, and entering final grades.

Undergraduate teaching assistants do much of the routine and menial tasks around the laboratory, such as washing of dishes, duplication of materials in booths, tearing down the booth, and demonstration materials. They assist as undergraduate instructors in the independent study session at busy times and may take full charge of the learning center at slack times.

FIGURE 5.1–An instructor and an undergraduate assistant making a final check on materials for the next week's work.

The secretary does nearly all of the clerical work involved in the course. She records all grades on a master card which is retained in her office. At mid-semester and at the end of the semester she makes a tabulation of the scores of all students. She types up all mid-semester reports of unsatisfactory work and prepares the cards for entry of the final grade. Although attendance is not required in GAS and ISS and absences are not penalized by the lowering of the grade, still it is desirable under this system to keep close check on the activities of all students. Students who are doing poorly in the course and are absent excessively from IQS are reported to the Dean by the secretary.

The total number of teaching personnel and its composition are about the same as were used previously under the conventional approach. The kinds of responsibility and the nature of the work load, however, are somewhat different in that each category of individuals associated with the course now has become somewhat more specialized and can be more creative in developing their area of contribution. It is possible under the Audio-Tutorial system to teach as effectively as with the conventional system using fewer personnel. However, the use of audio-tape has in no way eliminated the desirability of having teaching staff available for personal contact with the student. The more instructors available to the student, the better the job will be done. There are many times when it is advisable to have two instructors on duty in the independent study session, especially during the busy hours. Undergraduate teaching assistants can be used on these occasions effectively, and it is feasible to have some of the better students taking the course act as special teaching aids. In situations where only undergraduate personnel is available, the Audio-Tutorial system provides the advantage of exposing all students to consistent information presented· by the senior instructor. Thus, while the Audio-Tutorial system affords an opportunity for reduction of total personnel, it does not mean that a reduction is a requirement. It enables the personnel to make more meaningful and direct contact with the pertinent problems of the students.

The reaction of teaching assistants to the approach has been thoroughly positive. The significance of their role in the progress of the student has not been reduced but has been enhanced through the use of tapes. Their activities are now creative ones in the planning and development of their unit of work, and the face-to-face teaching activities of the ISS and IQS are very satisfying (Fig. 5.2).

Teaching in the independent study session is an enlightening experience. The instructor is surrounded by a group of students, all of whom are in attendance because they have chosen to be there. They have guidelines for what they are doing, and all are setting about to complete their study as rapidly and as effectively as possible without trying to impress anyone. When a student requests assistance, he has a specific problem in mind and is in a receptive mood for the answer. As soon as he has become properly informed, he is ready to continue his work without further attention from the instructor. The instructor has an opportunity to deal with difficult concepts and to try a variety of approaches to their presentation. The instructor's technique of teaching is either rewarded immediately and on a face-to-face basis with recognition and understanding by the student or he is at once aware of the student's failure to understand. In either event, the instructor learns immediately whether his technique is productive and can make alterations, if necessary. Often teaching assistants have discovered particularly effective sequences of presentation of a given concept and passed these along to the rest of the teaching personnel in the weekly session. All of this has contributed to the personal development and satisfaction of the teaching assistants.

Assistants who have had one semester of experience in the independent study session obtain teaching experience of a different dimension through their supervision of an integrated quiz session. Here they are exposed to the true nature of students and are

FIGURE 5.2—An instructor discussing a problem with a student. Questions are answered when they arise and the student is not forced to proceed to the next study activity only partially prepared.

made aware of the problems of communication and evaluation. Thus, contrary to the prediction of many colleagues, the morale of assistants has been unusually high and their contribution to the success of the program has been considerably greater than under the conventional system.

All people assisting in the course meet for a one-to two-hour session each week to discuss the activities of the past week and to prepare for the work of the coming week. It is not expected that the total preparation of each individual for the coming week is to be included here. It is anticipated that everyone will have listened to the tape on his own time prior to the staff meeting. The person setting up the ISS for the week should have checked out all the experiments. All instructors are expected to have read the *Scientific American* article and text assignments and have done the study problems. It is good practice at this meeting for the senior instructor to go through the objectives, the study guide, the special problems, and discuss the rationale for the methods and content. The person who sets up the ISS should have an opportunity to point out what difficulties might arise, where special reagents or stocks are stored (refrigerator, cold room, etc.), how frequently fresh materials need to be put out, and what general upkeep is necessary. A good meeting program might be (1) Discussion of the oral quiz for the next IQS, (2) Discussion of the new ISS setup (using the study guide and objectives), and (3) Discussion of administrative matters. Most of the meeting should concern the new ISS setup and include a discussion of the appropriateness and effectiveness of the methods and materials in accomplishing the week's objectives. Listening to the tape and covering the forthcoming ISS work in staff meetings gives consistent preparation for all the teaching assistants and results in more consistent dissemination of information to the students.

A "brainstorming" session at the end of the semester with all the staff is useful. First, a list of topics which need improvement is made. Then, one at a time, each topic is discussed and everyone presents modifications or alternative ways of doing it. This session works best when "anything goes" and no suggestion is ruled out by cost or improbability. One person's complex idea may turn out to be an excellent and simple solution when slightly modified by someone else.

Before leaving this section, it is pertinent to ask whether the Audio-Tutorial system can be used in schools where the staff is small, each member has charge of several courses, and/or little or no graduate teaching assistant help is available. This question cannot be answered easily and directly. One of the major questions is the compatibility of permanent staff and how much of the program is to be modified. It is conceivable that one learning center could accommodate several courses and that ISS time might be shared by the instructors of these courses. The number of booths and time open would depend on the number of students to be served and the amount of subject matter included. A theoretical case might involve three courses, conventionally taught as follows: Course A—2 hours lecture, 1 hour recitation, and 3 hours laboratory—enrollment 20; Course B—3 hours lecture, 4 hours laboratory—enrollment 15; Course C—6 hours laboratory discussion, enrollment 48. Assuming course C involved two sections and the other courses one section each, the total instructor time required would be: Course A—6 hours, Course B—7 hours, and Course C—2 sections, 12 hours, or a total of 25 hours. The requirement for the same courses under the Audio-Tutorial system would be: Course A—1 hour GAS, .5 hour

IQS; Course B–1 hour GAS, 1 hour IQS; Course C–1 hour GAS, 3 hours IQS, and approximately 11 hours ISS (assuming 32 tape players available) or a total of 19.5 hours, a saving of 5.5 hours per week. The 11 hours of ISS could be supervised either by senior staff, less qualified personnel or, in some schools, it might be practical to leave the learning center unattended part of the time. Possible sources of ISS help and alternatives include undergraduate majors, undergraduates who have completed the course, an undergraduate or someone on hourly wages acting as a monitor during the unmanned hours, housewives, or retired people interested in teaching. Other alternatives include use of unattended hours in the learning center (but post a schedule of times when assistance will be available), or optional or required small informal meeting sessions to talk over problems with an instructor.

PLANNING AN AUDIO-TUTORIAL LESSON*

One of the advantages of the Audio-Tutorial system is that it enables the instructor to reevaluate his procedures and reconsider his objectives. The reading of R.F. Mager's *Preparing Instructional Objectives* (1962), Fearon Publishers, Inc., Palo Alto, California, as a prelude to preparing a course and weekly objectives is highly recommended. A common fault of many instructors is that little time is spent in carefully planning the presentation of a course. We do many things with limited preparation and depend on our earlier experience of teaching the subject to cause us to do and say the right things at the right time. Most of us are resistent to change and sometimes we cling to ideas which have outlived their usefulness, thereby handicapping the kind of progress that should be made.

The following steps are suggested as a procedure for the development of an Audio-Tutorial lesson:

Step 1. List all of the objectives of the unit. The teacher should list as carefully as possible each achievement which he expects the student to accomplish, specifying the minimum acceptable performance. The list should include skills, concepts, vocabulary building, problem solving, creative activities, etc. It is a good idea to write test questions concurrently with the writing of objectives.

Step 2. List individually on cards all study activities useful in accomplishing the above objectives. These include the available media and teaching aids such as paragraphs to be read from the text and periodicals, exercises to be completed from a manual, specimens to be observed or examined, experiments to be completed, study problems to be worked, films to be viewed, points to emphasize on tape, and the many other items useful in this regard.

Step 3. Edit the list from step 2 and decide the method by which they can best be done. Some items might be included in the general assembly session, some in a special small assembly session, some in the independent study session, and some as outside activities.

Step 4. Arrange the study activities in their proper sequence. Consider carefully those

*The availability of prepared Audio-Tutorial material in many subject areas should not be overlooked. These usually consist of student study guides, suggested audio scripts which may be edited to suit the objectives of the instructor's course, teachers' guides, and associated audio-visual materials.

items which can be used as a foundation for subsequent ones and align each item in a properly programmed sequence. Sometimes this can be accomplished best by use of a planning board. The planning board and cards as described in step 2 enable one to visualize the entire unit of study and the cards can be easily shifted about until the best sequence is obtained.

PREPARATION OF TAPES

Be sure to make your final recording in a room which provides maximum isolation from outside noises. There may also be inside noises which normally go unnoticed, such as air-conditioners, fans, heaters, and so forth. A good preliminary check is to set the recorder in the record position and let it run for a while without saying anything and then relisten to the tape to see if it contains annoying background noises.

Step 5. Assemble the actual materials (experimental equipment, text, study guide, etc.). With these materials and a tape recorder, make a trial tape. Perhaps it would be helpful to have a student do each study activity as the instructor tutors him through the program. If the student helper is an average student, his questions should be useful in determining what points need to be elaborated and items to be reduced or eliminated. Further, this approach should give the tape a tutorial flavor, making each student feel the instructor is talking directly to him.

Step 6. Transcribe the preliminary audio tape and edit it critically. This step should enable the instructor to use precise words and avoid much of the redundancy which occurs in ordinary conversation.

Step 7. Make the final tape. It is probably better for most of us to make a final tape from a manuscript which has been edited and typed in capital letters. Emphasis marking and other helps can be entered at the discretion of the instructor.

Some points to keep in mind while making a tape.

- Regarding the voice:
    1. Use a conversational tone.
    2. Vary the tone of voice frequently.
    3. Speak cheerfully.
    4. Enunciate clearly.
    5. Speak rapidly—most people can listen faster than the average person talks. Slow students can always stop the tape but rapid students are limited to the rate of the tape.
    6. Avoid uh's and other distracting speech habits.

- Regarding the content:
    1. A basic aim of all education is to create the habit of critical thinking.
    2. The tape is NOT a lecture.
    3. The tape is NOT a substitute for written laboratory directions.
    4. Involve the STUDENT in the study program. Have him looking at diagrams,

specimens, tables, photographs, through the microscope, taking data, or SOME-THING—never just listening.

5. Variety is usually desirable.

6. Simple and direct activities are commonly more effective than complex, involved ones.

7. Proceed from known to unknown.

8. Students can synchronize the tape and movie for narration of short movie segments.

9. Repetition can be achieved by the student through a replay of the appropriate tape segment. Therefore repetition by the tape narrator is usually unnecessary.

10. Specially recorded sounds, voices of outstanding people, short dialogues, etc., when used functionally provide variation and add realism to the study.

11. Don't extend a lesson needlessly.

12. Make sure critical points are clarified. A brief statement often can provide the immediate reinforcement necessary to help the student proceed confidently.

● Regarding the mechanics:

1. Make a few practice runs to determine the volume level and the treble/bass balance. Usually it is better to record at the maximum permissible volume—or just below the distortion level. Also, record slightly on the treble side of a satisfactory treble/bass range (male voice).

2. Maintain a constant distance and direction from the microphone.

3. To make corrections stop the tape recorder, note the record-volume control setting, reverse to a segment of tape containing a natural pause in the conversation, turn the record-volume setting to zero, engage the record mode, quickly return the record-volume to the original setting, continue recording.

4. It is impractical to let the tape run during the interval while the student is performing certain study activities. Instead, the student should be signaled to stop the tape on these occasions.

5. A signal to stop the tape can be prearranged. This will reduce the monotony of repeating this suggestion and provide the student with a positive stimulus. A brief musical interlude is good for this purpose. (The musical interlude can be inserted easily by using two recorders or a recorder and record player. One recorder or record player supplies the music and plays continuously while the master tape is being made. Music is added to the master tape through manipulation of the volume control of the second tape player.) See also Appendix E.

USE OF FILMS

It would be impractical to include a detailed account of 8mm films and their production. In recent years there have been numerous studies on the effectiveness of film use and procedures for production. The topic is included here merely to give the author's viewpoint on certain aspects of the use and preparation of 8mm film and to report our experience with a few 8mm projection devices.

First one should question if a film is necessary for presenting a specific bit of subject matter. Is communication enhanced or best accomplished through the use of motion and color? It is a common practice for many teachers to follow a fad or trend toward the use of some new teaching device. The use of 8mm film has been no exception. Often the subject matter presented in movie film can be presented better in a series of still photographs. Black and white photographs have the advantage of being duplicated readily and are useful to students for review. However, the authors feel that so much subject matter demands motion and color, or at least is enhanced by it, that the effort and expense to include this equipment and materials in the classroom are well warranted.

There are some specific study activities which are best done through the use of 8mm film: (1) The steps in how to perform some procedure can be illustrated on 8mm film and the student can be individually guided as he performs the procedure. The film can be turned on, the student can view the first step, turn off the film, do that step, turn on the film, view the second step, turn off the film, do that step, etc. Where the film is provided on an individual basis as in the Audio-Tutorial system, the student can regulate the pace of the demonstration to suit his own skill and see the demonstration without looking over the heads of other students. Use of a projector facilitates this study activity through repetition of any segment or step of the procedure without delay, single frame projection, slow motion, and fast film viewing. (2) Time lapse and high speed photography permit the telescoping or expansion of a series of events. Certain obvious things, such as the growth of plant organs taking place over a period of several weeks, can be compressed into a few seconds and the events, thus magnified, are more understandable. On the other hand, high speed photography of rapidly moving objects, such as the motion of humming bird wings, permits the motion to be viewed at a slower rate and with greater clarity. In the Audio-Tutorial system these sequences can be incorporated into the study procedure at the precise time when the knowledge is complementary to other study activities. (3) Movie films can provide some experiences vicariously. These include studies involving dangerous or expensive equipment or studies producing benefits not worth the time investment. For example, it is a common practice to have students in a botany course study a median or near median section of a coleus stem tip. This study requires only one microscopic section through the middle of the coleus tip. The study of this one section does not give the student the full perspective of the plant apex. Ideally, he ought to view several hundred sections, but this is impractical because of time and costs. The series of stem tip sections photographed on 8mm movie film can be viewed in just a few seconds and is relatively inexpensive. (4) Movie films can provide students an opportunity to collect data from a recorded experiment and view problem situations for analysis. With some projectors it is conceivable that problems can be designed in such a way that the students can stop the projector to take measurements on the projected image, read dials, or obtain data in other ways and use these data to make graphs, tables, or other appropriate records. In cases where expensive equipment is involved, or where the collection of data would involve too much time, or the experiment involves conditions under which many students could not participate, the film can provide a visualization of the activities associated with the production of the data. The students can then collect the data and make an analysis. (5) Further use of film is for enrichment or to provide greater depth to areas of special interest. Films of investigators doing research and films that treat subject matter in depth frequently are good for this purpose and are often best presented with sound. Many of the current projectors are being constructed with sound capabilities, so it is feasible to have some booths set aside within the learning center for these enrichment potentialities. The loop film projectors have been useful in this regard.

The making of 8mm films is an overwhelming task for many teachers and it is unlikely that the average teacher will produce a commercially useful film. At best, a teacher can produce only an 8mm film which might serve as a pattern for a film to be commercially produced at a later time. The reel-to-reel feature of some projectors permits one to prepare a film for study by splicing together the segments of film which are critically related to the subject matter being presented.

Several movie cameras are available which are relatively simple and foolproof for the amateur. When the teacher makes only one film, naturally it will have to be placed at a central location for viewing. The students will need to interrupt their study and go to the appropriate location. This, of course, involves almost constant usage of the film and the film life is short. When a teacher has made some trial runs of a film and finds that he has the content and sequence appropriately structured, it is best that the film be made on 16mm film. This film can be used as the source for making multiple copies on 8mm film. Reproductions from 8mm originals are not very satisfactory.

As an operational procedure it has been found satisfactory to provide one projector for every two booths with the projector placed on top of the booth (Fig. 5.3). Projection is made into an inexpensive rear screen projection unit. A complete week of film viewing is placed on a single reel by splicing together those segments of film which are appropriate

FIGURE 5.3—One projector is adequate to provide for two booths when arranged as shown in this photograph.

to the sequence of study. The film segments are obtained from a great many sources. In each case a series of films are spliced together after severe editing and include only those portions which are significant or relevant to the student's study. This means that for 600 students it has been necessary to have 16 copies of each film to be viewed at the booth. An attempt is made to provide this many films for all subject matter which should be incorporated specifically into the sequence of study. An example would be a film showing the student how to perform some procedure. An occasional exception is only one available film to show how to operate some piece of equipment. In this case the projector is located alongside the piece of equipment at some central location.

In summary, the use of 8mm film provides an important dimension to the study activity. It is highly desirable that films be relevant to the nature of the objective and that students have an opportunity to control the pace at which these films are viewed. Irrelevant and extraneous motion picture materials are sometimes merely distracting and wasteful of students' time and should be eliminated from the study program. Films which are enhancement type should be clearly marked and made available at some central location so that students are not required to waste time with these interesting but time-consuming activities.

PREPARATION OF PRINTED MATERIALS

Printed materials have served an important function in communication for several hundred years and perhaps little or no space should be given to the subject here. However, in the Audio-Tutorial system printed material can be incorporated into the study program in a unique way and some consideration of the kinds, sources, and functions may be in order.

Basically, texts, outlines, lists, drawings, graphs, photographs, tables, diagrams, charts, short explanatory paragraphs, and items of this nature will help the student visualize or understand the subjects discussed on tape. The instructor will find many of these already available but it may be necessary to make some materials of his own. A good plan in the beginning is to use all materials one can find from any source and prepare only those additional ones necessary to the presentation. After the program has been tested a few times, the useful items, and those which need modification or redoing, will have been identified. When one has determined those which provide satisfactory results, these items can be offered for commercial publication in the form of a study guide. The procedure used at Purdue has been in this pattern, and over a period of some years of testing and revision student study guides,* suggested audio scripts,* and teachers' guides,* as well as a series of super 8 loop films, have been developed for a botany course.

The study guide for a unit of study contains a series of items sequenced as nearly as possible in the pattern in which the items will be programmed by the tape. Photographs, drawings, and diagrams may have arrows or other markings (labeled with numbers or letters) used to direct the student's attention to specific points of importance. For

*Copyright 1966. Available from Audio-Tutorial Systems®, Division of Burgess Publishing Company, Minneapolis, Minnesota.

example, a photograph of a transverse section of a root may have structures identified by numbered arrows and this photograph serves three purposes: (1) as a guide to help the student use the microscope to locate the structures on his specimen, (2) as a visual representation of the structure during the taped discussion of functions or other points the instructor wishes to emphasize, and (3) as a study aid for an exercise in labeling and recording information for future review.

Naturally, the number and kinds of items included in the study guide will depend on the nature of the subject matter, study activities involved, and the imagination of the instructor. A few possibilities are:

1. A series of photographs: (a) to show critical steps in the performance of a procedure, (b) to emphasize important steps of an event which will also be viewed as a movie, (c) to provide a source of data for analysis of some problem (students might be expected to extract the data by measurement on reading of dials), and (d) to show any other sequence which under a conventional lecture situation might have been presented by film strip or slides.

2. Conventional directions as typically included in a laboratory manual.

3. Summary statements or short explanatory paragraphs.

4. Forms, graphs, charts, and diagrams for collection of data or as a guide to the taped discussion. (The kinds of items which commonly are produced on the blackboard or overhead projection during a conventional lecture.)

5. Outlines, key words, questions, glossary, or similar information which will make the taped discussion more meaningful and informative (again, these are items often listed on the blackboard or overhead projector during a conventional lecture).

In addition to the study guide some special printed materials are made available to accompany the study either by placing one copy in each booth, by mimeographing enough copies for each student, or by asking the students to purchase copies. In many cases, copies of articles from magazines or journals should be placed in each booth. These copies are usually laminated with plastic to preserve them for use from year to year. In addition, some photographic prints are placed around the learning center as a part of the regular decor and the student is referred to them whenever they are appropriate to the context of study. The textbook assigned to the course and a library of texts either included in the booth or at a central location provide additional sources of printed material. Special photographs are often made to illustrate some procedure or experiment and arranged alongside the equipment at some central location. A Polaroid Land Camera is useful to provide these pictures. When the functional aspect of several items of printed material is established they should be assembled in a study guide arrangement and published for purchase by the student. Thus, the student can have his individual copy as a source of guidance for collection of data and study as well as for review purposes. Perhaps this is the goal for which one should strive; however, it is highly recommended that the study guide be the product of a few semesters' experience rather than an initial effort.

In summary, the printed materials should in no way be a replacement for the use of real specimens or real materials but should be supplementary materials which will help the student learn and serve as a guide in his approach to learning. It is felt that one should provide as many photographs, charts, tables, graphs, and other kinds of guidance as possible within the limits of feasibility of costs and preparation.

OTHER MATERIALS

The nature of botany and similar subjects requires student involvement with plant specimens, equipment for experimentation, models, and other materials. The procedure for their use is very often dictated by the nature of the content itself. Again, as with the other components of the Audio-Tutorial system, one should use as many kinds of substantive materials as practical within the limitations of space and costs. The most important consideration is the incorporation of these items into the study sequence at a time when they are relevant to the study. When feasible, the best situation is to have one of each item available in the booths. This permits their use with a minimum of distraction and effort on the part of the students. However, many items are of sufficient size or cost to make this distribution impractical and the placement of these materials at a central location is a better approach. This is especially true with large plants or with specimens which demand considerable attention in their production. For example, plants which have been subjected to a variety of photoperiod and temperature regimes, yeast cultures for growth curve studies, genetic demonstrations, etc., can be placed at a central location and all students can be asked to turn off the tape recorder and go to this location for collection of data (Figs. 5.4 and 5.5). Also, experimental equipment and materials are sometimes best located centrally so that all students can obtain their experimental setups from this source. This is especially true where the techniques may require the assistance of an instructor or where a single source of supply is a more practical situation. In any event, one should maintain maximum flexibility and allow the particular situation and subject matter to dictate the procedure which should be followed. The pegboard panel provides an opportunity for adjusting the arrangement of materials in the booth to make a pleasing display and a functional arrangement of substantive materials.

STUDY SESSIONS

The operational procedures for the study sessions are flexible and change with the nature of the subject presented. The next few paragraphs describe in detail some of the approaches used at Purdue University. However, the authors want to emphasize that these procedures serve as a basic pattern and not a rigid format.

1. Scheduling

Under the scheduling system for the botany course at Purdue University, the students are enrolled for one hour lecture, one hour recitation, and four hours laboratory. (The conventional terminology is used to identify class sessions in order to avoid unnecessary problems with school records.) The Audio-Tutorial equivalents are: one hour lecture—the general assembly section (GAS); recitation—the integrated quiz session (IQS); and laboratory—the independent study session (ISS). Since the enrollment is approximately 600 students and because of the size of the lecture hall (420 seats), two lecture sessions are scheduled for the general assembly sessions. Nineteen recitation sections (32 students each) must be scheduled to accommodate the integrated quiz sessions. The independent

FIGURE 5.4—A student using a spectrophotometer. One expensive piece of equipment at a central location can serve many students since each student is proceeding independently and seldom is there more than one student at a given point in the study at a given time.

FIGURE 5.5—A student determining the genetic ratio of segregating corn seedlings. One such flat is adequate for a class of 600 students.

study session is unscheduled. However, if one is beginning the Audio-Tutorial system for the first time, it might be easier if at least part of this session were scheduled. A good arrangement is to schedule two hours and leave two hours unscheduled (arrange hours). This permits students a gradual transition from the conventional structure to the freedom of the Audio-Tutorial system.

The general assemblies are scheduled to meet at 3:30 on Wednesday afternoon and at 3:30 on Friday afternoon. All students who are scheduled for the Wednesday afternoon general assembly are also scheduled for the small assembly (IQS) on Thursday. Students who are scheduled for the Friday afternoon session are scheduled to a small assembly (IQS) on Monday. This scheduling forces half of the students to complete their study by Thursday and the other half to complete their study by the following Monday. It results in a better distribution of utilization of the learning center. Also, since the general assembly is at the end of a week's work, it permits the senior instructor to discuss the preceding week's work making corrections or going into greater depth on certain subjects, or he can introduce the subject for the following week with very little overlap of the two weeks' subject matter.

One of the major problems of the Audio-Tutorial system is getting the first week's operation under way. When classes for the semester begin at Wednesday noon, the schedule arrangement suggested above works out as follows: (1) Half of the students are contacted on Wednesday afternoon and the other half Friday afternoon in a general assembly session; (2) half of the students are contacted again on Thursday and the other half again on Monday in small assembly sessions; and (3) if there is partial scheduling of the independent study session, additional contacts are made at these times. At the GAS meetings the students are introduced to the program and encouraged to begin their independent study right away. The initial sessions in the small assembly and independent study are also used for orientation. The subject matter for the first unit of study remains set up during the first week and a half. This permits the students extra time to become orientated to the system. Thereafter the subject matter is treated on a weekly changeover basis.

2. The Operation of the Independent Study Session

The independent study session is in the learning center, which is open from 7:30 in the morning until 10:30 in the evening Monday through Friday. During the first few weeks of the semester this time may be extended to include Saturday morning to provide more time for orientation to the new method of study. The student comes in at his convenience and checks in on a specially prepared record card (Appendix B). The card is placed in a numbered slot which assigns him to a specific booth for the duration of this time of study. The amount of time spent in study is left to the initiative of the student. He is free to come and go as he pleases. This freedom creates problems of crowding at favored times so that it is necessary to provide some methods to assist in the distribution of usage of the learning center. This is done by the scheduling procedure indicated above. In addition, a record is kept of the number of students at the learning center at hourly intervals and is made available to the students on the bulletin board. This enables them to check the busy times and arrange their schedules accordingly.

Some other possibilities, although not used by the authors, may provide some assistance. For example, if one were to schedule students for at least part of the independent study session (two or three hours) this could assure the student of having in his class schedule at least two or three hours of continuous time available and, on occasions where desirable, the student could be required to study in the learning center at this specified time. Even though the students were scheduled to attend the independent study session at a specified time they could be free to study on an unscheduled basis but with priority on the study space given to those students who are scheduled. Others have used an alternate method in which the student has earned his freedom of independent scheduling through a demonstration of doing satisfactory work. In other words, all students are scheduled to the independent study session but those students who are doing passing work are free to study on an unscheduled basis. Once the semester's work is under way, there is little difficulty in its operation and many of the problems solve themselves through student cooperation.

The learning center is set up on a weekly work basis; however, the first week is rather difficult, and either should be set up over an extended period of time or should cover a rather small amount of subject matter. As indicated earlier, when the semester begins on Wednesday, the first general assembly session can take care of a considerable amount of orientation. As the student arrives at the independent study session he is met by the instructor on duty and is requested to fill out the appropriate cards if this has not already been done in the general assembly session. The student is given brief instructions on the equipment and materials located in the laboratory and then is free to begin his independent study.

The duties of the instructor in the independent study session are outlined in detail and included in Appendix C. Basically, the functions of the instructor are: (1) to assist the student in the learning process, and (2) to prepare materials and set up the learning center. The assistance to students may take many forms depending on the nature of the subject matter and the needs of the individual. The instructor is expected to circulate within the learning center constantly, giving help when needed. Also, he will try to maintain a pleasant and studious atmosphere, keeping the noise level down, supervising the experimental equipment, etc. All instructors are required to dress in a white coat for identification purposes and male instructors are required to wear a tie. All instructors are expected to contribute to the smooth operation of the activities in the learning center.

Each instructor supervises the setup of study materials for one or more weeks. This means that during a semester each instructor will be responsible for one or two learning center preparations. Occasionally two or even three instructors might be assigned to a specific week's preparation, with one of them having the overall responsibility while the others assist him. In any event, the responsibility for any given week's preparation is assigned to one individual. In certain weeks, where the subject matter is varied or conditions seem to warrant, several instructors in the course may contribute to some aspects of the preparation. Credit for the quality of the preparation is recognized by placing on the inside of the learning center a small sign which says "This week's material courtesy of instructor John Doe." These assignments are made during the first general staff meeting with each instructor being given some opportunity to select the area of greatest interest to him.

The procedure for setting up the learning center begins with an examination of the materials from preceding semesters. These are stored as a unit in categories of weeks, along with photographs of preceding setups. Each instructor is requested to investigate the content of his week carefully and very early in the semester. He is then urged to meet with the full-time instructor and the senior instructor for information concerning any difficult aspects of his setup and to explore any suggestions for alternative ways of presenting the subject. Thus, the instructor is not robbed of the opportunity to use his own initiative for developing new materials, and, in addition, he receives the full range of experience in materials preparation. He is responsible for ordering any special equipment or specimens necessary for his week and for the planning of materials which require critical timing of their development. In other words, each week's work becomes a creative effort on the part of some instructor in the course and each instructor will have an opportunity for this type of activity.

Assistance to the instructors is provided whenever possible. A greenhouse man, who is a departmental appointment and serves for many courses in the department, gives assistance in the planting and potting of plants for a specific week's work. A full complement of equipment for making labels and signs is available as part of the prep room equipment and all instructors are encouraged to use this to make their setup neat and reasonably inviting. Undergraduate assistants help with the setting up and taking down of the week's materials.

All instructors are asked to make some special contribution to the improvement of the course during the semester. These contributions may be a special experiment which may be set up for observation during the semester, care of a terrarium and/or aquarium, or any kind of activity which may contribute to the decor and better operation of the independent study session (Fig. 5.6).

The assignment of instructors to serve as the independent study session instructor is done on a semi-lottery basis at the beginning of the semester. Each instructor draws from a hat a number which establishes the sequence of his opportunity to select the hours which would be most convenient for him to serve. Most instructors, depending on seniority, will

FIGURE 5.6–A student checking his progress on an electronic quiz board. An instructor may choose the maintainance of this board as his special contribution to the course.

be serving up to ten hours in the independent study session. The experienced instructors will be serving two or three hours in IQS and commensurately less in the ISS. The first round of selections, the instructors assign themselves to time intervals of two or three hours. During the second round they may assign themselves to a shorter time interval but not longer than a three-hour session. The selection is continued in this pattern until all instructors have been assigned their total time and all open time for the learning center is covered. In certain cases, where an adequate number of instructors are available, additional instructors are assigned for the crowded or busy times. Frequently, undergraduate students are used for some of these sessions.

3. The Operation of the General Assembly Session

The operational procedure of the general assembly session differs very little from that of the conventional lecture session. The senior instructor of the course is in charge of the general assembly session. The materials used in this session are the responsibility of the senior instructor and may include a variety of items depending on the nature of the subject matter.

The first general assembly session is an introduction and orientation session. For this session the senior instructor introduces himself and the other members of the staff. The students are asked to fill out a permanent record card and a learning center record card, and are given a number of handouts (descriptive materials and assignment sheets, Appendix A). All students are assigned to a specific seat in the lecture hall for the purposes of collecting data and to assist the senior instructor in becoming acquainted with the students. Attendance is not required except for special occasions of guest lecturers or for subject matter which will not be covered elsewhere in the course.

In addition to the trivial introductory activities, the students are shown a film "The Audio-Tutorial System—an Independent Study Approach." This film is composed of scenes from the classrooms depicting the various activities in which the students will engage during the coming semester. The mimeographed handouts are discussed in detail and the students are urged to assume responsibility for their own study. The problems of overcrowding are discussed frankly and the means of avoiding these unpleasant situations are explained. Since this is the first occasion of student meeting, the students are urged to visit the learning center at an early date and begin study immediately.

The second general assembly session is a very important one since it comes after the students' first week of independent study but precedes their first IQS. A useful and effective program for this general assembly has been to demonstrate the procedure of the IQS. From the audience of three hundred students, eight are selected randomly to come to the front of the lecture hall where they are seated around a table on which are placed the various items from the preceding week's study. Since these students are selected at random, one gets a full spectrum of preparation which enables one to demonstrate how each step in the IQS procedure will take place. All three hundred students, realizing that the following day they will be participating in a similar situation for grades, are very attentive and vicariously much involved. Since the materials are from the preceding week's work it also serves as a time for review and to establish a standard of expectation for the semester. The senior instructor, now serving as the instructor for the simulated IQS, begins by selecting items in the appropriate sequence and delivers the items to one of the eight students. The student performs and the senior instructor discusses his performance in a very frank way, establishing critical points both of content and procedure. All students in attendance have an opportunity to ask questions for clarification of any of these events.

Subsequent general assembly sessions will involve more routine types of discussion. Basically, the sessions will be help sessions in which the senior instructor will be approaching the subject matter in a slightly different way than in the independent study session. They will be attended only by those students who desire this assistance. However, for occasions of the showing of long films, or the presentation of a guest lecturer, the students are expected to attend. They are informed by bulletins published in the learning center and through the original schedule of activities on the hand-out sheet received at the beginning of the semester. For all general assemblies the common tools to facilitate communication, such as blackboard, plastic models, overhead projection, slides, and equipment of this nature will be used.

In summary, the general assembly session is operated on a flexible basis. It would depend on the need and on the senior instructor's opinion as to what contributions would be most important to the student's learning of the subject matter or the achieving of objectives. The session is not scheduled to provide a lecture in the conventional sense and seldom should be treated as such. However, there are some kinds of things which can be best accomplished in a large group and a provision for these should be included in a restructured course.

4. The Operation of the Integrated Quiz Session (Small Assembly Session)

The operational procedure of the small assembly session has changed considerably from the original pattern. Initially the small assembly session was designed to provide an opportunity for discussion and for a written quiz. The result of this procedure was that many of the students were not really concerned with the questions raised but merely used this occasion as a last-minute cramming session prior to taking the written quiz. Because of this attitude and because all serious students have an opportunity to have their questions answered at the time they arise in the independent study session, it seemed logical to alter the procedure. An alternative small assembly, called the integrated quiz session, was conceived which has proven to be a very fruitful activity. Some of the implications of this session have already been discussed, so the comments here are confined to the operational procedure.

Thirty-two students are scheduled to a one-hour recitation. The first meeting of this session is after the students have had the first general assembly orientation meeting. The procedure involves a continuation of orientation activities. The students are greeted by the senior instructor just outside the entry to the recitation room. Inside the room, the student writes his name on a large sheet of paper and is photographed on 35mm film with his name held in front of him. These photographs are later processed to four contact prints which serve several purposes in the course. One print is placed on the permanent record card, one on the learning center card, one on an IQS record sheet, and one on a large seating assignment chart for the general assembly session.

Following the photography students are divided into four groups of eight each to meet in the future as four integrated quiz sessions. These groups are designated as A1, A2, B1, and B2. A1 and B1 groups will meet simultaneously with different instructors and in different locations. They will take an oral quiz during the first half hour, after which they will take a 20-point written quiz. The A2 and B2 sections also will meet simultanously and immediately following their counterparts A1 and B1. They are scheduled to arrive at the beginning of the second half hour. During this time they will take their oral quiz and at the end of the second half hour they will take their 20-point written quiz. This means that the students in the A2 and B2 groups must be selected from those who do not have a conflict the following hour. Thus far, the few problems encountered in rescheduling have been taken care of on an individual basis by assigning nine students to some sections, or by shifting some student from this hour to some other hour in the course. This procedure permits the instructor for groups A1 and A2 to supervise the oral exam for group A1 during the first half hour and the oral exam for A2 during the second half hour. While the instructor supervises the oral quizzes, he also can proctor the written quizzes. If the instructor is replaced at the end of one hour, the replacement supervises the previous instructor's students while they do their written quiz during the time he gives his own A1 section their half hour oral quiz. This procedure has been mechanically satisfactory and by using a number of different quizzes there seems to be little or no problem of "carry-out" even with multiple sections.

After the details of assignment to the IQS the students are then engaged in a discussion of "what is science?" The remaining portion of this first meeting of the small assembly session is devoted to the definition of a problem, the designing of an experiment to give relevant data, and the decision on what data to collect. At the meeting's conclusion, all 32 students are taken to the greenhouse to set up the problem 1 experiment.

All subsequent meetings of the IQS are then the responsibility of the IQS instructor, and meet in groups of eight. Almost every time following this first meeting, the IQS follows the procedure described earlier in chapter 2. However, for some special occasion such as field trips or planning of problem 2, all four groups, A1, A2, B1, and B2 may meet together.

Instructors for the IQS are selected on the basis of experience and capabilities. They are assigned at a general staff meeting preceding the beginning of the course. Seldom is any individual assigned more than three hours, or three IQS except for the senior instructor in the course and the full-time instructor in the course, each of whom may take more if the situation appears to warrant it. Each instructor keeps his own record on a specially prepared form, grades his own 20-point written quizzes, grades the problem 1 projects, prepares unsatisfactory reports, serves as a counselor, and makes up the final grades for his sections. This does not mean that the student does not have an opportunity for contact with the senior instructor in the course, for the senior instructor has office hours, a weekly coffee hour, the general assembly session, and scheduled times in the independent study session.

In summary, the IQS is a variation of the old type small assembly session. Other possibilities exist for the small assembly session such as use as a recitation period, field trips, help sessions, or many other type sessions requiring 32 or less students.

5. Other Activities

Other study activities are included as necessary to supplement the formal study session. These are directed as the occasion may demand through any one of the three study sessions. These activities include the special research problems, field trips, outside readings, and study of this nature.

As indicated earlier all students are required to do a miniature research project. Project 1 is initiated at the first IQS as discussed in the preceding paragraphs. However, data may be collected on a class-wide basis and these data discussed in a general assembly session. Occasionally, a specialist is invited to help analyze the data statistically or discuss some special aspect of the problem. Commonly, the experiments are completed in four or five weeks and involve the growing of plants under greenhouse conditions. Each student is responsible for growing his own material except for routine watering which is provided by the greenhouse staff. The project is written in the style of a research paper following the format of the *American Journal of Botany* or the *Journal of Plant Physiology*. The finished paper is turned in to the IQS instructor and is either accepted or rejected. No grade is given but each student must have completed an acceptable paper to receive a passing grade in the course. When a paper is rejected, it is returned to the student and he is informed of the nature of the deficiency. He is given additional instruction if necessary and asked to resubmit a corrected paper within a specified time.

Problem 2, although primarily administered by the IQS instructor, is sometimes discussed at a special meeting of all "A" students during an evening session or at a general assembly session. On this occasion the mechanics and philosophy for the project are discussed. The same procedure is followed as with problem 1 except that all initiative is left with the student, who is told that he must "ask a plant or plants a question," design an experiment that will provide relevant data, analyze these data, and write an appropriate paper. The only limitations imposed are the available facilities and time. The student develops his project in close association with the IQS instructor. The problem must be clearly defined, and the experiment designed and approved by the IQS instructor before the research is begun. The completed paper must be turned in and accepted by a certain deadline. Any student in the course may do the paper but no additional credit is given to "D," "C," or "B" students. Students who have enough points for an "A" grade but do not do a problem too, receive a grade of "B."

Field trips are occasionally included in the study program. These are administered in two ways: (1) The excursion is composed of a competent instructor and 16-32 students. (The students are scheduled either through volunteers signing on a time schedule sheet posted on the bulletin board or by substituting the field trip for the study activities in IQS or a scheduled portion of the ISS.) or (2) the instructor's field trip commentary is recorded on a portable tape recorder and the student may check out the recorder from the secretary or the ISS instructor and take his field trip at his own convenience (Fig. 5.7). Although both systems have been used, the latter has been especially effective.

FIGURE 5.7—**A student listening to the instructor's tape re-corded commentary while examining a plant structure during an independent field trip.**

Outside reading has been encouraged through a limited bonus system, making a library available within the learning center, distribution of mimeographed copies of pertinent journal articles, and as a necessary activity connected with problems 1 and 2.

Perhaps a brief explanation of the bonus system is in order. A list of *Scientific American* articles is provided each student as a potential source of bonus readings. These selected articles are made available in the learning center and can be purchased at the bookstore if the student wishes. A two-point bonus question covering information obtained directly from the assigned article for the week is provided at the time the student takes the 20-point written quiz in the IQS. Answers to these questions are graded by the IQS instructor along with the 20-point quizzes.

One can conceive of other activities required in certain subjects for which no pattern has been included in the discussion in this chapter. These must be taken into consideration as a course is restructured. Many of the "once-a-semester" events can be handled easily and sometimes more effectively through the "sign up" process described for the field trip. In any case, a clear definition of objectives often suggests several possible ways for helping students achieve them.

TESTS AND GRADES

The grading system is based upon the approach that all students achieving a specific level of accomplishment shall receive a commensurate grade. The objectives for each week's unit of study are mimeographed and made available to each student at the beginning of the study. Many educators disagree with this approach and express considerable concern when the percentage of failures is small. The Audio-Tutorial system is not a method for alleviating the strain on university facilities by eliminating students or a screening mechanism for students who are clever at "beating the system." This system will appeal only to those instructors who are anxious to enable as many students as possible to achieve their highest level of accomplishment.

Grades are calculated on the basis of the number of points accumulated by the student in relation to an arbitrary number of possible points. The grade level established is: 90% or above equals A; 80% equals B; 70% equals C; 60% equals D; and less than 60% equals F. Students accumulate points through a series of quizzes, exams, and bonus points (Appendix A). Weekly quizzes given in the IQS include an oral exam (10 points), and a written exam (20 points), with a potential of a 2-point bonus question based on the reading of a *Scientific American* article. One 200-point final exam is given at the end of the semester. All students with the exception of those who are excused because of extenuating circumstances are required to take all quizzes and exams. The total number of points is as follows:

	Points
14 oral quizzes	140
14 20-point written quizzes	280
1 final exam 200 points	200
	620
Potential bonus points	28

The circumstances surrounding the oral quiz have been described earlier. Each student, selected randomly, receives an item from the preceding week's work, and is expected to identify the item, relate it to the objective on the objective sheet, and then demonstrate that he has achieved the objective. The instructor's responsibility does not involve asking questions. Instead, he is to disperse the items in the appropriate sequence, randomly select a student to perform, and assign the student a grade upon completion of his presentation (Fig. 5.8.). These grades are assigned subjectively by placing the student

FIGURE 5.8–An IQS instructor conducting an oral quiz.

in one of three categories. If the instructor is much impressed, the student is placed in a category of excellent and given 9 points; if the instructor is not very much impressed, the student is placed in the category of mediocre and given 7 points; if the instructor is disappointed, the student is given 5 points or less. At the end of the half hour oral quiz, the students who have made additional contributions may have their grades raised accordingly. Although some inequities exist between the evaluations of the instructors, the range of points over which the student may receive a passing score reduces the significance of this variation and there have been relatively few complaints.

The 20-point written quiz which is given immediately following the oral quiz provides all students an opportunity to prove their competence in a more conventional testing vehicle. In nearly every case the student is usually graded higher by the subjective approach. The 20-point written quiz is structured so that approximately 14 points of questions are closely correlated to the written objectives. The remaining points, which place the students in categories of A or B, are problem questions requiring the student to extrapolate from the information learned in achieving the objectives. The 200-point final exam is made up from the subject matter covered in the 20-point quizzes.

The 2-point bonus is given to those students who demonstrate a knowledge of certain *Scientific American* articles and are able to answer specific questions from these articles. Only a small percentage of the students avail themselves of this possibility. These questions are administered by the IQS instructor and are presented at the same time as the 20-point written quiz.

The 200-point exam is comprehensive, given at the end of the semester. It is made up of questions used on the 20-point quizzes or questions comparable to them. Most questions are multiple choice and responses are made on IBM cards. The score from this test is totaled with the scores from the quizzes and bonus points to provide a grand total of points from which the final grade is determined.

As indicated in previous paragraphs, the research projects do not affect the grade level. The first of the two research projects is required of all students if they are to receive a passing grade in the course. The projects are assigned a score of satisfactory or unsatisfactory. The second project is required of all students who anticipate an "A" grade. Students who receive enough points for an "A" grade but have not successfully completed their research project will receive a grade of "B."

In summary, the Audio-Tutorial system does not demand a specific grading method. However, it does seem to require short quizzes at frequent intervals to provide motivation and feedback to the students. When testing intervals are extended beyond that which coincides with a setup in the learning center, only strongly motivated and highly self-disciplined students avail themselves of the facilities for study. Therefore, it is strongly recommended that some routine checking of the student's progress be included in the system.

Chapter VI

MINICOURSES–A FURTHER POSSIBILITY

While serving (1965) on a panel for the Commission on Undergraduate Education in Biological Sciences investigating the role of laboratories in biology, Donald Bucklin and S. N. Postlethwait of this book became excited about the possibility of individualizing study through the use of a "pool" of study modules. It was not until the fall of 1969, however, when Robert N. Hurst joined the staff that it was possible to experiment with this concept at Purdue University. Since botany and zoology were both now to be taught by the Audio-Tutorial system, it seemed feasible to experiment with the implementation of two ideas—learning for mastery and minicourses. John Welser began a similar experiment in veterinary science at the same time. While these experiments were little more than a year old at the time of this writing, the results were encouraging and it seemed desirable to include these experiences in the revision of this book.

This chapter attempts to define the minicourse concept, elaborate some of the potential for its use, and describe the efforts to implement minicourses and learning for mastery at Purdue University.

THE MINICOURSE CONCEPT

The use of the modular approach to teaching is not new and has been attempted in many different settings. Several names have been applied to the modules such as: concepto-pack, ATPs (Audio-Tutorial Packages), Biotech's, Coursettes, Uni-Pacs, slates, etc. A minicourse can be defined as a unit of subject matter which can be dealt with conveniently both administratively and intellectually. The name minicourse has been applied to the modules developed at Purdue University to convey the idea of "small courses." The use of the term "course" to represent a relatively large module or unit of subject matter is a familiar concept. A college education is divided into courses such as chemistry, mathematics, physics, botany, zoology, psychology, political science, etc. This practice has permitted some degree of individualized college education and has been a convenient unit for grouping bodies of knowledge into curricula for specialized fields of study. The minicourse concept is an extrapolation of the conventional course concept to a lower order of magnitude. The improved resolution provided by smaller units of subject matter should result in even greater individualization of study programs and more precise identification of the content of a curriculum. Thus the minicourse concept calls for breaking courses into components which will allow unit mastery and flexibility plus the opportunity to tailor a student's education more closely to his needs (Fig. 6.1).

The parameters of a minicourse are as flexible as those for a conventional course. As with conventional courses, the amount and nature of subject matter included is arbitrarily decided by the instructor of the minicourse. The behavioral objectives for a minicourse

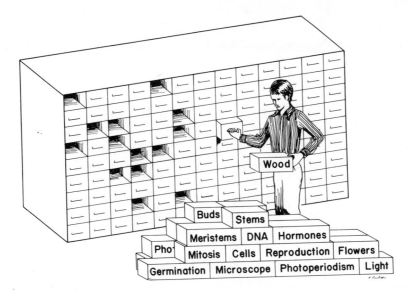

FIGURE 6.1—Minicourses can be structured to form the equivalent of a conventional course. These modules can provide individualization of the amount, nature and sequencing of study for a heterogeneous group of students.

should prescribe its length and content. A unit of subject matter which logically constitutes a coherent study of a topic or concept is a minicourse. From a practical point of view, minicourses should be short, permitting them to be completed in one study session; however, other alternatives are possible. In general, the shorter the module the more flexible it becomes. The concept does not eliminate the possibility of combining two or three short study programs into a larger unit and having it remain a minicourse. The content of a minicourse is mastered to a specified level before the student proceeds to another unit of study. Comprehensive examinations can be given on the completion of one to several minicourses, but basically it is anticipated that each module will be self-contained and may or may not be correlated to other minicourses. Obviously one could establish prerequisite minicourses or relate modules to one another in any logical combination.

The teaching strategy could be as varied as it is with conventional courses (a series of two or three lectures, a laboratory, a seminar, or a combination of these); however, most instructional material could also be packaged as Audio-Tutorial programs.

Minicourse Teaching Strategies

1. Self-instructional programs (A-T, programmed texts, etc.)
2. Lecture-lab series (three or four lectures and labs in the conventional pattern)
3. Seminars and small group discussions
4. Research projects (some projects might involve several weeks' study)
5. Combination of strategies

The amount of credit for a minicourse is related to an approximation of the amount of study time required by the student. Minicourse credit is expressed in fractions of an hour which can be totaled when appropriate to equal a larger, more conventional representation of the student's progress. For example: twenty five to thirty minicourses might be recorded as four semester credit hours in biology.

1. Application

Minicourses can be used in many contexts, especially when self-instructional programs are employed.

A. Course components – The self-instructional units can be used as components of a larger, more comprehensive unit or course such as botany or zoology courses. In this case the instructional materials can be maintained in a special facility and specific minicourse assignments made. The number of minicourses required would relate to the total semester credit hours for such a course. Completion deadlines and sequencing of subject matter is specified for the entire program in much the same pattern as described in the earlier chapters on the Audio-Tutorial system.

B. Educational browsing – Since each minicourse is more or less an independent study, these independent units can be maintained in a library system or learning center. Students can use them as a source of educational browsing, to investigate special interests, to update important areas of information, or for review.

C. Remedial studies – Self-instructional minicourses stored in a learning center can be made available to students for supplementary or remedial studies in courses taught in the conventional manner. Students can be assigned specific remedial minicourses based on diagnostic tests, or the information covered in certain minicourses can be prerequisite with each student responsible for making up his deficiencies. Minicourses stored in this way also can be used as a resource to investigate areas of special interest or for special projects.

D. Continuing education – Minicourses in the self-instructional mode housed in a library or learning facility can be used as a source for continuing education. Faculty could review and update themselves without the time investment and regimentation of auditing courses. The facility might also serve professional people in the community who desire to update or extend their college education but who cannot enroll in college courses.

E. Community education – The materials necessary for self-instruction are often portable and potentially useable in individual study at home or in other situations disassociated from the conventional college facility. A variety of methods for dispensing or distributing minicourse programs could permit individuals to achieve many of their educational goals almost totally detached from a university. If these were the same materials used in a university context, college credit could be established by some appropriate testing procedure, and the individual could acquire a considerable portion of a college education at home. Compatible individuals could form study groups or clubs to concentrate on a specific cluster of minicourses and through mutual assistance and encouragement master the subject matter for college credit.

2. Advantages

Several benefits can be anticipated with the use of the minicourse concept.

A. Pacing — The use of self-instructional minicourses provides an opportunity for individual pacing at two levels—within the minicourse and within the traditional "course" designation. Students can be totally independent in their rate of study for a minicourse if they so desire. With few exceptions, it is not necessary to meet specific schedules or progress at a specific rate. On a more expanded basis, such as the semester credit hour equivalent of a conventional course, a student can begin and complete a series of minicourses at any time during the year instead of being locked into a semester time block. More emphasis is placed on acquisition of the information than on the time or rate of accomplishing the task. This is an especially important advantage for open colleges where students with little academic training are attempting to do college work. The magnitude of a conventional semester load of course work may be overwhelming and a student who fails to complete it in the prescribed time may become so humiliated and frustrated by the experience that his status is worse at the end than at the beginning.

B. Evaluation — Because of the compact and repeatable nature of a minicourse, the effectiveness of the learning strategy can be critically examined and evaluated. Components of a study program can be analyzed and eliminated, enlarged upon, reorganized or resequenced to provide the most efficient and effective study activities.

C. Flexibility — Sequencing of subject matter can be more flexible than with the conventional course. Not all students should begin at the same level or with the same topics. Some individuals may wish to start their study of biology from a chemical orientation whereas others may be more interested in a taxonomic approach. Each student beginning his study with his own area of interest would probably become more aware of the necessity for study in the other areas of his discipline—an awareness which might never have surfaced in a conventional lock-step sequencing. It is feasible then to allow students to begin by studying their primary interest and spread their base of knowledge as their interest grows.

D. Multi-courses — Subject matter can be adjusted to individual needs. For example, the veterinary science major may need to develop a great many skills in biology that differ from those needed for an English major. A student can take those minicourses particularly adapted to his own needs. The number of overlapping minicourses in an individualized curriculum will vary depending on the requirements or needs of the students.

E. Success orientation — The concept of learning for mastery can be satisfactorily implemented through the use of minicourses. No student need fail any minicourse since the size of the unit and the use of specifically stated and measurable objectives permit adjustment in study procedures related to individual needs. Failures can be pinpointed to specific subject matter (behavioral objectives) and remedied. The student can spend whatever time is necessary for him to achieve the minimum requirement. Since grades are not based on competition, students are free to help each other. The instructor becomes a coworker as the student strives to master the stated objective.

F. Team teaching — Minicourses provide an opportunity for using the very best teachers and subject matter experts to produce the instructional programs. A "pool" of these instructional programs provides a modified team-teaching approach with the potential for selecting the team of teachers from a great range of experts.

G. Increased personal contact — The use of minicourses provides an excellent opportunity for personal contact between students and staff. Instructors, freed of the repetitive activities of dispensing information, can deal with student problems on an individual basis. Teachers have time to give guidance to students who wish to go into greater depth, and to elaborate important and interesting points for those students who may desire it.

H. Frequent revision — Minicourse programs can undergo frequent revisions without a major overhaul of the entire biological curriculum. Each revision of a given topic can be based on the need for change, whether to update content or to improve the program's effectiveness. Revision can be approached intelligently on the basis of a careful analysis of both content and method.

I. Increased reinforcement — Since each minicourse is a complete unit and is tested at the end of the study, the student will receive immediate reinforcement or correction before progressing to the next unit of study. This reinforcement may be of considerable consequence for both attitude and "readiness" for subsequent study. This is in contrast with some conventional courses where the student is evaluated only after several weeks of study. A lack of feedback to the student can often result in frustration and, in some cases, a false sense of security. Basic ideas may be only partially or poorly learned and later cause the student insurmountable problems.

J. Multi-approaches — Many principles can be approached in a great variety of ways. With the minicourse concept it is possible to provide alternate programs for certain subject matter and to permit students to select the program which is best suited to their own particular interest, background and capacity.

K. Greater adaptation to varied teaching strategies — Minicourses provide a greater opportunity to adapt the teaching strategy to the subject matter being taught. Conventional courses commonly use only lectures and a lab and all subject matter is forced into this format. By using minicourses, one can employ the teaching strategy best suited to the nature of the content.

L. Multi-sensory — Minicourses make it possible to use instructional strategies which involve all of the sensory stimuli. One can structure a program involving sound, touch, taste, and sight. It seems logical that a correlation must exist between the extent and variety of stimuli and the amount of learning that occurs.

M. Multi-use — Once a minicourse has been well established, its content clearly identified, and its program known to be effective, the minicourse may be useful in a great variety of courses.

For example, a minicourse on mitosis can be useful for botany, zoology, horticulture, agronomy, and many other courses as well.

N. Lower cost — If minicourses can be used in this great variety of contexts and offer the advantages listed above, the cost of the total educational program for a student should be decreased. In addition, burden on educational facilities ought to be lightened since a substantial percentage of educational material could be studied while disassociated from the university facilities.

3. Disadvantages

No educational system operates without certain disadvantages and compromises. The minicourse approach will also have some major problems or disadvantages. Some of those expected at this time are as follows:

A. Major themes — There is a possibility that major themes might be overlooked by subdividing a discipline into small units of information. Under the conventional approach the same potential problem exists since subject matter is usually presented in lectures or laboratories separated in time and space. However, this eventuality has not been demonstrated to occur under either system and there are several possibilities to make adjustment if it did. Under the conventional system the major themes are often the subject of a single lecture or are referred to as a part of each study unit. This same strategy can be used to integrate and establish continuity among minicourses. Periodic comprehensive examinations can cause students to review and elaborate broad themes, e.g., final exams.

B. Administration — Logistics for administering minicourses is indeed a problem. If one has six hundred students and all are progressing at different rates and if the completion of a minicourse series does not coincide with the end of the semester, record keeping and maintenance of perishable materials are major problems. These administrative difficulties may be offset, however, through the more efficient use of materials since students are at different points in their programs at different times and one item of equipment can serve more students. Keeping records of each student's progress is a major task and certainly much more difficult than under the conventional system.

C. Facilities — The use of university facilities on an unscheduled basis may cause some problems. Students may find all the facilities in use at favorite times, and may waste considerable time trying to complete their study. This can cause much distress and frustration.

D. Change — The use of minicourses establishes a new role for the teacher, student, and administration. Any change from the normal procedure requires some adjustment time for all involved. Some students, having been conditioned over the years to taking little or no responsibility for their own education, find this new relationship to their progress rather frightening and overwhelming. Under this concept, the student's progress depends directly on the individual and his own initiative. Students who have entered college to acquire a degree merely by attending class find the requirement to master subject matter upsetting. Mastery is a new experience and the prospect of having to achieve above a 50 or 60% level is unfavorably received by some students. It may take a great deal of experience before they can appreciate that mastery of basic ideas will pay dividends in the long run. A whole new set of study habits is required and motivation becomes a critical factor.

The new role of the teacher is to seek ways in which to motivate students and assist them in a more personal way. The teacher is no longer a "dispenser of information"; rather he is a facilitator of learning. He is a strategist who attempts to maneuver students into situations which will cause them to accomplish specific objectives. This role is often less "ego inflating" and may expose his lack of capacity to deal with people on a personal basis. He must also be creative in the design of learning programs—a procedure which requires more than simply rehearsing what he knows. His programs are available for the scrutiny and criticism of his colleagues and students. This can be an uncomfortable position for many of us.

The new role of the administration is one of modifying the system to accommodate student needs in a less routine way. Scheduling is more difficult, record-keeping problems increase, and accounting for staff and student time becomes a major task. Many of the routine procedures will require revision and a major overhaul may be necessary.

Other disadvantages may also exist that are not yet recognized. However, the potential advantages far outweigh the disadvantages and solutions to the problems come fairly quickly. It is not for the "packages" that minicourses have been developed but for the multitude of innovative possibilities they present. The description of the two pilot studies at Purdue University which follows will further emphasize and elaborate some of the potential and the problems involved in utilization of the concepts of learning for mastery and minicourses.

Pilot Study I — Botany and Zoology
By Robert N. Hurst

Identification of Minicourse Categories and Topics

Prior to the fall of 1969 Biology 108 and 109 (Botany and Zoology) had been taught as separate entities. Though 108 was listed as a prerequisite to 109 and though there had been interaction between the senior instructors of these sequentially numbered courses, they had not actually been taught as sequential courses. The sequential nature was in reality an artifact of the catalog.

During 1968-69, it was decided to integrate the two courses, to adopt the concept of learning for mastery and to convert 109 to A-T. The first steps were to define the course content and identify the conceptual packages or "minicourses." Though this task appeared Herculean, it was in reality a rather pleasant and enlightening experience. The content of the two courses subdivided naturally into conceptual packages, and minicourse topics were easily established.

Four categories of minicourses were generated; the first three (common minicourses, plant minicourses, and animal minicourses) were obvious delineations of already-existing topical content in the two courses; the fourth represented an enhancement made possible by elimination of the redundancy which resulted from the courses being taught as separate entities.

The common minicourses were those which covered concepts common to both plants and animals such as cells, respiration, mitosis, meiosis, protein synthesis, and genetics. Common minicourses also included topics of such import that if a student took only a single semester of biology he at least would be introduced to these important concepts. Examples of this latter type of common minicourse were photosynthesis and succession. The elimination of redundancy alluded to earlier occurred in the generation of common minicourses. Many common concepts were being taught by both senior instructors. A series of minicourse topics pertaining primarily to plants made up the second category and a series pertaining primarily to the animal world made up the third.

The fourth and most flexible category which continually changed as topical minicourses were added and deleted was one containing so-called optional minicourses.

This was the bonus category mentioned afore. A student had to complete a specified number of these minicourses if he enrolled in and completed both 108 and 109. The optional aspect of these minicourses was his decision to complete specific minicourses from an extensive list of units available. Students usually chose those of special interest or value to them. Pre-vet students, for example, typically elected to complete an optional minicourse on the vertebrate skeleton. This minicourse was of value to them when they took the veterinary medicine extrance exam as sophomores. In fact, this optional minicourse and several others were and will continue to be produced specifically at the request of students. These optional modules, then, enhanced the role of the student in determining to some extent his curriculum while in the courses. Typical optional minicourse titles included flowers, fruit and seeds, population, birth control, wood anatomy, and more than twenty others at this writing.

If a student enrolled in either 108 or 109 as the first course in the sequence, he completed all the common minicourses plus all the plant or animal minicourses depending on his enrollment in 108 or 109. In his subsequent enrollment in the second course of the sequence, he completed all the plant or animal minicourses and a specified number of optional modules. Upon completion of the sequence, he had achieved mastery on all of the common and plant or animal modules and a specified number of optional minicourses.

Facilities, Scheduling, and Quiz Format

The facilities for the two courses were not significantly different (except in terms of size) from the physical arrangement which was already in existence for Biology 108. Two rooms connected to the main hall and to each other by a prep room served as the Learning Center. Each room had 32 booths and students entered either room from the common prep room. This brought students from both courses into frequent contact with one another and perhaps broke down barriers commonly found between members of two different courses. It was hoped that students would begin to think of their enrollment not in terms of a conventional course, but as a contract with the senior instructors for the completion of specified numbers and categories of minicourses.

A master panel near the front of the prep room was programmed each week to show the location of specific minicourses and availability of the minicourses booths. The booths were numbered sequentially from 1 to 64 and minicourses used primarily by one course might be found in either room. Typically, however, to assure the greatest amount of instructional help for the student from the Graduate Teaching Assistants working in the Learning Center, most of the minicourses used by 108 were housed in one room and those used by 109 students in the other. Flexibility remained, however, and occasions arose when an increased booth requirement in one course was solved by simply moving needed minicourses into the other room.

A schedule of the minicourses which were available each week in the Learning Center was given to the students and the specific minicourses over which the students were to be quizzed were listed for each week. Students were urged to follow the suggested time schedule, but provisions were made to allow those for whom the pace was too fast to move more slowly through the course. Minicourse setups scheduled in the Learning

Center during a specific week were always held over for at least one additional week to enable slower students (or those who had not satisfied their oral quiz instructor or who had not reached the mastery level on their written quiz) to continue their study.

Oral quizzes were scheduled at a specific time each week for each student, who then met in a session similar to the oral quiz portion of the conventional IQS. The format was virtually the same. The major change was to a complete-incomplete evaluation by the instructor instead of points equating to grades of A, B, C, D, F. Students who received an incomplete on their oral were cycled through a re-study, re-take program in order to complete this requirement.

A written quiz was also prepared for each minicourse, and, depending on quiz item and minicourse difficulty, a mastery level was set for each minicourse quiz by the instructor. To achieve mastery a student had to reach or exceed that level. This might mean 9 correct answers out of 10 questions on one minicourse, 13 out of 15 on another, etc. The level of mastery was arbitrarily determined by the senior instructor based on past experience. Though the mastery level varied among minicourses, it averaged between 85 and 90%. An early attempt at 100% mastery was abandoned when it became obvious that the best prepared student even on a short quiz may accidentally read a question incorrectly or make an incorrect mark on his answer card.

Written quizzes could be taken prior to the scheduled oral quiz session or for a two-week period after the scheduled oral quiz. Students were encouraged, however, to take the written quiz immediately after their oral, and because it was convenient to do so (they were held in the same room), they usually did. If the mastery level was not achieved, the student was cycled through a re-study, re-take program which included an extensive oral quiz on a one-to-one basis with an instructor to determine the student's readiness to attempt the written quiz a second or third time.

Record Keeping and Personnel

A sign in-sign out card upon which students recorded time spent in the Learning Center was used for booth assignment as in the earlier conventional A-T format. In addition a single card listing the numbers for all minicourses in all four categories (about 85 minicourses) was used by a secretary in the quiz room to record a student's progress. Next to each minicourse number there was a space for recording the results of both the oral and written quizzes. The only symbols used were "I" for incomplete and "C" for complete. When a student demonstrated to his oral quiz instructor that he had an adequate grasp of the information and concepts presented in a given minicourse, the instructor recorded a "C" on his own worksheet and transferred it to this permanent record card. A "C" was also recorded by the secretary when a student reached the mastery level on a written quiz for a given minicourse. Each time a student received an incomplete on an oral quiz or failed to reach the mastery level on a written quiz an "I" was recorded. A check on an individual student's progress and a record of any difficulty he might have been encountering was available from this card. It was also easy to run a quick check on the effectiveness of a given minicourse program or the difficulty of a written quiz by observing the I's and C's recorded.

This same card was used to record completed minicourses which were to be "banked" by students for later use. Students enrolled in either course could study minicourse units they would normally take while enrolled in the other course and "bank" them until their enrollment in that course. A student could in reality complete both courses while enrolled in one. When he registered for the second course, it would have already been completed. Though students were slow to accept the idea of "banking" minicourses during the first and second semester the system was used, several students in the third semester "banked" courses, and two students completed over half of the minicourses required for the second course. The "banking business" will undoubtedly increase, and this option will very likely help the extremely capable student maintain interest and motivation.

There was a logistical problem of maintaining individual records for each student. These records had several entries made each week and some were carried over into the next semester when students failed to complete the course. In spite of its appearance, the problem was not insurmountable. In fact, during the first semester of the experiment, record cards were maintained by the individual oral quiz instructors for each of their own students. It was awkward, but operable. It was "discovered" before the start of the second semester that a full-time secretarial clerk could be hired at the same cost as one Graduate Teaching Assistant. Thereupon, one assistantship was turned back into the department and one clerk was hired. This secretary sat in the quiz room, handed out written quizzes, graded answer cards, gave students *immediate* feedback on quizzes, told them which behavioral objectives the questions they missed were related to, recorded the quiz results and did all this for 800 students enrolled in the two courses during a normal five-day work week. The burden of record-keeping was removed from the instructors, and uniformity of records was achieved. Thus the program already operating in a conventional A-T format was converted to the minicourse-mastery format with no increase in personnel.

Study Sessions

No basic change was made in the study session format from that of the Biology 108 course. Students were still scheduled into a General Assembly Session one hour a week, a weekly oral quiz session, and they were still expected to arrange to study in the Learning Center (the Independent Study Session) for approximately four hours per week. If a student followed the suggested schedule of minicourses set up in the Learning Center, it would require about four hours of work each week to complete the ISS. Some weeks three or four shorter minicourses might be scheduled, other weeks only one or two longer modules.

Grading Procedures

Students were told in the first General Assembly Session that no one could fail the course (see Appendix G for student handout). Furthermore, when they completed the required minicourses by satisfying the oral quiz and achieving mastery on all the written quizzes, they received a C. The grades of A and B were awarded to students who chose to work for those grades and who accumulated A-B points by the various means outlined below. Students who failed to complete all the required minicourses were given an Incomplete on their grade report. When the students completed the unfinished mini-courses the Incomplete was changed to the A, B, or C they had earned. There was no time limit placed on the student to complete the course. It is conceivable that a student's education might be interrupted by military service, pregnancy or whatever, for a period of several years. The student would still be given credit for any minicourses already completed when he or she returned to complete the course.

Grades of A or B were earned by accumulating designated numbers of points assigned to activities beyond the completion of the oral and written quizzes for required minicourses. About 60 per cent of all the possible A or B points was associated with three special A-B exams given during the General Assembly Sessions to students working for an A or B grade. Questions on these exams were hopefully not the type C level students could answer. They could not be answered by rote memorization of factual information, but were structured to force the student to synthesize, transfer learning, interpret, or design (some of the kinds of activities one expects from A or B level students).

About 14 per cent of the total A-B points possible was associated with the oral quiz. Students presenting outstanding contributions to the presentations of others could earn one or two points each week towards an A or B.

The remainder of the total possible A-B points (26 percent) was associated with the activities outlined below. The grade of B (which obviously required fewer points than an A grade) could not have been earned by accumulating points only from this last category. So many opportunities were afforded the students to earn points in this category that any student willing to put forth the effort could have earned the maximum number of allowable points. About 60 per cent of the points necessary to earn a grade of B could have been earned then from this last group of activities. The rest of the points for a B would have had to be earned from the first two categories. (See the table below for clarification.)

Source of A-B Points and Points Needed for an A or B

Category	Total Points Available	Total Allowable
1. A-B Exams	110	110
2. Oral Quiz Bonus	26	26
3. Multiple Activities		
Supplemental Readings	42	
Bonus Operations	14	
Quests	17	50
Extra Optionals	34	
Projects	50	
	Total Points	186
Total Points Needed for a B —	85	
Total Points Needed for an A —	110	

1. Students could read assigned supplementary articles and summarize them in a writing session each week in the quiz room.
2. Students could perform so-called Bonus Operations in the Learning Center when they appeared in the Study Guide for a given minicourse. These were activities such as additional dissections, supporting readings, and additional information that could not be fitted into the minicourse because of time limitations or specific appeal only to special interest groups. Students performed the study and then took an oral quiz with the instructor on duty in the Learning Center and earned up to a specified number of points. This was a favorite activity of many students.
3. Students could complete Quest assignments found in the Study Guides of particular minicourses. Quest topics were those of a controversial nature, or topics treated differently by different authors, or topics not adequately covered in the text which were worthy of further study or of interest to particular groups of students. Quest assignments were library oriented, and students were required to use at least three references for the paper they submitted for possible A-B points.
4. Students could complete extra optional minicourses beyond the number necessary to complete the required number for the course, and A-B points were awarded on the basis of the unit value of extra optional minicourses completed.
5. Finally, students could become involved with any worthwhile biological project after consultation with the senior instructor, and earn up to the number of points agreed upon by the student and senior instructor. These projects could take any form including laboratory work, library work, involvement in an ecological project, etc.

Results

The information presented above outlines the program as it operated at the time of this writing. This section of the paper will summarize some of the early results which caused the senior instructors to adjust and alter the program to its present format. The format will continually be revised, but early experiments have indicated that the program is not only operable, but well worth the extra effort required to implement it.

1. Freshman students are probably not ready to discipline themselves completely and accept total responsibility for individual pacing. They appreciate suggested schedules and time limits. When students during the first semester were told they could repeat a minicourse quiz until they reached the mastery level, they either never got around to trying it a second time or they did not study between attempts and began to try to "luck out" on quizzes. By limiting both the time during which they could complete the minicourse and the number of times they could try, while requiring them to pass an oral quiz before subsequent attempts, the problem was virtually eliminated. When they realized the re-take system almost guaranteed success, they accepted it.
2. Students preferred the idea of minicourses being optional to them. They seldom complained about the length or the poor quality of an optional minicourse, yet

never hesitated to do so via the suggestion box for minicourses in the other three categories. Many minicourses were removed from the three required categories and converted into optional modules. Careful scheduling can almost guarantee that students will take specific optionals which the senior instructor feels are most important. In time a student may have the option of choosing at least 50 per cent of his program in the two courses.

3. Students preferred shorter minicourses. It was advantageous to fractionate a long module into two modules, even when total study time for the two modules was greater than the original. Several long minicourses were split whenever shorter modules could still meet the criterion for a minicourse. For example, a minicourse on excretion which had an original unit value of 3.0 (the average student would take three hours to complete the entire program) was split into two minicourses, (1) excretion—with a unit value of 2.0, and (2) kidney function—with a unit value of 1.5. Although both minicourses were scheduled the same week and students actually spent more time in the ISS to complete the two modules than the original mother module, they did not complain about the length of the two units as they had about the mother module.

4. Students preferred a greater variety of ways to earn A-B points. They enjoyed taking the A-B exams, and almost every student took all three exams though many had no chance of improving their C grades with the last exam even if they had every answer correct.

   They were also quite willing to have the total number of points necessary for an A or a B grade raised as long as more options for earning points were given. The oral bonus point system was adopted at the suggestion of several students. The quality of the oral quizzes increased several magnitudes with this change. Students did more outside reading and were more prone to offer additional contributions to try to have 1 or 2 A-B points awarded them each week in IQS.

   As indicated in the section on Grading Procedures, several other options for earning A-B points were introduced and undoubtedly several others will be added. Each option usually meant an increased performance needed to achieve the higher grade, but students were pleased with each new option.

5. It was thought some students who did not finish the course might request the senior instructor to award them a D grade in the course rather than be forced to earn a C. The grade of D is a passing grade, and it is the only grade some students look for in courses distasteful to them or difficult for them. No student has made this request; therefore, the concept of learning for mastery may not be too antagonistic to the student mind.

6. A major complaint heard often about students is that it is difficult to get them into the library except to sleep or study class notes. In Biology 109 about 35 per cent of the students attempted one or more quests which involved them at least one time with three or more different library books. This is a beginning in a course which pushed few if any students into the library before the introduction of the quest. It is anticipated more will choose to earn A-B points in this manner in future semesters.

7. The grade breakdown for the first complete year of the experiment was as follows:

A	20%
B	23%
C	37%
*Incomplete	20%

8. The average number of hours spent in the Learning Center each week by letter grade received is indicated below. Keep in mind that the minicourses were scheduled so the average student would spend about four hours in the Learning Center each week.

A students	3 hrs. 48 mins.
B students	3 hrs. 49 mins.
C students	3 hrs. 19 mins.
Incompletes	2 hrs. 58 mins.

A considerable amount of outside study apparently was involved with the earning of A or B grades, since A students spent less than thirty minutes more than C students in the ISS each week.

9. Finally, with the minicourse and mastery package, a greater amount of peripheral teaching and learning took place. After just one or two weeks of the course, students formed study groups (most commonly their oral quiz groups). These units could be found in the prep room, in both rooms of the Learning Center, in every empty room near the Learning Center, and in the halls outside the Learning Center. Much information was being transferred and a good amount of incidental teaching and learning. Discussion in these groups revolved around the behavioral objectives. If these instructional objectives are properly written they can demand appropriate behavioral responses from the students whether learned from a minicourse program or from a peer in an informal study session. If this is the case, is it not most complimentary to the entire concept of individualized instruction that these sessions occur? Perhaps more teaching and learning takes place in these sessions than through the audio tape and all the supporting media.

If minicourse packaging and the concept of learning for mastery help students learn biology better and if at the same time these students enjoy it more, their senior instructors could not be more pleased. Preliminary experiments indicate this might be the case.

Pilot Study II — Comparative Veterinary Anatomy
By J. R. Welser

A comparative gross anatomy course** provided an opportunity for application of the

---

*This high percentage is rather distressing at first glance. However, if one considers that in a freshman course 20 per cent D's and F's is not uncommon and that the students receiving an incomplete under this system may have only two or three minicourses yet to master to obtain a C grade in the course—20 per cent incompletes is reasonable. Further, a potential now exists for giving variable credit depending on the amount of minicourses mastered.

**VAN 421 Gross Anatomy of Domestic Species—Semester II, 1969-70, Purdue University.

educational concepts of minicourses, learning for mastery,* and A-T instruction in veterinary medicine. The traditional 16-week semester course was subdivided into 12 minicourses based upon the topographical areas of the animal (head, neck, thorax, abdomen, etc.). The length of time devoted to each minicourse was based on past experience and the amount of material to be presented. Specific behavioral objectives were written for each minicourse and distributed to the students. Along with the objectives, the students were provided with a variety of learning activities (A-T programs, dissections, demonstrations, handouts, suggested readings, and live animals) to aid them in attaining the stated objectives. The objectives directed the structuring and production of the learning activities. For each minicourse an A-T program which integrated basic knowledge with dissection in the laboratory and surgical applications was provided. The A-T programs consisted of audio tapes, 2 × 2 slides, loop films, video tapes, preserved specimens, demonstrations, handouts, and suggested readings. The programs were set up in a multi-media study room in booths equipped with a cartridge tape recorder and a 2 × 2 slide projector. Ten study booths were used for the class of 60 students.

For evaluation purposes and for assignment in the dissecting lab, students were randomly divided into ten groups of six students, and each group selected a leader. In the dissecting laboratory, each group had a horse and a cow cadaver assigned to it for dissection. A live horse and cow were available for palpation in a room adjoining the dissection laboratory. It was suggested that the group work together by discussing, quizzing, and explaining concepts to one another. However, students did not have to work together since the laboratories (multi-media and dissection) were open 24 hours per day. Instructors were available in the learning laboratories to answer questions at specified times, usually three hours per day, five days per week. In addition to the senior instructor, two graduate instructors assisted in student evaluation and staffing of the learning laboratories. An artist/secretary/record keeper and a photographer/equipment manager composed the rest of the staff.

The evaluation of each minicourse was based solely on the stated objectives for that minicourse and was in the form of a tag (identification) test and an oral exam. The oral exam was given to a total work group, with the group leader making an appointment with the assigned instructor when the group was ready for evaluation. The students were expected to complete the objectives for each unit (mastery level was set at 90% on the tag test, along with an accurate and complete answer on the oral exam as judged by the evaluating instructor). The oral exams were conducted in a method similar to that described earlier in this volume. It was expected that each student would be prepared on all the objectives for each minicourse. The item each student discussed was chosen at random at the time of the oral exam. Following a student's presentation, he was graded incomplete (I), complete (C), or plus (+), based on his performance on both the oral and written exams. A plus rating was awarded to students for superior performance (above minimum), on both the oral and written exams. The other members of the group were expected to provide corrections or additions and to ask any questions that they felt were pertinent at the end of a presentation. Each oral evaluation was scheduled for one half hour. A 4 × 6 card listing the minicourses was maintained for each student to record his progress.

*For further material on Mastery see Benjamin S. Bloom. Learning for Mastery: Evaluation Comment. University of California, Los Angeles, California, 1968.

Upon achieving the required mastery level on evaluation of each unit, the student was given a complete (C), indicating that he had satisfied the objectives for that unit. If a student failed to meet the objectives for a minicourse, he received an incomplete (I), and could submit himself for reexamination whenever he felt ready. The (I) was replaced by a (C) if the student met the required mastery level upon reexamination. In order to satisfactorily complete the course, the student had to complete all the minicourses by the end of the semester. Failure to complete any minicourse by semester end resulted in an incomplete (I) for the semester. The completion of all 12 minicourses assured the student of a grade of "C" in a course. Thus, a student could not fail the course per se, but rather, he could only fail to complete the course.

Completion of seven minicourses by the end of the eighth week, and the subsequent completion of five additional minicourses before the scheduled final exam, permitted the student, if he so desired, to take the mid-term and final exams. By taking both the mid-term and the final exam, the student attempted to earn a grade of "A" or "B" in the course. This did not jeopardize the grade of "C" the student had already earned by meeting the mastery level for the 12 minicourses. The basis for awarding a grade of "A" or "B" in the course is illustrated in the table below. A student scoring better than 85 per cent on the mid-term and final exams and receiving at least 7 plus ratings (+) on minicourse evaluations was awarded a grade of "A."

Final Course Grade Determination
A-B Exam Score

	Up to 75%	75% and up	85% and up
<5	C	C	C
5	C	B	B
7	C	B	A

Results

In minicourse evaluations throughout the semester a total of 71 incompletes (10 per cent) were given. These incompletes were distributed among 67 per cent of the students with one-third of the students meeting the mastery level for all 12 minicourses on their first attempt. Very little conflict occurred with the students over the judgment concerning their performance on the minicourse evaluations. In several instances the students volunteered to return after additional preparation. In all cases the incompletes were made up before the semester and deadline and no student received an incomplete for the course. The use of the plus rating on the oral and written exams was found to be cumbersome. It will be dropped from usage in future courses.

Cognitive

At the semester end the students had been asked to master the identification of 672 anatomical structures, as well as be able to orally describe or discuss 122 topics. The 672 items represented separate anatomical structures, and did not include the multiple identification of the same structure on the cadaver, skeleton, or live animal. To evaluate total course achievement (mastery) of the objectives, a 60-item laboratory identification test (chosen at random from the 672 items) was given at final exam time. In addition students were asked to answer questions requiring application of the identifications for 40 of these 60 items. The test mean was 87.2%, with a high of 98% and a low of 75%. There were only three scores in the 70s. The level of performance (mean 87.2%) at the completion of the course compares favorably with the level of mastery (90%) required on each unit evaluation throughout the semester.

Finally the cognitive level of the students was compared with that of students who had previously taken the course utilizing more traditional methods of instruction. The comparative exam consisted of 100 multiple choice questions and was constructed by using two exams given by other instructors in 1968 and 1966. The 1968 exam consisted of 60 items and was used on part I of the 1970 exam. Part 2 of the exam included 40 of the 50 items used in 1966. Ten items of the 1966 exam were similar to the 1968 exam and were discarded. To the author's knowledge, the exams were not available to the students. A one-way analysis of variance among classes (1966, 1968, 1970) on Student Aptitude Test scores indicated no significant differences among the classes, $F=1.21$(ns).

As is apparent in Figure 6.2, supported by statistical analysis, the different course design and method of presentation of instructional materials resulted in no significant difference in student learning on final examination.

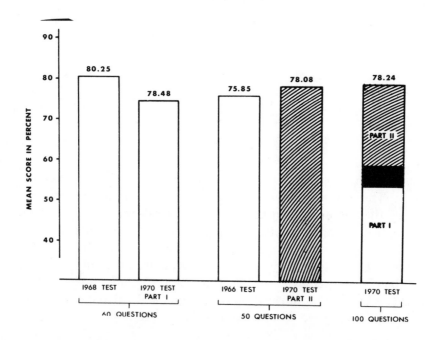

FIGURE 6.2—The final exam for the experimental course was made up of the 1968 (part 1) and 1966 (part 2) final exams. Ten questions which were similar on the 1968 and 1966 tests were discarded. A comparison of the mean test scores showed no significant differences.

Affective

The students completed three separate opinion evaluation forms on the course: (1) The Purdue Rating Scale for Instruction—a course evaluation form with a reliability of .91 when completed by more than 20 students; (2) Veterinary Student Course Evaluation—a form developed by the veterinary students to evaluate their professional courses; (3) Instructor's Evaluation Form—prepared by the instructor. There was close correlation of the opinions registered by the students on each of the evaluation forms. For example, the student reaction to questions on the usefulness of the course produced "favorable" results on all three forms. Thus replies to questions on "How the course is fulfilling your needs" were in the 99 percentile on the Purdue Rating Scale. "Did you feel this course was useful in your personal development as a professional?" produced results of Yes 59 No 0 using the Veterinary Student Course Form; while "My overall rating of the usefulness of this course" showed up as 91 per cent (median) (0-100 per cent) on the Instructor's Evaluation Form. The suitability of methods by which subject matter of the course was presented was in the 99 percentile on the Purdue Rating Scale.

One of the frequent criticisms of automated instruction is that it will result in less student/faculty contact. On the precourse questionnaire 86 per cent of the students felt that they would see less of the teacher using Audio-Tutorial (A-T) instruction. This criticism was not supported by student opinion on the course evaluation form (items A, B, C in the table below). Since the contact between the instructors and students was on a one-to-one or small group basis, the students felt more time was spent with them and that the time spent was more relevant.

In comparison with the other courses I have taken, the methods used this semester resulted in				
	Percent Replying			
	Much More	**More**	**Less**	**Much Less**
A. Formal contact with instructors	27	33	29	11
B. Informal contact with instructors	62	36	2	0
C. Time spent in discussion with instructors	43	47	10	0
D. Time spent in discussion with students	57	41	2	0
E. Learning from fellow students	47	49	0	3

The allegation that the specification of objectives will limit what the students learn was not borne out by student opinion. In response to the statement, "I used the objectives as a guide to what I learned, " 100 per cent of the students replied "always" or "sometimes." However, in response to the question, "Did the objectives limit what you learned?" 26 per cent replied "never," 29 per cent replied "seldom," 45 per cent replied "sometimes," and none replied "always." In response to the question, "What was the objectives sheets' biggest advantage?" 41 per cent replied, "As an outline to important topics for study."

As is apparent in the table below, the students were in agreement that it was their fault if they failed to perform satisfactorily on a unit evaluation. This fact was due to several reasons. The primary reason was that learning for mastery calls for specifying what is to be learned by the students and basing evaluation on these specifications. In addition, the students were asked for input for each unit's objectives and the group leaders were consulted concerning their group's progress. Thus, specific objectives used in evaluation focus the responsibility for learning on the students and aid them in directing their activities.

If I failed a unit evaluation, in my opinion

	Percent Replying			
	Always	Sometimes	Seldom	Never
A. It was my fault	72	26	2	0
B. It was my group's fault	6	18	27	49
C. It was my instructor's fault	0	9	26	65
D. It was the objectives' fault	4	17	13	66

The students were asked to rate the course activities on a scale of 0-100 per cent by evaluating their effect on amount of learning, motivation, long range value, and development of attitude towards veterinary medicine. The results, shown in Figure 6.3,

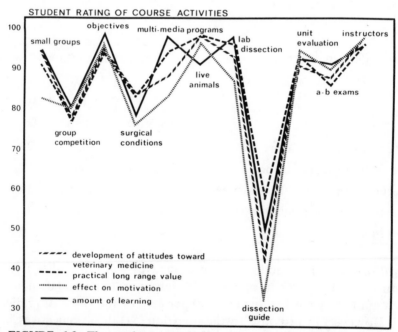

FIGURE 6.3—The students rated the various course activities on a scale of 0-100% concerning their contribution to the amount of learning, effect on motivation, practical long range value, and development of attitudes toward veterinary medicine.

indicate that those factors which had learning value were also rated favorably in motivation, long range value, and development of attitude. The dissection guides, group competition, and surgical conditions were downgraded relative to the other activities. The poor rating of surgical conditions is difficult to explain since many students felt that they were useful in illustrating applications of basic scientific knowledge to clinical veterinary medicine, thus serving as an advanced organizer. The instructors were especially pleased with the high ratings received by the objectives, multi-media programs, and unit evaluations.

The failure to attain any significant cognitive gain utilizing the developed model of instruction should not discourage its application or overshadow the positive ratings in the affective domain. The possibilities presented by minicourses, learning for mastery, and A-T instruction are many and warrant further application.

Chapter VII

THE USE OF AUDIO-TUTORIAL METHODS IN ELEMENTARY SCHOOL INSTRUCTION

GENESIS OF THE PROGRAM

By 1965 it was clearly evident that the Audio-Tutorial approach was highly successful with college students, not only in botany but also in other sciences and a wide range of disciplines. We had begun some research on cognitive learning processes using students in the A-T botany course at Purdue University, and some promising results were evident. Since much of the learning occurs in the A-T center, and study time was recorded as shown in Chapter IV, some measure of learning efficiency was possible.

Most evaluation has been for grading purposes with testing conducted to array students for grade assignment. High test scores may be the result of high motivation for protracted study, evidence of prior knowledge, good genic aptitude, or all three factors in some combination. Efficient learning calls for rapid acquisition of new knowledge as well as high performance. The critical variable of time needed by individuals for acquiring knowledge is rarely measured in educational research. A-T instruction, then, provided a means for obtaining data on this highly significant parameter in the study of cognitive learning; the method provided a way to assess the amount of knowledge acquired per unit of study time. However, college students may study for varying intervals outside of the learning center. They may have widely different backgrounds in related areas, e.g., chemistry or zoology, which can influence the rate of learning in botany but not be detected in pretests or other approaches assessing the "starting point" for individual learners. For these reasons it was evident that elementary school children taught in school would make much better research subjects, and it remained to be seen if A-T methods could be devised which would function with young children.

With the time and freedom of a sabbatical leave at Harvard University in 1965-66, the second author commenced development of A-T programs for first and third grade children. Some financial support was provided by the Research Development Center at Harvard University, and a technician as well as a research assistant cooperated with the author. By November, 1965, two 15-minute lessons dealing with plant growth (corn and beans) were developed and tested with children in Bishop Elementary School in Arlington, Massachusetts. An RCA cassette-type tape recorder (now extinct) was employed for simple, one-knob operation of the recorder. Now there are dozens of smaller, more effective cassette recorders on the market, and we are moving away from the Technicolor loop film projector to other types of projectors. Figure 7.1 shows a child working at an early A-T lesson. Four lessons on plant growth were developed during 1965-66 and several lessons on electrostatics for use with third grade classes (cf. Bridgham 1969). Evaluation showed that an A-T approach was effective in teaching children concepts of plant growth and electrostatics. Programs were tested in three Boston area elementary schools.

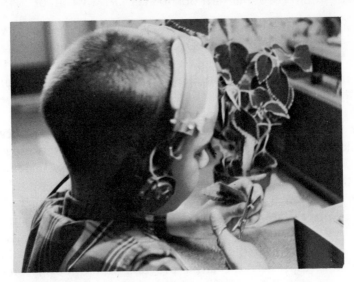

FIGURE 7.1—First grade student working at an early Audio-Tutorial lesson on plant growth.

Upon returning to Purdue University with some good evidence that the A-T method could be effective in teaching science to elementary school students, one might expect that financial support to continue the work would be easy to come by, especially with the recent passage of the Elementary and Secondary Education Act with millions of federal dollars targeted at improving school learning. Not so. Numerous phone calls, personal visits, and written proposals to various agencies proved fruitless. Then, as so commonly happens, some support for a demonstration program was secured at home in West Lafayette, Indiana, through the Wabash Valley Education Center. Successful use of the plant growth programs designed in the Boston area by students in Otterbein, Indiana, a small rural community, suggested that A-T science lessons could be used by a wide range of students. At this time, the second author moved to Cornell University.

With continuing support from the Wabash Valley Education Center and from Cornell University, a series of A-T lessons were designed and tested in some fifty schools located in Indiana and New York. The teachers involved were enthusiastic about the A-T elementary science lessons, and none requested to drop from the demonstration programs. Following termination of support from the Wabash Valley Education Center in 1969, research work and lesson development were continued largely with support from Cornell University. Our experience had shown that carefully prepared A-T instruction in science not only was an effective, practicable approach to elementary school science teaching, but the programs provided a powerful research tool for the study of cognitive learning processes. The future financial support of this program now appears to be dependent on its salability through commercial channels.

PROGRAM DEVELOPMENT

Typically, the planning of curriculum for elementary science has been centered on layout of a "scope and sequence chart" showing at what grade levels and in what sequence science topics will be ordered. Of course, in this planning, careful consideration is given to topics presented in competing elementary science programs. If Company X has a unit on rocks in grade four, then Company Y authors are likely to plan a rock unit into the grade four program. Up to the mid-1960s, elementary science textbooks and associated "lab kits" were monotonously similar.

Federal support for elementary science curriculum development began in 1960 with funding of the Elementary Science Study (ESS). In addition to this program, the National Science Foundation provided support in 1961 for the Science Curriculum Improvement Study (SCIS), the American Association for the Advancement of Science Program (Science–A Process Approach) in 1963, and several other smaller projects. The ESS program sought to place emphasis on children's work with materials in such a way as to encourage "inquiry" or learning by "discovery." No sequence of units was planned nor was sequencing considered desirable. The SCIS program and the AAAS program did plan sequences for lessons, especially the latter program where lessons present a sequential hierarchy of "process skills" or "inquiry skills" such as observing, classifying, inferring, and experimentation.*

Until the mid-1960s, elementary science programs were all topical in organization. Topics such as weather, rocks, plants, planets, transportation, etc., were presented in successively greater detail at higher grade levels. In contrast, concept organization of material would present living systems, energy and energy transformations, molecular kinetics, etc., not with these labels, but with deliberate emphasis on these scientific concepts with progressively more sophisticated exemplars and pupil activities at higher grade levels. The move to concept organization of elementary science was given impetus by the National Science Teachers' Association's Committee which recommended that sequential science programs should be planned around the major "conceptual schemes" of science with coordinate attention to the processes of science (cf. Novak 1964 and 1966).

The ESS program continued the topic approach to science but improved on earlier programs in the quality of material developed and the heavy emphasis on direct experience with materials, rather than memorization of facts. The AAAS program is topical as to content organization, but the heavy emphasis on "inquiry skills" minimizes the importance of the content presented. Karplus, the director of the SCIS program, placed emphasis on the concept organization, with teacher guides designed to explain both the concept organization and the importance of children's manipulations of material.

Our work with Audio-Tutorial science has been based on a conceptual organization of content but with careful attention to "inquiry skills." As a base for planning new lessons, we have used the organization of The World of Science Series (Novak 1966) which was developed over a six-year period of writing and testing. Audio-Tutorial methods so greatly enhance the quality of science that can be presented, as contrasted to textbooks with associated teacher-led activities, that the A-T elementary science program probes more

---

*For further information on these programs see Paul DeHart Hurd, and James Joseph Gallagher, New Directions in Elementary Science Teaching. Belmont, California: Wadsworth Publishing Co., 1968.

deeply and broadly those concepts present in The World of Science Series. Nevertheless, it is necessary to consider curriculum goals for more than a month or year, and the set of concepts developed progressively in the Series has been more than helpful in aiding graduate students and other staff members who have been involved in A-T lesson development.

By way of illustration, the curriculum model proposed by Johnson (1967) may be helpful. He points out that curriculum planning begins with assessment and selection of knowledge in the "teachable" culture. Curriculum planning involves more than selecting content, albeit even this had been poorly done in many early science programs; it also involves decisions on ordering that content and in planning instructional strategics (Fig. 7.2). It is the latter area where A-T methods provide important advantages although content selection and sequencing have also been carefully considered in our work. In addition, A-T methods provide a useful way to assess whether or not "desired pupil behaviors" are being attained, for errors in performance are easily observed and the defective segment of the A-T program can be modified accordingly.

Planning a new A-T lesson has been a complex process. First, consideration is given as to what major concept (or concepts) are to be extended by the lesson. The next step usually involves planning an appropriate activity through which the concept may be illustrated. This step may take days or weeks. Very early in the planning we discuss with children the concepts or activities we are considering for a lesson. The need for interaction with children at all stages of lesson development is absolutely critical. Sometimes a new piece of apparatus is designed, such as that shown in Figure 7.3. The apparatus shown was designed for lesson 6 in our first grade lesson series to allow a child to observe how addition of "energy producing units" (i.e., dry cells) increases the amount of change observed, such as the speed of the motor or the brightness of the light bulb. We

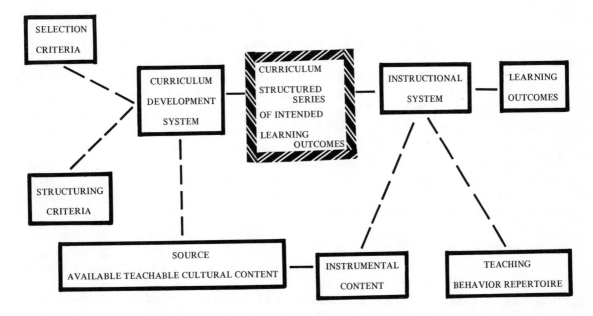

FIGURE 7.2—Johnson's (1967) model for curriculum design.

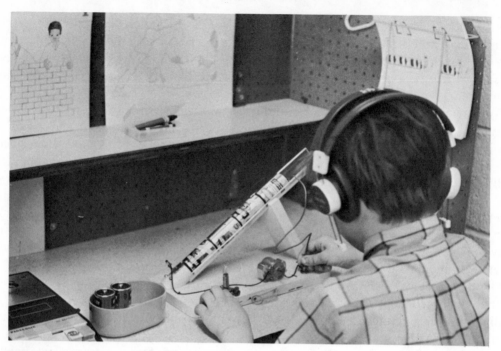

FIGURE 7.3—Child working with apparatus to illustrate relationship between amount of energy and amount of change.

are extending the child's concept here that changes in matter don't just "happen," but rather that energy exchanges are involved in changes. To be sure, no one lesson or even a series of lessons will establish clear, fully assimilated concepts of energy or the relation between energy and changes. However, these experiences will be remembered, and the ordered sequence of experience together with appropriate language development has been shown to develop substantial, stable concepts in the children we have studied.

Once the content and activities for a lesson have been selected, a program is written and then recorded. Next, we try out this new program with four or five children at the appropriate age and experience level and observe them as they are guided by the audio-tape. Immediately, it becomes apparent that some major or minor changes are needed. Sometimes the children fail to manipulate the apparatus in the proper way. When stopping the tape and showing children how to perform the manipulations proves unsuccessful, we sometimes have to scrap the apparatus and begin all over again. More often, changes in the language used, slowing the pace of audio guidance, or minor modification of the apparatus will suffice to solve the problem. With every lesson at least three or four revisions are necessary before it will be relatively trouble-free and successful with most children in the target population.

At this point we commence extensive field testing with lessons placed in classrooms, learning centers, and other locations (Fig. 7.4). Periodic observation of students is still needed, but now a trained technician might be employed to identify possible trouble spots. We use "behavioral checklists" to record observations as well as interviews with students to determine why they had trouble with segments of the program. A sample behavioral checklist is given in Appendix H. When 90 per cent or more of the students are

FIGURE 7.4a–Carrel in a self-contained classroom.

FIGURE 7.4b–Carrels set up in a learning center.

successful on all of the critical items of our checklist, we consider the lesson to be "operational" and move on to other work. However, long term evaluation and careful analysis of children's learning has shown areas of program deficiencies, resulting in scrapping of some lesson sequences and redesign of others. The process of program writing, field testing, long term evaluation and revision can go on endlessly, but practical necessity requires that program sequences be "ready" for mass tryout at some point.

Our experience has been that four to six revisions are needed for each lesson. Planning, writing, and pilot testing of a new program ordinarily require 50 to 100 hours of staff time. Some of our programs have been revised much more than this, with input of up to 200 hours of staff and technician time. Consequently, each 15-minute A-T program we have developed cost about $2000, even employing graduate students and other comparatively "cheap" labor. Clearly, the development costs for quality A-T science programs at the elementary school level is completely out of range for individual schools or even large school systems. However, once developed and mass produced, the A-T approach to elementary science is economically feasible. Present market information suggests that a 30-lesson (one lesson per week) A-T science program can be available to schools for about five dollars per pupil per year. Moreover, special "science" teachers are not needed, and we have found teacher acceptance of A-T science to be unanimous.

Although planning and developing an entire A-T science program requires resources available only at the national level, additional A-T lessons or planning of related class activities can be and have been done by individual teachers. The A-T approach to individualizing elementary science teaching will be best where teachers add their creative talents and human presence.

LESSON EVALUATION

Lesson evaluation begins at the time of lesson development. Even early exploratory work with children using a new piece of apparatus or a novel demonstration is part of the evaluation process. We wish to maximize student learning of key science concepts, and one necessary requisite is that every element in a lesson must make some sense to the children. With young children, motor dexterity is occasionally a limiting factor, and early, informal tryout of a new device may indicate the need for redesign of a piece of equipment or a game board. Similarly, the student's cognitive limitations, such as inadequate vocabulary, may mean special care must be devoted to presenting new concept words or selecting adjectives to describe a procedure or phenomenon.

In the design of A-T programs for children, the same strategy applies as is indicated throughout this book. The name of the game is to help all students acquire knowledge and skills efficiently, not to see who will succeed and who will fail. For each activity, each description, and each illustration we seek to determine if changes can be made that will reduce or eliminate student failure. As indicated in the previous section, this process requires up to 200 hours of staff time for the design of a single 15-minute lesson. Though too often we think of evaluation as occurring with students only after a learning episode, Scriven (1967) has pointed out the need for careful evaluation during the curriculum design process. By the time a lesson sequence is ready for wide-scale field testing, we already have good evidence that significant learning will occur simply because the instruction has been refined to the point where learning is assured, much in the same manner that manufacturers can guarantee performance of a product as a result of design and quality control procedures. To be sure, we must expect some failures or partial failures, and evaluation during program design is not sufficient.

Another form of evaluation we have used is paper and pencil tests with children. Picture-test items are developed which abstract to some degree the concepts illustrated in the lessons. We have used two basic forms of picture-test items. One type requires that the child recognize and mark on the appropriate picture or segment of a picture. This is basically a recognition-type item where the child is required to see in the drawing a relationship, object, or phenomenon illustrated in the lesson. Some measure of the child's cognitive competence is indicated by simple recognition of elements essentially identical to those in the A-T lesson; success in correctly marking items where similar but novel relationships, objects, or phenomena are illustrated is suggestive of more adequate concept acquisition. Direct recognition and recognition of similar but novel elements are shown in items illustrated in Figure 7.5.

A second form of picture-test item we call production items. These are drawings that are in some way incomplete and the child is instructed to mark the picture in such a way as to illustrate a relationship or phenomenon. Examples of production-type items are

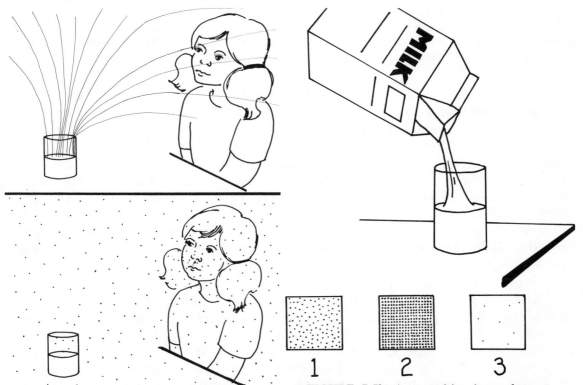

FIGURE 7.5a—A recognition item where students are to mark which picture best represents a smell, as they did during instruction.

FIGURE 7.5b—A recognition item where student may recognize which model (box) best illustrates molecules in a solid, liquid or air, similar to tasks in two lessons.

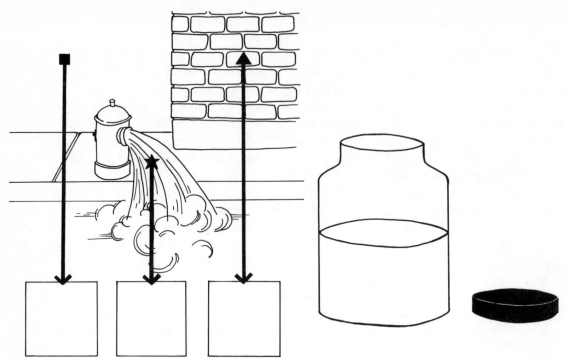

FIGURE 7.6a–A production item where students are to represent molecular patterns for solids, liquids, and air, similar to tasks in lessons.

FIGURE 7.6b–A production item where students are to represent a smell coming from the jar, a task not in the lessons.

shown in Figure 7.6. These items can also be of two types; some require marking in a way similar to illustrations given in lesson sequences, whereas others require transfer, or illustration of relationships in new ways or phenomena not previously considered. Scoring production-type questions requires special procedures. We usually identify types or categories of response and record the "category" represented by a student's response, not whether the answer is right or wrong. Some response categories indicate better concept acquisition whereas other categories suggest some type of cognitive deficiencies. Examples are shown in Figure 7.7.

Picture tests are comparatively easy to administer. We have used two procedures, both involving audio-tape instructions for the test items. Group testing can be done with simple portable cardboard carrels or by using carrels in learning centers where possible. In this format, a single tape player is connected to the headsets of all booths and children are given test instructions item-by-item as they proceed through the test booklet. To reduce errors due to sticking pages, etc., color-coded booklets are used with six or eight different colors in succession, thus minimizing errors due to children marking correctly according to audio instructions, but on the wrong page. Color coding permits easy inspection by the test administrator to assure that children are marking the correct page.

Where group testing is not feasible or desired, individual testing can be done using the same audio instruction but with students working independently. The use of audio instruction standardizes timing, voice, and environment and thus reduces error variance when comparisons between students and groups of students are desired. This has some

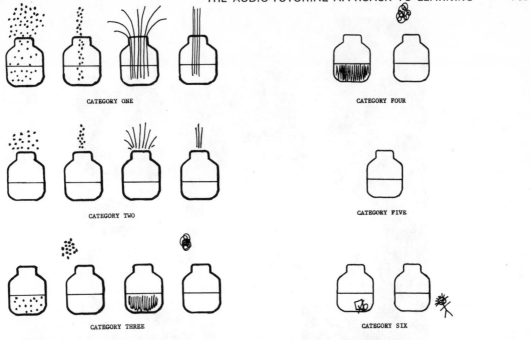

CATEGORY ONE

CATEGORY TWO

CATEGORY THREE

CATEGORY FOUR

CATEGORY FIVE

CATEGORY SIX

FIGURE 7.7a–Sample student responses to question in 7.6b as categorized for scoring purposes. Low number is most "scientifically correct."

FIGURE 7.7b–Continuation of 7.7a.

practical value as well as implications for statistical analysis. Picture tests may also be administered by the teacher, but for research purposes we have employed audio-taped instruction almost exclusively. Figure 7.8 illustrates our testing procedures.

Our most valuable information for program revision as well as for analysis of children's cognitive growth has come from structured interviews. The clinical interview or structured interview requires that the evaluator work with one student at a time, proceeding through a series of questions. Obviously, this is much more difficult and time consuming than picture test evaluation. However, we have found that more useful information can be obtained through individual interviews, and these have also served as a good validation mechanism for our picture tests.

Interviews may deal with objects or phenomena identical to those in A-T lessons, or novel materials can be used. As with picture tests, the best indication of concept acquisition is when a child can describe the behavior of novel objects or novel phenomena and associate these with similar observations he made in A-T lessons. Figure 7.9 shows a child being interviewed.

The promise of interview evaluation is that flexibility· in questioning is possible. Sometimes from the mere expression on a student's face, it is possible to recognize that a word or phrase is not understood. The experienced interviewer can rephrase the question or change the illustration used. Our objective is to assess the upper limits of the student's knowledge of concepts taught, not his ability to understand our questions. We have found that picture tests and similar paper-and-pencil tests tend to underestimate a student's knowledge gains by 20 to 50 per cent. Due to lucky guessing or responding to spurious

FIGURE 7.8—Group testing using audio-tape questioning.

FIGURE 7.9—A first grade child being interviewed on knowledge of smells as related to molecular movement.

cues that accidentally lead to correct answers, some children score high on picture tests. This can be misleading in lesson evaluation or in research on comparative gains of experimental groups.

Efficient Audio-Tutorial instructional design requires that we estimate as well as possible the maximum knowledge the learner acquires, or we may introduce unnecessary repetition or redundancy in learning tasks. We sometimes observe that only a small percentage of students have acquired key concepts even with probing interview assessment. Chance success on objective-type questions or spurious cuing to the correct answer may mislead us to think some elements of a learning sequence are adequate in the form developed when in reality important revision is called for.

To illustrate the power of interview evaluation, data is provided in the table below for second grade students. These students had completed five 15-minute Audio-Tutorial lessons dealing with forms of energy and concepts of energy conservation. The instruction occurred over a five-week interval. The data show that most or the majority of the youngsters could recognize forms of energy when novel examples were provided, what McClelland (1970) called "first order transfer." The success pattern was highest for examples of kinetic energy and lowest for potential and elastic forms. This pattern is consistent with the types of energy usually observed by children and hence in line with the total range of experience. This illustrates that success in Audio-Tutorial learning is a function of the students' prior experience, and the data are consistent with our learning theory expectations described later in this chapter. It would be very difficult reliably to assess student's knowledge of each energy form on paper and pencil tests.

Number of Subjects Responding to Interview Questions Categorized by Form or Energy and Answer Acceptability*

Energy Form	Satisfactory	Dubious	Unsatisfactory
Kinetic	28	2	2
Potential	18	6	8
Elastic	20	2	10
Heat	25	3	4

*From J. A. McClelland, 1970, p. 93.

PATTERNS OF A-T UTILIZATION

Through the past five years we have found Audio-Tutorial instruction in science to be widely accepted in elementary schools. In cooperation with the Wabash Valley Education Center in West Lafayette, Indiana, and the Finger Lakes Regional Supplementary Education Center in Cortland, New York, A-T programs were field tested in over eighty different schools. More than two hundred first and second grade teachers have participated in field trials of A-T lessons. To date, no school administrator nor teacher has wanted to discontinue use of A-T lessons. This is one kind of evidence that elementary school science teaching can be done effectively with the Audio-Tutorial approach.

One reason A-T has proved to be successful with teachers is that most of the work in planning for science instruction has been done. With the heavy emphasis on reading and language skills now characteristic of the primary school, teachers can rarely find time in their busy schedule to plan science lessons, gather necessary materials, try out experiments or demonstrations, and study subjects with which they are not familiar. Moreover, some primary grade teachers have only limited training in science and feel not only inadequate but sometimes frightened of science. The school syllabus may include science, but organized science instruction is seldom seen in the primary grade classroom.

We believe that the veritable absence of science instruction in the primary school is almost tragic. Frequently, we have had teachers remark how surprised they were that so-and-so did well on our science evaluation. We have found correlation between science achievement and achievement on other school tasks often to be very low and sometimes negative! Informed educators increasingly recognize that the primary school is for many children a destructive experience. Holt's *How Children Fail* and Kozol's *Death at an Early Age* are only two of the many popular descriptions of the tragic consequences children experience when success in school is denied to them. Even if we were to say that science is unimportant as an area of study in the elementary school, the fact that some students we have observed (one or more in every class) have almost no success in school except with science could be reason enough to include this as part of the primary school program.

How can Audio-Tutorial methods be used? We will try to illustrate some instances we have observed where A-T has been effective. In every case, the teacher has an important role, even though that role may require a minimum of preparation and class time.

Most commonly we observe that a carrel in the classroom with a new lesson supplied each week can serve as the backbone of a good science program. In the self-contained classroom (still the most common type although "open" schools are rapidly appearing), the teacher plays a vital role in organizing activities. For A-T lessons to be effective, children must have one or more opportunities to perform the lesson. Most teachers manage this by making a roster and attaching this to the carrel. As a student completes a lesson, he or she places a check after his or her name. New rosters can be posted each week, or a single form might serve for several lessons. Once a protocol is established, children manage very well to have their turns at lessons and to keep things running properly. Students should have an opportunity to repeat all or portions of a lesson. The teacher should perform the lesson once to become familiar with the concepts presented (this also proves to be an effective form of "in classroom" in-service teacher education at no extra cost). Children may perform lessons any time during the day other than during periods of group instruction. Most teachers provide various forms of "seat work" to occupy students while the teacher works with small reading groups or individual students. This "seat work" time is ordinarily the occasion for A-T work as well.

If a new lesson is set up each Monday morning, by Wednesday most students will have completed the lesson at least once. This is a good time for the teacher to lead a class discussion on the content of the lesson. If the lesson deals with "how plants grow," the teacher can effectively draw out many additional examples of plant growth that relate to those supplied in the lesson. This increase in the number and kinds of examples helps to fix the concepts in the children's minds and also to broaden the range of experience the children see as relevant to the concept. Examples can be used that are directly relevant to their experience (perhaps drawing on examples from plants in the room or in the children's home) and thus heighten personal involvement with exemplars of concepts. In short, both the opportunity for verbal expression and the addition of new examples can aid what Piaget calls "assimilation" of new concepts.

Some teachers use bulletin boards, science tables, reading corners, and similar devices to increase the depth and breadth of experience children may have with concepts presented in A-T lessons. Additional experimentation or "inquiry" activities are not only possible but desirable. For example, children "plant" seeds in a plastic vial during lesson 8 in our first grade series. It is relatively easy for the teacher to expand this experience and to have children plant other seeds in similar ways; in fact, our Teacher's Manual for the lesson provides suggestions as to how this can be done and where materials can be easily obtained by the teacher or the students.

As learning centers become more common in elementary schools, we thought A-T carrels might be used in these centers, for space limits usually require that only a single lesson can be available at any one time in a classroom. In the learning center, several lessons in a sequence can be set up simultaneously and students can move ahead or go back and review lessons. Some modification of protocols would even allow for students to check out lessons from a storage room, and set up the lesson and proceed in relatively unbridled independent study, somewhat as suggested for the IPI model at Pittsburgh (Lipson 1966). This has too frequently proven to be unsatisfactory. Here are some of the problems we have observed when A-T science lessons have been provided in learning centers.

First, we believe that the teacher's role can be very important for effective instruction. When A-T lessons are available in the learning center, the observation "out-of-sight, out-of-mind" usually applies. The teacher busy with her classroom activities may never see any of the A-T lessons. Obviously, she cannot and does not provide discussions, follow-up activities, or tutorial guidance. This is not due to perversity; elementary school teachers are very busy. In cases where the school principal has decided that A-T carrels shall be in the learning center, we have frequently found that teachers request that these be in their classrooms instead, especially teachers who have had carrels in their classrooms in the past. The reasons they give are almost all positive and in line with good A-T practices suggested above.

Another difficulty we have observed is that A-T lessons in a learning center may be unattended for days at a time with no check to see that all necessary materials are in order. Of course, this can and does happen in the classroom as well, but with several lessons set up at the same time, the chance for misplaced items increases, and some schools experience a considerably higher "disappearance" rate. In this respect, we should point out that our loss ratio has been unbelievably small—we have never lost a tape recorder or headset or any larger pieces of equipment in five years and some 100,000 student exposures. Vandalism has been almost nonexistent.

Perhaps the most serious limitation we have observed is that, unlike in the classroom, students seldom stand around a carrel in a learning center and talk about things in the lesson. Partly this is due to what is regarded as "orderly" learning center management. However, lunchtime, recess time, and various breaks in the day's schedule usually offer more opportunity for children to gather around a carrel and talk about things when the carrel is in their classroom. This limitation may be only transitory. As schools move from classrooms and "learning centers" to open schools with only learning areas, all of the advantages of A-T in classrooms plus the advantages of A-T in learning centers can be combined. We have not had enough experience with "open schools" at this writing to evaluate adequately the results of this type of organization. We are, however, optimistic and highly supportive of the "open school" concept (Wing 1970).

At this point it is important to note that A-T instruction is more than a method of teaching science; it is also a method of modifying teacher behavior. To illustrate, we first pilot-tested some lessons in a rural Indiana elementary school because the superintendent of the system wanted to inject some new ideas into the school. Two pleasant, very experienced teachers (over twenty years in teaching) were to be the first to use the A-T programs. To say that they were apprehensive at first is gross understatement. But they were dedicated professionals and they agreed to try the "system." As they observed their children silently leaving their seats for a turn at the A-T carrel, the joy on the children's faces as they recognized their success with the lesson materials, and they saw the meaningful way in which the students could discuss as a group what was in the lessons—these things had the impact you would expect. Not only did these teachers become strong proponents of A-T science, but they welcomed planned arrangements that doorways be eliminated from the new school, making it easier to share A-T carrels with adjoining rooms. We later visited these teachers in their new building. What a surprise! No more rows of chairs, little recitation in unison, no asking for permission to move to the A-T carrel. Instead: a reading corner, clusters of tables for art and science, and a completely different attitude toward students.

Our example is not an isolated case but is the most striking example carefully observed. Most of the enthusiasm and support we have received from school administrators for our A-T science programs has not been a result of the effectiveness of this approach for teaching science (in fact, seldom do they inquire about this). Administrators have supported this effort for what they have seen it contribute to positive changes in teacher behavior.

A-T science instruction is not incompatible with other elementary science approaches. Many teachers who have used our programs also use some other science materials. We have found our lessons used together with SCIS, ESS, and Science—A Process Approach lessons, as well as with some more traditional published materials in elementary science. In twenty Indiana schools we conducted a demonstration where both Science—A Process Approach and A-T lessons were provided, but to different classes. The evaluation of teacher feedback showed that both programs were accepted, but teachers who were familiar with both much preferred A-T science to the SAPA program (Wabash Valley Education Center 1970). We do not hold the position that A-T science is the only way to present the subject in elementary schools; we do believe it is unfortunate that so little federal support has been available for this development in contrast to other teacher-dependent approaches supported by multi-million dollar grants. As more evidence becomes available on the impact and acceptance of the various elementary science programs, we may observe some redirecting of federal resources as has already occurred at the college level.

HOW CHILDREN LEARN

Much has been written about what is wrong with elementary school education. Most of the criticism has been leveled at what Skinner calls our "aversive" methods whereby we force children to do what we wish under threat of punishment (Skinner 1968, p. 95). He argues that we resort to aversive methods not because they are the most effective or most favored, but for want of alternatives. Although the hickory switch is gone, various forms of ridicule, scolding, sarcasm, criticism, and incarceration (kept in for recess or after school) continue as aversive devices that force students to behave as the teacher desires. Effective classroom control often means skillful employment of aversive measures. But what alternatives are there?

We all recognize that children must want to learn if we are to succeed in teaching. Motivation for learning, we say, is necessary. Aversive methods of motivation do work, but unfortunately learning tends to stop when the aversive pressures cease. We can employ ego-enhancing motivation (praise, group recognition, "gold stars," status advancement), but this kind of motivation works only when some students are denied it, or are subjected to aversive motivation. The most common practice is to combine aversive and ego-enhancing motivation to achieve some level of student commitment to learning.

Far more desirable motivation results from cognitive drive. This is the motivation which occurs when a learner recognizes that he has acquired some new knowledge or a new mental competency. We see this conspicuously when youngsters recognize that they have mastered the solution of a type of mathematics problem. We also see this when a child recognizes that the heat energy of boiling water is just another form of energy converted from the red-hot coils of the range or flames of the burner. In short, the motivation that comes from cognitive drive is intrinsic to the learning task and operative in similar future learning, whereas aversive or ego-enhancement motivation is not relevant to the specific learning task and has little carry-over potential to new, similar learning tasks. The consequence is that when motivation is via cognitive drive, the learner becomes effectively self-motivated for continuing learning, whereas other forms of motivation require continuous effort on the part of the teacher (or system), as we indeed observe to be the case even with many graduate students!

What do we know about the learning process that can be used to help students succeed in learning so that cognitive drive can result? We know that rote learning, i.e., the acquisition of new information without association to prior concepts in cognitive structure, is useful only for very limited purposes. Usually we rote learn a telephone number only well enough to retain it until the number is dialed. If it is the number of a close friend, we may "overlearn" it sufficiently to recall the number from day to day or for a few weeks. But rote learning has very little value for most of the knowledge we wish to transmit in school. Instead, our goal is to effect new knowledge acquisition in such a manner as to associate this new knowledge with prior concepts and concomitantly to embellish those prior concepts. This kind of learning is referred to as meaningful learning by David Ausubel (1968), and it is meaningful learning we strive for in our teaching. Ausubel has developed a reasonably adequate learning theory that has significant value for the design of instruction. Our Audio-Tutorial elementary science program has utilized elements of Ausubel's theory in planning and evaluating lessons and lesson sequences.

To learn meaningfully, a student must have in his cognitive structure some relevant concept, or as Ausubel refers to it, a "subsumer." Subsuming concepts function to facilitate the acquisition of new information so that both the rate and the quality of learning are affected. In contrast to rote learning (where information is arbitrarily incorporated into cognitive structure) knowledge acquired through meaningful learning is not only more rapidly acquired, but it is also retained for impressively long periods of time. Let's look at some evidence. The table below shows students not only gained substantially from pretest in September (X = 14.02) to posttest in June (X = 28.33), but they retained this knowledge one year later (X = 28.54) and even two years later (X = 29.33) without additional biology instruction! (Cf. Novak 1970, pp. 66-67.) Contrary to popular opinion, facts are not rapidly forgotten when learning is meaningful, rather than rote.

**Mean Scores for Students on BSCS Biology
Exam in a Milwaukee High School**

Test	N	Mean Score	Percent of Total Possible
Pretest	39	14.02	28.0
Posttest—1962	39	28.33	56.7
Posttest—1963	39	28.84	57.7
Posttest—1964	39	29.33	58.7

In a study of students enrolled in elementary botany at Purdue University, we found a marked difference in achievement for those students characterized as high in "analytic ability" as compared to those scoring in the middle or lower one-third of the group on a measure of analytic ability. Our criterion test for analytic ability was a test dealing with answers to problem situations. In 1961 when the study was done, we characterized this as a measure of a student's "analytic ability," but now we would say that the test could be considered a measure of the relevant subsuming concepts (not factual detail) a student has in the area of botany. Figure 7.10 shows that students with high analytic ability (good subsumers) scored better on the final botany exam with only nine hours study time in the learning center than did students with poorer subsumers after twenty hours of study. Moreover, the results cannot be attributed simply to differences in initial factual knowledge of botany, for little difference existed between the groups on pretest means. In the area of chemistry, we have also found evidence that possession of subsumers is critically important to knowledge acquisition (Ring 1969).

We have surveyed over one hundred studies of school learning and have found these to be generally consistent with predictions one might make on the basis of Ausubel's learning theory (Novak, Tamir and Ring 1971). Most of our current research is designed to test specific hypotheses derived from Ausubel's theory, unlike the research surveyed where we constructed hypotheses post hoc, with all the attendant risks. So far all of our data is strongly supportive of Ausubel's theory.

It is important to recognize that subsumers do not operate to facilitate any kind of

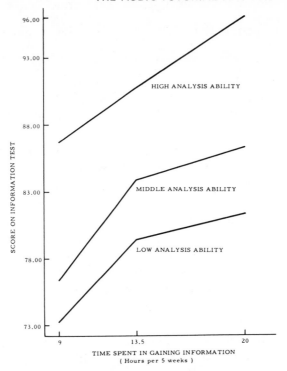

FIGURE 7.10–Achievement in college botany as a function of learning time for high, middle, and low analytic ability groups.

new learning. Only that new knowledge which is specifically relevant to subsumers in cognitive structure will be more readily acquired. Where relevant concepts do not exist, new knowledge must be rotely learned. However, careful design of instruction can allow for rapid development of elemental subsuming concepts. Ausubel (1968) suggests that advance organizers can be provided, i.e., learning more general and more abstract than that of the material to follow, thus serving to provide "anchorage" from which subsuming concepts will be formed.

With children we must give more than passing attention to the development of new subsumers. In many areas of science, the children have no appropriate concepts (or even erroneous concepts) through which meaningful learning may proceed. Indeed, frequently children lack important concept terms and concrete experience with objects or phenomena to which these terms apply. Partly, for this reason, we must provide children with carefully selected concrete ("hands on") experience with things, or meaningful learning may never occur. It is this fact that has led the ESS and SCIS groups to emphasize the importance of direct experience with materials, especially for primary school children. To illustrate that air is matter, we have children squeeze sealed plastic tubes, blow on a windmill, invert a jar of air in a pail of water, and do other things that may convince them that air is matter and all matter takes up space.

Piaget (see Ginsburg 1969) has carefully studied children's growth in cognitive competence and has described developmental stages. He and his co-workers have found that certain kinds of learning are not possible until a child reaches a developmental stage sufficiently advanced to permit the new experience to be meaningful. For example, most children at age six or seven do not "conserve volume"; that is, they will not recognize that a tall, thin container may contain less liquid than a short, wide container or vice versa. Even when shown the levels of liquid poured from one container into another and back again, they will still mispredict which container holds the larger "drink." It is not until ages 9 to 11 that most children recognize and can explain which container holds the larger volume of liquid.

Conservation of volume is only one area Piaget and co-workers have investigated with children. Taken together, these studies provide important boundary conditions as to the kind of mental competencies that can be reasonably assumed at a given age and what should not be assumed. For example, we illustrate in our first level lessons that substances like plaster are made of smaller particles, and children break up a plaster "cookie" to observe the smaller units. Since small pieces of plaster can be broken into even smaller units, we can lead the child to believe that solids are made up of tiny units or particles which we call molecules. However, we cannot assume that he will recognize that if all the plaster chunks were put back together, the same volume of plaster would result. But this is not critical to the development of the concept we are presenting, i.e., solids are made up of very small particles called molecules.

Another important principle we obtain from the research of Piaget and others is that new concepts are not quickly assimilated into cognitive structure. A child may believe that solids are made of tiny units called molecules, but the full import of this is not to be expected for years. We can say to the child that substances which feel heavy are made of heavier molecules or have molecules packed more closely together; this statement may be repeated by children at age six or seven, but it is hardly more than a fairy tale to him at this time. The point is, however, that what may be learned essentially as "fairy tales" in grades one or two will be seen to correspond to reality the child observes. In time these original "fairy tales" become powerful explanatory models. Our interest is not to accelerate mental development of children; our interest is to provide experience which can lead to the child's development of scientific models for explanation of natural phenomena and not the otherwise acquired mystical models, or no models at all. It will take several more years before we can determine what effect A-T science training will have on children's concepts of causality at, say, the junior high school level. We do have adequate data to suggest that A-T instructed children respond in very significantly different ways to some kinds of questions or demonstrations than do uninstructed children. This provides at least one necessary condition for potential differences in the cognitive capacities of 12- or 14-year-old students who have had early, effective science instruction.

While high school and college students generally possess the necessary mental operations characterized by Piaget, they still require appropriate sequencing of experience to effect concept learning. Moreover, concrete experience with objects of study is essential for children, but this kind of experience is equally essential for adults and young adults when dealing with concepts related to novel objects or phenomena. The greater experience range of older students may require only a quick manipulation of an instrument or object to be studied and too often conventional laboratory work monotonously extends concrete experiences when neither increase in manipulative skill nor referent experience for concept terms is needed. Not only does this waste time (and money), but it impedes growth of cognitive drive motivation.

The organization of the instructional sequence is critically important. The psychologist Gagne (1970) places primary emphasis on the hierarchical ordering of learning experience. We agree with this but reject the rigid adherence to hierarchical ordering. For example, to recognize that the size and complexity of the sporophyte generation increases as we move up the plant phyletic scale would be a higher-order element in Gagne's structure. However, rather than postponing presentation of this concept until late in a botany course, we would advise that it be introduced early to function as an "advance organizer" to relate more specific concepts of plant life cycles. According to Ausubel's theory, one may proceed almost simultaneously to teach several levels of knowledge hierarchy. The key consideration is that sequencing should be planned progressively to differentiate and add meaning to each concept or set of concepts of the hierarchy.

There is much to learn about learning and a great deal of research is needed. We believe that current psychological theories are adequate for planning and interpreting research with actual classroom instruction. The scientific process of deduction-induction and theory revision can proceed in the analysis of learning. To this end, we believe Audio-Tutorial methods present an enormous and promising research tool and, concomitantly, an effective, practicable instructional regime.

REFERENCES

1. Ausubel, David P. Educational Psychology: A Cognitive View. New York: Holt, Rinehart and Winston, 1968.
2. Bridgham, Robert. "Classification, Seriation and Learnings of Electrostatics," Journal of Research in Science Teaching 6 (1969): 118-27.
3. Gagne, Robert M. The Conditions of Learning. New York: Holt, Rinehart and Winston, 1970.
4. Ginsburg, Herbert, and Sylvia Opper. Piaget's Theory of Intellectual Development: An Introduction. Englewood Cliffs, N.J.: Prentice-Hall, 1969.
5. Johnson, Mauritz, Jr. "Definitions and Models in Curriculum Theory," Educational Theory 17 (April 1967): 127-40.
6. Lipson, Joseph I. "An Individualized Science Laboratory," Science and Children 4 (December 1966): 8-12.
7. McClelland, J. A. Gerald. An Approach to the Development and Assessment of Instruction in Science at the Second Grade Level: the Concept of Energy. Ph.D. dissertation. Ithaca, N.Y.: Cornell University, 1970.
8. Novak, Joseph D. "Importance of Conceptual Schemes for Science Teaching," The Science Teacher 31 (October 1964): 10.
9. _____. "A Model for the Interpretation and Analysis of Concept Formation," Journal of Research in Science Teaching 3 (1965): 72-83.

10. _____. "The Role of Concepts in Science Teaching." In Analysis of Concept Learning, edited by Herbert J. Klausmeier and Chester W. Harris, pp. 239-54. New York: Academic Press, 1966.

11. _____. The Improvement of Biology Teaching. Indianapolis: Bobbs-Merill, 1970.

12. Novak, Joseph D., Morris Meister, Warren W. Knox, and Dorothy W. Sullivan. The World of Science Series. Indianapolis: Bobbs-Merrill, 1966.

13. Novak, Joseph D., Pinchas Tamir, and Donald Ring. Interpretation of Research Findings in Terms of Ausubel's Theory and Implications for Science Education. Mimeographed. Ithaca, N.Y.: Cornell University, 1971.

14. Ring, Donald G. An Analysis of the Cognitive Influence of High School Chemistry Instruction on College Chemistry Achievement. Ph.D. dissertation. Ithaca, N.Y.: Cornell University, 1969.

15. Scriven, M. "The Methodology of Evaluation." In Perspectives of Curriculum Evaluation, edited by R. W. Tyler, R. M. Gagne, and M. Scriven. AERA Monograph Series on Curriculum Evaluation, 1967.

16. Skinner, B. F. The Technology of Teaching. New York: Appleton-Century-Crofts, 1968.

17. Wabash Valley Education Center. Final Summary of 1969-1970 Field Evaluation of Elementary Science Instruction for First Grade Students. Mimeographed. West Lafayette, Indiana: Wabash Valley Education Center, 1970.

18. Wing, Cliff, and Patricia Mack. "Wide Open for Learning," American Education 6 (November 1970): 13-15.

Chapter VIII

IN CONCLUSION

The Audio-Tutorial system must not be confused with the use of audio-tape as a substitute for the lecturer or teacher in the classroom. It is a programming of a sequence of study activities in the voice of the senior instructor. In contrast to *other media,* the student has control of the rate at which he proceeds with his study, an opportunity to replay as often as he desires, but most importantly, all of the conventional experiences involving handling specimens, doing experiments, manipulating the microscope, and other items of this nature are retained. There is no attempt to substitute the sound of an instructor's voice for the performance of an experiment, collection of data, and the analysis of these data. Many of the modern gadgets for teaching have attempted to use one medium of communication as the only source of all of the student's learning. Most subject matter, by nature, requires a variety of approaches; therefore, attempts to reduce student involvement to one or two sensory organs have met with unsuccessful results. These experiments have prejudiced many teachers against adopting or experimenting with the use of modern communication media. While these experiments have been unfortunate, we must not let them blind us to the true advantages of the teaching aids which can give us real assistance in helping our students learn.

In the Audio-Tutorial approach:

1. Emphasis is placed on student learning rather than on teaching.

2. Students can adapt the study pace to their ability to assimilate the information. Exposure to difficult subjects is repeated as often as necessary for any particular student.

3. Better students are not a "captive audience" and can use their time most effectively. Their interests are not dulled by unnecessary repetition of information already learned but they are free to choose those activities which are more challenging and instructive.

4. The student can select a listening time adapted to his diurnal efficiency peak.

5. Tapes demand the attention of the students. Students are not distracted by each other.

6. Students have more individual attention, if they desire it.

7. Scheduling problems are simplified. The four hours of scheduled time from which the students are relieved under the new system can now be distributed throughout the week as necessary to adjust to the student's activities.

8. More students can be accommodated in less laboratory space and with less staff.

9. Makeup labs and review sessions can be accommodated with a minimum of effort.

10. The student feels more keenly his responsibility for his own learning.

11. Each student is essentially "tutored" by a senior staff member.

12. Potentially, the system can be used to standardize instruction where desirable, *e.g.,* between the University and the University Centers.

13. Opportunity for research on learning processes is enhanced.

SAMPLE ORIENTATION MATERIAL FOR DISTRIBUTION DURING THE FIRST WEEK OF SCHOOL

BIOLOGY 108   Calendar, First Semester, 1967-1968

WK	UNIT TITLE	SUN.	MON.	TUE.	WED.	THUR.	FRI.	SAT.
1	Introduction to Plants	Sept. 10	11	12	7:30 AM 13 Classes Begin	14	15	16
1	Introduction to Plants	17	18	19	20	1st 21 IQS Quiz	22	23
2	Matter and Mechanics	24	1st 25 IQS Quiz	26	27	28	29	30
3	Plants and Water	Oct. 1	2	3	4	5	6	7
4	Transformation of Energy	8	9	10	11	12	13	14
5	Transformation of Energy	15	Last 16 Drop Day Freshmen	17	18	Pro. 19 I Due In IQS	20	21
6	Mineral Nutrition and P. Structure	22	23	24	25	26	27	28
7	Structure of Tracheophytes	29	30	31	Nov. 1 Yellow Slips Due	IQS 2 Quiz Pro. I	3	4
8	Structure of Tracheophytes	5	IQS Quiz 6 over Pro. I	7	8	9	10	11
9	Ecology	12	13	Last 14 Day for Freshmen to Drop W/O grade	15	16	17	18
		19	Last 20 Day to Select Pro. II Topic	21	11:30 22 AM Vac. Begins	23 V	24 V	25 V
10	Plant Growth Development	26	Classes 27 Resume: No IQS	NO 28 IQS	29	30	Dec. 1	2
11	Plant Growth Development	3	4	5	6	7	8	9
12	Reproduction	10	11	12	13	14	15	16
13	Reproduction	17	18	19	11:30 20 AM Vac. Begins	21	22	23
		24 V	25 V	26 V	27 V	28 V	29 V	30 V
13	Reproduction	31	Jan. 1	2	11:30 3 AM Vac. Ends	4	5	6
14	Plant Kingdom	7	8	9	10	11	12	Classes 13 End: Pro. II Due
		14 STUDY	15 PERIOD	FINAL 16 WEEK	17	18	19	20

BIOLOGY 108—ASSIGNMENTS

A. Lab Manual: Plant Science, by S. N. Postlethwait, H. D. Telinde, and D. D. Husband.

B. Text: Botany, 3rd ed., by W. W. Robbins, T. E. Weier, and C. R. Stocking.

C. Workbook: Study Problems in Plant Science, by H. T. Murray, Jr.

D. Scientific American offprints—optional reading, except those in parentheses, which will be provided in the laboratory.

Lesson Week	(A) Postlethwait, et. al.	(B) Robbins, et. al.	(C) Murray	(D) Sci. Am. Reprint
1	Introduction of Plants	Chap. 1, 2, 3, & 15	2-1, 3, 4, 5; 3-1; 27-3A	Germination
2	Matter and Mechanics of Cells	Chap. 4 & pp. 48-56	4-1, 2; 5-1, 2	The Living Cell
3	Plants and Water	pp. 155-159, & Chap. 11	6-1 to 6 7-1, 3	How Sap Moves in Trees; (Life and Light)
4	Transformation of Energy-Photosynthesis	pp. 37-45, & Chap. 12	8-1, 2, 6, 8, 9, 10, 11	(How Cells Transform Energy, pp. 2-9). The Path of Carbon in Photo., and the Role of Chlorophyll in Photo.
5	Transformation of Energy-Respiration	Chap. 13	9-1; 10-1 2, 4, 5A, 5B, 8, 10	(How Cell Transforms Energy, pp. 9-13)
6	Mineral Nutrition in Plants; Introduction to Plant Structure	Chap. 10; pp. 45-48; Chap. 6; pp. 73-81	11-1 to 4 12-1, 3, 6; 14-1, 2, 3	(How Sap Moves in Trees, pp. 6-10); How Cells Divide; The Genetic Code II
7&8	Structure of Tracheophytes	Chaps. 7 & 8	15-1 to 75	The Next, New Biology, by J. Bonner (reprint provided in lab)
9	Ecology	Chap. 18	16-1, 2, 3; 17-1, 2, 3, 6, 6, 7; 18-1 to 5	World Population; Man's Ecosystem by LaMont Cole (reprint provided in lab)
10	Plant Growth and Development	Chap. 17	19-1 to 8; 20-1, 2, 3	The Control of Growth in Plant Cells
11	Plant Growth and Development	Chap. 17	3-2; 21-1 2, 3; 22-1, 2	Plant Hormones & Regulators by Van Overbeek (reprint provided in lab); Light and Plant Development
12	Reproduction - Sexual & Asexual	Chap. 14	24-1, 2, 5, 6, 7, 8, 9, 10; 25-2, 3	The Fertilization of Flowers
13	Reproduction - Genetics	Chap. 16	26-1 to 15, 20, 22	The Fine Structure of the Gene
14&15	The Plant Kingdom	Skim over chaps. 19 to 29, reading only what interests you	27-1, 2, 3; 28-1 to 5 8, 9	The Genetic Basis of Evolution

GENERAL INFORMATION SHEET

Code Used: GAS—General Assembly Session
ISS—Independent Study Session
IQS—Integrated Quiz Session
Room Numbers: GAS 1-105; ISS G-415; IQS G-418 and G-422;
Dr. Postlethwait G-308; Mr. Husband G-305.
ISS Hours: 7:30 AM–10:30 PM Monday through Friday
Grade Scale: A—90% B—80% C—70% D—60% F—Below 60%

Approximately 14 IQS Oral Quizzes @ 10 points each	140
Approximately 13 IQS Written Quizzes @ 20 points each	260
1 Final Exam @ 200 points	200
	600

Texts: *Plant Science,* by S. N. Postlethwait, Harvey D. Telinde, and
David D. Husband.
Botany, 3rd edition, by W. W. Robbins, T. E. Weier, and C. R. Stocking

Weekly Oral and Written Quizzes: A 10-point oral quiz will be given each week during your Monday (or Thursday) IQS. It will concern anything covered the previous week in ISS. A three-step method of oral presentation posted in ISS will be used. The oral quiz will be followed by a 20-point *written* quiz which will cover (1) study problems assigned, (2) reading assignment in Robbins, et al., and (3) information learned in ISS but which does not lend itself to oral quizzing. (See Handout "BIO 108 Study Procedure" for more information about the Oral Quiz.)

Final Exam: A final exam will be given during the scheduled time which the University will publish near the end of the semester. The exam will be worth 200 points (1/3 of final grade) and will consist of questions taken from the weekly written quizzes. Learn the rationale used for each question you miss, and use them to study for the final.

Scientific American Articles: Bonus points may be gained by those students who read certain articles assigned each week (see Assignment Sheet). A total of 2 points per article will be possible. No points will be given for reading parts of an article, as may be assigned for a particular week. Bonus quizzes must be taken immediately following your weekly written quiz. You will be asked to summarize the article; one point will be given if you convince the grader that you read the article, and one point will be given if you seem to have clearly understood what you read. Approximately 30 bonus points may be earned during the semester.

GAS: At this session you will meet with Dr. Postlethwait at 3:30 PM Wednesday or 3:30 PM Friday. Come to the one you are scheduled to attend. This time will be used to clarify, integrate, and direct your study in the course. Announcements will also be given here. A schedule of what is to be covered in each General Assembly Session will be provided so that you can determine for yourself whether the session would be valuable to you. Although roll will not be taken, it is emphasized that there are times when the GAS is essential for the fullest understanding of the subject matter, and we are leaving it up to the student to determine this. When in doubt it is best to attend!

IQS: You are signed up for one (1) Integrated Quiz Session. Of the 4 hours "to be arranged," one hour will be used the first week for the beginning of Problem 1, and then all 4 hours are to be devoted to independent study. When you meet in your scheduled IQS you will become oriented to the course and begin Problem 1. The group will then be divided into smaller IQS of eight students each and an instructor will be assigned to each group. This session will be used for the weekly quizzes.

Study Problems: Each week certain problems will be assigned from your Study Problems Manual. We will not require you to hand any of the work in; however, material covered in the problems will appear on the weekly written quizzes and final exam.

PROBLEM 1 and 2 (Miniature Research Problems)
  Problem 1—required of all students
  Problem 2—"A" students must earn the required number of points and must do
    Problems 1 *and* 2 in order to receive an A in the course.

BULLETIN BOARDS: It is each student's responsibility to check the bulletin boards in ISS each week for announcements.

ABSENCES: It is the responsibility of any student who is absent to find out what he missed as far as announcements, subject matter, etc. If you have an "excused absence" you must notify your IQS instructor and present proper documentation to that effect. Unexcused absences, or failure *to notify your Instructor* (you may call the secretary's office, Mrs. Booth, 92-4086, and leave a message) will result in your being given a zero for both the oral and written quizzes. (It doesn't take a math major to see that just one unexcused absence is difficult to overcome, grade-wise.)

Makeup written quizzes can be taken if done so before noon Tuesday of each week. At noon Tuesday the quizzes will be returned to the students in the "microscope cabinets," and a key will be posted in the glass case outside G-415. Arrangements can be made with either your IQS Instructor or Mr. David Husband (92-4081) to take a makeup. If you cannot locate these persons, call 92-4086 and explain your situation to our secretary (Mrs. Booth).

ISS: Most of your weekly study should take place in the ISS LEARNING CENTER (G-415, G-416). Bring your text, *Study Guide* and *Study Problems Manual.* Each week you should pick up a copy of the *OBJECTIVES* in ISS. These should act as your guide for the week's ISS study and for the oral quiz. Room G-415 is the *LEARNING CENTER* for Biology 108. It is a place where a student can exchange ideas with other students and the instructor, practice quizzing himself or others, see if the instructor can stump him with a *practice* oral quiz, work study problems, read assignments, take a study break with a coke or cup of coffee, etc. ISS hourly attendance will be posted each week so you can see when it is not crowded.

YOUR RESPONSIBILITY: A good deal of money and thought has gone into making the LEARNING CENTER a pleasant, attractive place to study. We plan to help you as much as we're able. Help us . . . take care of the tapes, tape players, microscopes, movie projectors, lab equipment, booth, etc. We will *NOT* tolerate thoughtlessness!

GENERAL ISS INFORMATION

1. Procedure for entering lab:
   a. All students must enter (and leave) the lab through the northwest door only.
   b. Every time a student enters lab, he must go to the desk and find his card in the alphabetical file.
   c. Pull your card out of the file.
   d. Check the booth assignment file for an empty booth containing a tape player in good working order.
   e. Write on your card—the day, the booth number you have chosen, and the time you are signing in. There is a clock in the lab.
   f. Place your card in the booth assignment file.
   g. Go to your booth and begin your independent study.
2. When you have completed your study:
   a. Clean up your booth.
   b. Turn off the tape player; there is no need to rewind the tape.
   c. Go get your card.
   d. Sign yourself out on the card.
   e. Refile your card in the box.
3. An instruction sheet on how to operate the tape players is posted in each booth. If you need any help, please ask the lab instructor. Anytime you think something is wrong with the tape or the tape player, call the instructor. An instructor will always be in the lab to answer any questions you may have about the week's material.
4. In keeping a lab open for long periods of time as we do, we must require certain things of the students:
   a. Put any equipment that you use back where you got it.
   b. Wash all the glassware you use before returning it.
   c. Clean up your booth before you leave.
   d. Stop the tape and flip the off-on button on your tape player to *off* whenever you leave the booth to look at a demonstration or leave the lab.
   e. Do not touch the tape player, especially the reels, while you are listening to the tape.
   f. Please help us keep the booths free from pen and pencil marks. If you must doodle, use a piece of scratch paper.

STUDY PROCEDURE

A. Take text, study problems, and Study Guide to ISS. Pick up a copy of the week's objectives.
B. Do each exercise in sequence and thoroughly before proceeding to the next step!
C. Ask for help whenever necessary and check progress with lab instructor frequently.
D. Prepare a short oral presentation for each demonstration, experiment, or procedure in ISS. If this step is properly done, you can be sure to get at least a B in the course. Include:

1. A statement as to what the item, apparatus, specimen, setup, experiment, etc., is.
2. Talk about its role or significance in the week's study.
3. Give specific details about it.

Example: If you were handed a twig during Week 6 and asked to discuss it—answer:

1. This is a buckeye twig.
2. The basic theme of this week's study is cell replication and the twig is an example of an end product of many cell divisions. In a living twig, cell division is associated with its further growth. The twig structure displays evidence of growth activities. One of our objectives for the week is to be able to identify and name the function of eight structures visible on a twig.
3. Specifically—The bud at the tip (point to the bud) is a terminal or apical bud. It contains next year's leaves and stem. It is protected by modified leaves called bud scales (point out) which fall off during the emergence of the leaves and stem in the spring. They leave scars called terminal bud scale scars (point out previous year's scars) and one can determine the age of a twig by counting their distribution. When last year's leaves fell off, they left leaf scars (point to one), and within each leaf scar the vascular bundle scars can be seen (again, point to them). The portion of a twig which produces leaves is referred to as a node, the parts in between the nodes are called internodes. The twig is covered with small pores, called lenticels, which function in allowing gasses to exchange between the inside of the twig and the outside.

SCI. AMER. OFFPRINTS FOR 1967-68

6. Dobzhansky: The Genetic Basis of Evolution. January 1950.
12. Grant: The Fertilization of Flowers, June 1951.
90. Bracket: The Living Cell. September 1961.
93. Mazia: How Cells Divide. September 1961.
107. Butler & Downs: Light and Plant Development. December 1960.
117. Koller: Germination. April 1959.
120. Benzer: The Fine Structure of the Gene. January 1962.
122. Bassham: The Path of Carbon in Photosynthesis. June 1962.
153. Nirenberg: The Genetic Code. March 1963.
154. Zimmermann: How Sap Moves in Trees. March 1963.
167. Steward: The Control of Growth in Plant Cells. October 1963.
616. Huxley: World Population. March 1956.
1016. Rabinowitch and Govindjee. The Role of Chlorophyll in Photosynthesis. July 1965.

RECORDS

To satisfy the requirements of the registrar's office and to keep from losing the identity of individual students, it is necessary to have an effective system of records. While grades are not based on the amount of time spent in ISS it still seems desirable to have a reasonably accurate record of the activities of all students. To facilitate this in the independent study session a check-in check-out card is used which is manipulated by the student and doubles as an efficient means of assigning booths. Affixed to each card is a picture of the student and blanks are on the card for entry of times that he checks in and checks out. A record of quiz grades indicates student attendance in the integrated quiz session.

Photographs are taken of each student at the first small assembly session. Each photograph is identified by having the student hold a large card bearing his name. Four photographs are produced from the 35mm negative by contact prints. One photograph is placed on the ISS learning center check-in check-out card, one on a permanent grade record card in the secretary's office, one on the IQS instructor's record sheet, and one is used to make up a large chart showing the seating arrangement in the general assembly session. All grades are turned over to the secretary on a weekly basis for recording on the permanent record card kept in the secretary's office.

In addition to these cards, each instructor of an integrated quiz session is expected to keep appropriate records and information concerning the progress of each student.

Students are urged to keep a personal record of their progress in the course. The following forms are used.

LEARNING CENTER "CENTER-IN CHECK-OUT" CARD

NAME_____

Last   First   Middle

Wk. Day	Booth No.	Time In	Time Out
1			
2			
3			
4			

Wk. Day	Booth No.	Time In	Time Out
5			
6			
7			

PERMANENT RECORD CARD

NAME_____

Last	First	Middle

	M	T	W	T	F	S
7:30						
8:30						
9:30						
10:30						
11:30						
12:30						
1:30						
2:30						
3:30						
4:30						
5:30						
6:30						
7:30						
8:30						
9:30						

LOCAL ADDRESS_____

HOME ADDRESS_____

Street

_____

City   State

LOCAL PHONE_____

STUDENT NO. _____

Major Area of Interest_____

FUTURE OCCUPATION_____

SMALL ASSEMBLY SESSION_____

DATE_____

COMMENTS:

Total absences

GAS   _____

SAS (IQS)_____

ISS   _____

NAME_____ School_____ Semester_____

Last	First	Middle

ORAL QUIZ WK.	WRITTEN QUIZ WK.	SCI. AMER. WK.	HOUR EXAMS	PROBLEMS
1 ___	1 ___	1 ___	1 ___	1 ___
2 ___	2 ___	2 ___	2 ___	2 ___
3 ___	3 ___	3 ___	3 ___	3 ___
4 ___	4 ___	4 ___	4 ___	
5 ___	5 ___	5 ___	5 ___	
6 ___	6 ___	6 ___		

_____ MID-SEM. POINTS

FINAL_____

_____ MID-SEM. GRADE

7 ___	7 ___	7 ___		
8 ___	8 ___	8 ___		
9 ___	9 ___	9 ___		
10 ___	10 ___	10 ___		
11 ___	11 ___	11 ___		
12 ___	12 ___	12 ___		
13 ___	13 ___	13 ___		
14 ___	14 ___	14 ___		
15 ___	15 ___	15 ___		

_____ SEM. POINTS

_____ Grade

STUDENT PERSONAL PROGRESS RECORD FOR BIOLOGY 108*

WEEK	ORAL QUIZZES	WRITTEN QUIZZES	SCI. AMER.	HOUR EXAMS
1	_____	_____	_____	1 _____
2	_____	_____	_____	2 _____
3	_____	_____	_____	3 _____
4	_____	_____	_____	4 _____
5	_____	_____	_____	5 _____
6	_____	_____	_____	FINAL
7	_____	_____	_____	EXAM _____
8	_____	_____	_____	TOTAL _____
9	_____	_____	_____	
10	_____	_____	_____	PROBLEMS
11	_____	_____	_____	1 _____
12	_____	_____	_____	2 _____
13	_____	_____	_____	3 _____
14	_____	_____	_____	
15	_____	_____	_____	
TOTALS	_____	_____	_____	

GRADE SCALE:

A—90%   B—80%   C—70%   D—60%   F—Below 60%

*(1) One or more of the above types of tests may not be given a particular semester. Information regarding this will be posted in ISS. If you miss a test, place an A, for absent, in the blank. If it is an absence *excused* by your *IQS instructor*, place an A Exc. in the blank. When a particular test is *not* given, place a dash (—) in the appropriate blank. Points may or may not be given for the problems (1, 2, and 3) and the Scientific American articles, depending on the semester.

(2) Students are responsible for recording their own points on this sheet each week during the semester. Neither the BIO. 108 teaching staff nor the secretary will look up your points for you from the official record at any time during the semester (and especially not at the end of the semester).

INSTRUCTIONS FOR NEW STAFF

Setting up an ISS for the first time will be, at least in part, a unique experience for most teaching assistants (T.A.'s). One T. A. is assigned to each of our ISS preps. This means that during a semester he will be involved with at most two or three preps. Alternatively two or even three T.A.'s could be assigned to a prep with one having the overall responsibility and the others assisting him. The former method has the advantages of not tying a person up for as many weekends and puts the responsibility more squarely on the person in charge. For our unit on the plant kingdom, however, we assign each T.A. one to several of the plant divisions since the setup is fairly extensive and comes at the end of the semester when everyone has final exams. The first prep of the semester is probably best done by the instructor since by doing an excellent job on it he can set the example. The assistants are motivated to do a good job because of pride in their work and the fact that their photograph and name appear on the bulletin board as having done that week's setup. The full-time instructor in the course should be present to assist and provide guidance for the T.A. when he sets up the ISS. The instructor and T.A. assigned to the prep should meet far enough in advance to make sure that all the materials can be prepared in time. A meeting between the senior instructor, instructor, and teaching assistant would also be helpful. The instructor would be wise to take photographs and make notations on each week's setup in order to start (or update) the course's teacher's guide and any additional notes or procedures. The T.A. must listen to the tape over his week before starting the prep so that he can take notes and make any changes, if they exist, from the procedures in the teacher's guide.

It is very important that each exercise on the center tables be clearly defined as to the exercise number and page in the study guide to which it pertains. Directions and labels should be typewritten or neatly printed on signs and organized in a logical stepwise sequence within the area reserved for the setup. A small item out of sequence or not clearly explained as to its purpose in an exercise, or lack of a simple definition of a term, can cause a great waste of time to the student. It is often these kinds of things which cause a student more trouble than understanding some concept like electron flow in photosynthesis.

Some of the materials which we use frequently or in large quantities for the ISS setups are as follows: white cards for signs, felt marking pens (assorted colors but mostly black), label gun, lettering set, masking tape and magic tape, styrofoam, pegboard holders, aluminum foil (to cover work area or prevent pots from leaking in a booth), tape player repair and maintenance items (pliers, screw driver, pipe cleaners, splicing equipment, electrical tape, etc.), paper cutter, poster paper (6 ply, white, 22″ × 28″), construction paper (assorted colors), spray paint, thin plastic to cover and protect posters, dixie cups, spare movie projector bulbs, cleaning equipment (broom, mop, dust pan, and brush), and brown or white paper (in rolls) to put on the center tables and in the booths. Stocks of frequently used items should be kept at certain minimum levels so the person doing a prep does not run out.

An old typewriter with large or pica type for the prep room can be very convenient for making signs.

The list of procedures given below is a useful reminder guide, especially for new assistants. It may be made in the form of a check list with sufficient space left below each item for notes.

General ISS Procedures for Teaching Assistants.

Graduate teaching assistants may delegate *duties,* but not *responsibilities,* to undergraduate teaching assistants.

I. ISS prep for week
    A. Prior to the Saturday setup
        1. Check the prep drawer and shelf to see what materials are on hand.
        2. Meet with Mr._____ as early in the semester as possible. Go over the study guide procedures and photographs together.
        3. Listen to the tape and take notes pertinent to the prep. Do this as soon as the tape is available.
        4. Collect and store (refrigerator, cold room, etc.) any out of season materials (twigs, autumn leaves, spinach, beets, pineapples, fruits, green beans, etc.).
        5. See that sufficient numbers of certain types of common greenhouse plants will be available when needed. Check with the greenhouse attendant. *(Coleus,* geranium, *Impatiens,* etc.)
        6. Give any required special planting instructions to the greenhouse attendant (for growth curves, mineral deficiency studies, genetic seed, anatomy materials, special plants for your prep, etc.).
        7. Have the necessary media and solutions prepared in advance by the undergraduate assistants. (For mineral deficiencies, Benedict's solution, stains, etc.)
        8. Set up any experiments which need to be ready by Saturday and germinate any seeds that may be required.
        9. Order the necessary materials from outside sources (grocery store, pet shop, flower shop, biological supply houses, etc.) sufficiently in advance using the proper requisition forms.
        10. Check out the necessary materials from the biology stockroom and obtain the necessary glassware from the washing room.
        11. See that sufficient copies of the necessary mimeograph materials have been run off (for booths, center tables, weekly objective sheets, etc.).
    B. Saturday 12:30 PM — Sunday
        1. The ISS prep must be completed by 7:30 AM Monday.
        2. See that the quiz board is set up.
        3. Set up a demonstration booth by 1:00 PM Saturday so the undergraduate helper can set up the rest of the booths.
        4. Booth setups should be completed by 5:00 Saturday.
        5. Check library reference materials for good illustrative materials, and make them available to the students.

6. Put out 2 X 2 slides appropriate to the week's work.

7. See that the movie projectors and appropriate cartridges are put in the booths and/or on the center tables.

8. ISS prep undergraduate assistance is available from Saturday 8:30 AM–5:00 PM and Sunday 2:00 PM–6:00 PM. Use this help or else you will have to do it yourself.

9. Check the appropriate prep room storage shelf, the miscellaneous shelves (for items which may be useful), the prep drawer, etc., for materials pertinent to your prep.

10. Make sure the tape-microscope-movie projector and cartridge cabinets are locked Sunday evening.

C. During the week your prep is in the ISS

1. Make daily checks on the center tables and in the booths. Replace and refresh.

2. Make sure everything is "ready to go" each morning.

3. Make sure items required from the stockroom are in sufficient quantities so we don't run out during the evening.

4. Place a note on the ISS instructor's note board on the front table with any special instructions, such as what materials are stored in the refrigerator, when to obtain or replace ice, when to change or refresh certain items, etc.

II. ISS Prep teardown

A. Saturday

1. Center tables and booths must be cleared and put away neatly by 5:00 PM.

2. Materials for IQS should be placed on empty prep room shelves until the carts are free from the current prep room setup (Sunday evening).

3. Place dirty glassware in the tray on the shelf.

4. Tear down the quiz board and put the materials away.

5. Put extra mimeographed sheets, demonstration signs, and booth signs away neatly in the appropriate prep drawer.

6. Put the posters on the old posters shelf.

7. Make sure none of your prep is left in the learning center or on the prep room table or in the sink area.

B. Sunday

1. Distribute the ISS materials on the two carts to be used for the IQS sections. Make duplicates where necessary. Include the three-step IQS presentation procedure signs and any special announcements, etc.

C. Tuesday evening

1. Put the IQS materials away neatly and put the dirty glassware in the tray on the shelf.

2. Leave the two carts empty and clean.

3. Put the dirty glassware tray on one of the carts and take it to the wash room.

III. Daily staff duties

A. 7:30 AM staff

1. Replace necessary items in the booths and on the center tables.

2. Make coffee.
3. Water all the plants in the learning center (booths, growth shelves, center tables, house plants, prep room, etc.)
4. Check the ISS instructor's note board for special instructions such as getting certain items out of the refrigerator, getting ice from the ice machine, etc.
5. Turn on the aquaria and terraria and growth shelf lights (unless they are on a timer).

B. 10:30 PM staff
1. Turn off all the lights (except those on a timer or which should be left on)—aquaria, terraria, demonstration microscopes, booth microscopes or lights which students forget to turn off, room lights, etc.
2. Make sure all the tape players are turned off.
3. Clean up all the booths and rearrange the materials neatly.
4. Clean up the center tables.
5. Clean up the study table.
6. Clean up the prep room table and sink area.
7. Turn out the greenhouse lights and lock the greenhouse door.
8. Make sure the coffee pot is unplugged.
9. Refile any cards left in the booth assignment file.
10. Lock up the learning center.

C. 7:30 AM—10:30 PM staff
1. Make coffee
2. Routinely check the ISS prep materials on the center tables and in the booths. Change or freshen-up when necessary.
3. Clean up the booths, center tables, floor, study table, prep room, etc.
4. Unplug the coffee pot when the coffee level is low so the heating element will not burn out.
5. Record the hourly ISS attendance.
6. Repair tape players, splice tapes, repair movie cartridges, etc. Tape players which you cannot fix should be noted on the instructor's note board with the trouble described. Unusable movie cartridges should be placed in the appropriate box "to be repaired" in the prep room.

IV. The following notice will be posted in the prep room.

NOTICE

To: Staff and students of Biology 108

This room will be cleaned on _____ at _____. All materials not labeled with NAME, *DATE, USE OR ISS PREP* will be put away, taken back to the greenhouse, or removed to the glassware washing room by the undergraduate in charge of the prep room. Items not stored in their proper place will be put where they belong. On most other days this room will be straightened up. Nothing will be put away but will instead be placed on the shelf reserved for this purpose. The sink area and the table in the prep room must always be kept clear except when someone is actually working so that students can use the table as a study or break area. When you complete your work, put all your materials back where you got them.

V. Possible undergraduate duties

1. Take and pick up glassware from the washroom.
2. Fill distilled water bottles on top of the cabinets in G-416.
3. Replace perishable booth items.
4. Grade quizzes, make quiz keys, post quizzes and answers.
5. Set up and tear down booths.
6. General cleanup—including washing glassware, sweeping the floors, returning coke bottles, washing windows, cleaning sinks, waxing sinks, drain boards, booths, and tables, emptying wastebaskets, etc.
7. Aquaria and terraria upkeep.
8. Greenhouse cleanup.
9. Make signs or posters.
10. Defrost refrigerator once a semester.
11. Keep carts clean and papered.
12. Water plants.
13. Help with ISS preps.
14. Teach in ISS.
15. Be in charge of an ISS setup.
16. Weekend cleanup; sweep, empty baskets, etc.
17. Check bulletin boards and message file and ISS instructor's note board.
18. Attend the weekly staff meeting.
19. Listen to the tape each week.
20. Run trial ISS and Problem 1 and 2 experiments.
21. Make solutions, media, stains, buffers, etc.
22. Collect twigs, seeds, pods, etc.
23. Collect discarded petri dishes from the microbiology labs.
24. Wash blackboard.
25. Keep storage cabinets neat.
26. Paint.
27. Meet with the T.A. in charge of each week's ISS prep.

STUDENTS RESEARCH PROJECTS

The research projects are turned in to the student's IQS instructor and graded by him. This instructor counsels his students, handles their problems, and checks on their progress. The full-time instructor in the course is in general charge of the problems. He designs the projects (except for those where this is left up to the student), sees that the necessary materials are available and in working order, and holds general meetings with the students about their questions. New projects must be devised every semester since the write-ups are returned to students and end up in dormitory and fraternity files.

Satisfactory completion of Problem 1 is a minimum requirement to pass the course. Certain problem write-ups are poor and must be rejected. Handling this situation can present difficulties. Several alternatives are possible:

Have students:

1. Rewrite the entire report.
2. Rewrite only the unsatisfactory parts.
3. Rewrite nothing, but make it clear that an unsatisfactory becomes a part of the IQS instructor's subjective evaluation.
4. Give a quiz over the problem and proper format.
5. Assign a special makeup such as a critical review of a journal paper, short research paper, etc.

The IQS instructor will oversee Problem 2 activities in his sections. He may conduct orientation and progress meetings, help students find a problem, help them when difficulties arise, hold informal discussions at different times each week (posted in advance), and demonstrate techniques and the proper use of special equipment.

Some of the following procedures may be helpful in administering the problems:

1. Keep only small vials of expensive or short supply chemicals (such as hormones) available to students to prevent cross contamination of your main stocks, large errors in amounts that students may calculate that they need, and to cut down on waste. Refill vials as needed.
2. Keep concentrated stock solutions and lanolin pastes of common growth regulators in the refrigerator. Allowing students to dilute down from these can prevent the waste and accumulation of large quantities of, for example, 10 ppm GA. Stock solutions should be replaced as they deteriorate, of course. If supplies of these chemicals are adequate, you may want each student to prepare his own stock solution.
3. Put maximum amounts allowed per student on certain expensive chemicals.
4. Have instruction sheets by each piece of equipment (including balances) and some mimeographed sheets describing certain useful techniques such as chromatographic bioassay.
5. Make up stocks of commonly used chromatographic solutions and spray reagents.

6. Have readily available such things as commonly used equipment, solvents, stains (anatomy and chromosome), instruments, etc.
7. Put molecular weights on growth regulator bottles or vials if they aren't already there, and put molarities on stock bottles of acids and bases.
8. Keep a master list of students, the titles of their projects, and their IQS sections.
9. Post a calendar of events with regard to the problems.
10. Make optimum use of helpful signs, and place equipment where it is easily found and used.
11. Have the student show his results and data to the ISS or IQS instructor so he can be checked off as having completed the project. If the ISS instructors do this, a master record book is kept by the instructor on duty in the ISS.
12. Have students turn their data in to a pool so it can be tallied with class data and placed on a large graph in the learning center or prep room. This will allow students to see the weekly progress of the experiment (if it is a growth experiment, for example).

The greenhouse is generally used for Problem 1 since it usually involves some sort of growth project, although the growth shelves in the prep room or learning center may be used if sufficient space is available or if ragdoll germinators are used. Materials and instructions for the other problem may be located on shelves or tables in the prep room. Sometimes, when a large number of students are doing a project and certain pieces of equipment (such as manometers) are in limited supply, we have made up individual numbered boxes of equipment which the students can sign up for or check out from the ISS instructor whenever a box is free. By having a fixed number of boxes, one can control the number of students working on the problem at any one time. The student is required to return the box in clean and unbroken condition to the place where he got it. The instructor then checks him off as having completed the project. If time is available, the instructor may go over the data with the student.

AN EXAMPLE OF PROBLEM I

(Handout for students)

BIOLOGY 108   PROBLEM 1

The Effects of CCC, Gibberellic Acid, and Salts on Wheat *(Triticum vulgar)* and Buckwheat *(Fagopyrum esculentum)*

PROBLEM

What are the effects of different concentrations of CCC, gibberellic acid, and salts on the germination and early growth of wheat and buckwheat?

INTRODUCTION

The discovery and application of new plant growth regulators is moving ahead at a rapid pace. Application of these chemicals to crops has often preceded the investigations into the far-reaching effects these substances may have on plant growth, crop yields, human consumption, etc. The late Rachel Carson, in her best-selling book, *Silent Spring,* condemned the indiscriminate use of chemicals without prior extensive investigations of their effects.

Wheat and buckwheat are two economically important crop plants. Today's farmer is faced with a whole host of new chemicals and soil enrichment mixtures. In this problem we will attempt to ascertain the effects of a naturally occurring plant growth hormone, gibberellic acid, a man-made growth regulator, CCC (or 2-chloroethyltrimethylammonium chloride), and salt concentration (using a commercially sold N-P-K mineral nutrient additive called "Take-Hold").

MATERIALS AND METHODS

Materials: Saran wrap or waxed paper; paper towels; wheat and buckwheat seeds (if these seeds have been dusted with fungicide, less mold will develop); Dixie cups; plastic squeeze bottles; masking tape; grease pencils; rubber bands; 1, 3, and 5% salt; 10, 100, 1000 ppm (parts per million) gibberellic acid; 10^{-4}, 10^{-3}, 10^{-2} M (molar); metric rulers; centigram balance.

Methods: The "ragdoll" method of seed germination as demonstrated by your SAS instructor will be used in this problem. Ten ragdolls, numbered 1 through 10 and labeled with your name and the treatments, will consist of paper towels moistened with—

ragdoll no.
1. tap water
2. 1% salt
3. 3% salt
4. 5% salt
5. 10 ppm gibberellic acid
6. 100 ppm gibberellic acid
7. 1000 ppm gibberellic acid
8. 10^{-4} M CCC
9. 10^{-3} M CCC
10. 10^{-2} M CCC

Dip the towels in the proper test solutions, let the excess solution drip off, and prepare your ragdoll. Place 10 wheat and 10 buckwheat seeds in each ragdoll. Check your ragdolls occasionally to make sure they don't dry out completely. If the paper feels dry, you may add a little water at the top of the ragdoll, using a plastic squeeze bottle. If the seeds remain too moist, however, they will rot or become moldy. Any water collecting in the bottom of the Dixie cup the ragdolls are in should be poured out.

RESULTS

Collect your data after two weeks. Note whether (a) the treatments stimulated or inhibited the germination and/or subsequent growth, (b) how great the effects were, (c) what parts of the plants were affected, and (d) any other pertinent observations. Part b will involve the collection of *quantitative* data, *i.e.,* length and weight measurements.

PROBLEM WRITE-UP

Follow the format and direction exactly as given on pages 2 and 3 of your study problem manual.

Problem 2 usually required that the students do some original research. Due to the heterogeneous nature of even a group of students all anticipating an "A" in the course, these projects may range from the relatively simple to the fairly complex depending on the capabilities and desires of the individual student. The following material, in the form of mimeographed sheets, is given to those students who plan to do Problem 2.

PROBLEM 2 HANDOUTS

General Considerations

1. Attend the orientation meeting(s).
2. Attend at least one of the informal discussion sessions.
3. Notices of all meetings will be posted on the bulletin board in ISS.
4. Do problems 1-1 through 1-15 in the study problems.
5. Problem 2 must involve some *original* research. You will not be permitted to repeat someone else's work exactly.
6. Problem 2 must involve the collection of *quantitative* data: length, dry or wet weights, volume, turbidity, number, etc.
7. At least one of the following pieces of equipment or techniques must be used (unless you have special permission to do otherwise): centrifuge, manometer, colorimeter, paper or thin layer chromatography, bioassay.
8. Some possible ideas for Problem 2 will be posted in ISS. You may select one of these, or, better still, use them to stimulate some ideas of your own.
9. Turn in an original *and* a carbon copy of your write-up. We will keep the carbon. (As an alternative we may just ask for a copy of your summary.)
10. Report write-ups must follow the same format as papers written for the journal *Plant Physiology.*
11. A sample write-up from the journal and one by a former student will be posted outside ISS.

Useful References for Problem Ideas and Techniques

1. *Plant Growth and Development* by A. C. Leopold.
2. *Plant Physiology* by J. Bonner and A. Galston.
3. *The Germination of Seeds* by A. M. Mayer and A. Poljakoff-Mayber.

4. *Environmental Control of Plant Growth* by L. T. Evans (Ed.).
5. *Research Problems in Biology* (Series 1 and 2) by A. Grobman (Ed.).
6. *Annual Review of Plant Physiology.*

The above books are on reserve in the Life Science Library. Certain books may be available on the ISS bookshelf. The journals below are all in the Life Science Library.

7. Scientific journals such as *American Journal of Botany, Plant Physiology, Botanical Gazette, Botanical Review, Plant and Cell Physiology, Physiologia Plantarum, Journal of Experimental Botany, Annals of Botany, Science, Phytochemistry, New Phytologist, Canadian Journal of Botany, Nature, Bulletin of the Torrey Botanical Club,* etc.

Materials Available

1. Large variety of seeds.
2. Paper and thin-layer chromatography equipment.
3. Analytical balance and centogram balance.
4. Buffers, pH paper and pH meter.
5. Greenhouse plants.
6. Genetic seeds.
7. Cultures of algae.
8. Red, green, blue, and far-red plastic light filters and large coffee cans for use as exposure chambers.
9. Centrifuge.
10. Bausch and Lomb Spectronic 20 Colorimeter.
11. UV light source and UV scanning light.
12. Sterile transfer chamber.
13. Ovens.
14. Light quality growth chamber.
15. Dark growth chamber.
16. Special plant materials such as pores, gemmae, pollen, plantlets, duckweed, bulbs, rhizomes, etc.
17. Microtome and slide-making equipment.
18. Autoclave.
19. Refrigerator and freezer.
20. Fans.
21. Ocular and stage micrometer.
22. Controlled temperature water bath.
23. Air pump.
24. Haemocytometer.
25. Concave slides.
26. Compound microscopes and stereo binocular microscopes.
27. Polaroid camera (instructor will take pictures; students provide cost of film.)
28. Styrofoam ice buckets.
29. Hot plates.

Chemicals Available

1. Indoleacetic acid (IAA).
2. Indolebutyric acid (IBA).
3. Naphthaleneacetic acid (NAA).
4. B-naphthoxyacetic acid.
5. 2,4-dichlorophenoxyacetic acid (2, 4-D).
6. p-chlorophenoxyacetic acid.
7. o-chlorophenoxyacetic acid.
8. 2,4,5-trichlorophenoxyacetic acid (2,4,5-T)
9. 2,3,5-triodobenzoic acid (TIBA).
10. Gibberellic acid (K salt, 10%) (GA).
11. Phosphon (0.3% paste or 10% aqueous).
12. 2-chloroethyltrimethylammonium chloride (CCC).
13. Coumarin.
14. Maleic acid hydrazide (MH).
15. Cholchicine.
16. 22 different amino acids.
17. Ninhydrin.
18. Assorted carbohydrates: sugar such as glucose, fructose, galactose, mannose lactose and maltose; dextrin; soluble starch, starch, and cellulose.
19. Glucose-1-phosphate (K salt).
20. 2, 3, 5-triphenyl-2H-tetrazolium chloride.
21. Invertase.
22. Pectinase.
23. Agar and nutrient agar.

POSSIBLE IDEAS FOR PROBLEM 2

1. What are the effects of various hormones and potato extracts on the growth of isolated potato "eyes" (buds) in starch-agar culture?
2. Is there a water-soluble germination inhibitor present in the pulp of "X" fruits?
3. Is phytochrome already in the active form (P_{730}) in certain non-light-requiring seeds?
4. Can the senescence of bean cotyledons be delayed or prevented?
5. Is IAA, GA, or kinetin the root growth hormone in "X" seeds?
6. Does chemical (volatile or water-soluble) competition exist between certain plants?
7. Is the formation of anthocyanin in mung bean hypocotyls light dependent?
8. What factors influence the development of plantlets on isolated Bryophyllum leaves?
9. What factors influence the nastic response of *Mimosa* pinnae in water culture?
10. If corn mesocotyls or bean hypocotyl hooks are prematurely signaled to stop growing using light, how does this affect their subsequent growth (if they are still below the soil surface)?

THE EFFECT OF MALONIC ACID ON AEROBIC AND ANAEROBIC RESPIRATION IN BAKERS' YEAST

By S. Kieselbach

1. Summary

A manometric study of the effects of malonic acid on aerobic and anaerobic respiration in bakers' yeast was made.

Although the results were far from definitive and further more sophisticated work would be interesting, several conclusions can be made, at least tentatively:

1. Malonic acid can increase the amount of aerobic respiration even though it is a known inhibitor of one of the steps of the Citric Acid Cycle.
2. In small concentrations the malonic acid inhibits the Citric Acid Cycle by competing with succinic acid for the enzyme and not being present in large enough quantities to cancel this effect by entering the respiration process itself.
3. Malonic acid may have some effect on anaerobic respiration although such an apparent effect may be due to the inhibition of the small amount of aerobic respiration taking place.

2. Introduction

The ordinary bakers' yeast is usually studied in an anaerobic situation because of its commercial applications which rely on this form of its respiration. This experiment was designed to examine malonic acid inhibition on the yeast's aerobic respiration. Since malonic acid is known to inhibit the Citric Acid Cycle by competing directly with succinic acid for the succinic dehydrogenase (7), malonic acid should be expected to inhibit only those steps of glycolysis which require succinic dehydrogenase and succinic acid. Since any inhibition at all should be noticeable in the total amount of carbon dioxide given off by the respiring plants, it is therefore possible theoretically, to examine anaerobic versus aerobic respiration of the yeast by systematically varying the malonic acid concentration and observing the products and relative amounts of them during the respiration.

In Figure 1 the two paths of respiration are shown in their commonly accepted form. The red indicates the final phases of aerobic respiration which occurs when oxygen is available to the organism for eventual transfer of an electron pair and the formation of water. The black is the commonly accepted anaerobic path in which carbon dioxide and ethanol are the common plant products when the oxygen supply is not sufficient. The balance between these two should be evident in the amount of or the pressure increase caused by the carbon dioxide given off.

3. Materials and Methods

One ¼-ounce package of standard commercial bakers' yeast was allowed to incubate in a lukewarm solution of 15 grams of glucose in 100 cc of distilled water. After approximately forty-five minutes 25 ml of well-stirred yeast and sugar solution were put

Figure 1

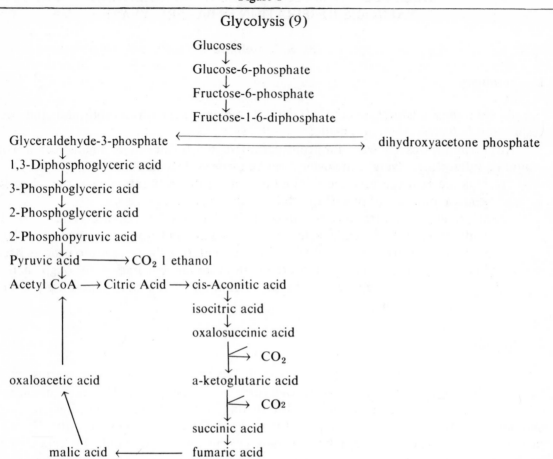

Glycolysis (9)

Glucoses
↓
Glucose-6-phosphate
↓
Fructose-6-phosphate
↓
Fructose-1-6-diphosphate

Glyceraldehyde-3-phosphate ⟵⟶ dihydroxyacetone phosphate
↓
1,3-Diphosphoglyceric acid
↓
3-Phosphoglyceric acid
↓
2-Phosphoglyceric acid
↓
2-Phosphopyruvic acid
↓
Pyruvic acid ⟶ CO_2 1 ethanol
↓
Acetyl CoA ⟶ Citric Acid ⟶ cis-Aconitic acid
isocitric acid
oxalosuccinic acid
⟶ CO_2
a-ketoglutaric acid
⟶ CO_2
succinic acid
oxaloacetic acid
malic acid ⟵ fumaric acid

Table I

Solution Number	Molar Conc. of Malonic Acid*	Prepared by
1	1×10^{-1}	1.04 gm. acid + 100 ml H_2O
2	1×10^{-2}	10 ml sol'n 1 + 90 ml H_2O
3	1×10^{-3}	10 ml sol'n 2 + 90 ml H_2O
4	1×10^{-4}	10 ml sol'n 3 + 90 ml H_2O
5	1×10^{-5}	10 ml sol'n 4 + 90 ml H_2O
6	1×10^{-6}	10 ml sol'n 5 + 90 ml H_2O
control	0.0	100 ml H_2O

*concentrations are based on a molecular weight of 104 gm/gm-mole for malonic acid in each of seven 50 ml Erlenmeyer flasks. Each of these was attached to a manometer and the system was allowed to stabilize. The flasks were then sealed and one milliliter of each of the malonic acid solutions (see Table I) was injected into a flask. Zero time readings were taken on the manometer. These readings were used as the base for all other readings.

The malonic acid solutions were prepared by a dilution series by mixing 10 ml of the weakest available solution with 90 ml of distilled water as described in Table I.

No buffer solution was added but it was calculated that 1 ml of even the strongest solution of malonic acid used would not change the pH of the system more than 1 pH unit. All flasks were shaken regularly every five minutes and readings were made until two of the flasks popped corks, both between 150 and 160 minutes.

The problem of carbon dioxide being absorbed by the system and forming carboxylic acid was not controlled. The pH of each of the flasks was, however, taken at the end of the experiment and all fell within the range of pH=5−6 which is within the optimal range for yeast growth (3).

4. Results

The readings were made by determining the change in mercury level as compared to the base reading. These readings may be found in Table II for each of the seven systems considered in this experiment. No corrections of these measurements were made to

Table II
Pressure Difference in Ml. of Hg with Time

Time	Solutions of malonic acid added						
(min)	10^{-1}	10^{-2}	10^{-3}	10^{-4}	10^{-5}	10^{-6}	·control
0	0.0	0.0	0.0	0.0	0.0	0.0	0.0
4	0.0	0.0	0.0	0.0	0.0	0.0	0.0
10	-0.1	0.0	0.2	0.1	0.5	0.55	0.0
20	-0.1	0.0	0.4	0.4	1.3	1.3	0.0
30	-0.1	0.1	0.7	1.1	1.7	1.9	0.0
40	0.3	0.4	1.5	1.7	2.4	2.5	0.4
50	1.2	1.1	1.5	2.2	3.1	3.2	0.9
60	1.8	2.1	2.7	2.8	3.6	3.8	1.3
70	2.4	2.7	3.3	3.6	4.7	4.0	1.3
80	3.1	3.4	4.2	4.6	—	—	1.5
90	3.8	4.2	5.3	—	5.0	3.9	2.6
100	4.0	5.1	—	5.0	5.7	4.1	3.8
110	—	—	5.5	5.8	6.0	4.1	—
120	5.4	5.6	6.5	6.2	6.5	4.5	4.3
130	6.0	6.4	7.0	6.6	7.0	4.4	4.9
140	6.6	6.7	7.5	7.2	7.3	4.8	5.2
150	7.2	7.4	8.1	popped	7.7	5.3	5.8
160	8.1	8.1	8.6	—	8.0	5.8	6.7
170	8.4	popped	9.1	—	8.1	6.1	7.2

Table III

Conc.	Initial rate	Final rate
control	.0531 ml/min	.0576 ml/min
10^{-1}	.0656	.0677
10^{-2}	.0795	.0639
10^{-3}	.0615	.0550
10^{-4}	.0591	.0445
10^{-5}	.0654	.0400
10^{-6}	.0676	.0462

account for carbon dioxide absorbed by either the yeast solution or the mercury, or for the variables in the equipment. The experiment had too many variables itself to justify the correction of the readings.

The rates in Table III were determined by taking the slope of the various carbon dioxide versus time graphs (Graphs I-VII) both before and after the discontinuity, which was interpreted as being due to the transition from aerobic to anaerobic respiration in the yeasts. The initial rates should, therefore, represent the aerobic rate of respiration and the final, the anaerobic rate.

5. Discussion

As stated in the introduction and illustrated in Figure 1, the carbon dioxide given off in the aerobic respiration would be twice as great as that given off in anaerobic respiration for each pyruvic acid produced. Malonic acid competes competitively with succinic acid for the succinic dehydrogenase. It would have been expected, therefore, that for the control the rate of carbon dioxide given off would have been relatively large while oxygen was still present in the system and then would fall off to approximately half of the original rate as the yeast was forced to use the anaerobic phase. This was obviously not the case. The two rates were approximately equal on both sides of the discontinuity. The only explanation can be that there was no change from aerobic to anaerobic and that the discontinuity was caused by other factors such as a leak which allowed a pressure drop.

Another similar peculiarity can be observed in the yeast system which was treated with 10^{-1} M malonic acid. Here also the rates are approximately the same, therefore leading to the same conclusion that either one or the other of the respiratory phases predominated throughout or that the balance between the two remained constant.

Only an oxygen leak would have allowed the aerobic phase to continue for this length of time. As stated above this might have been the cause in the control system, but in the 10^{-1} M system no irregularity in pressure occurred so it must be assumed that for some reason, such as complete inhibition of the aerobic phase, the anaerobic phase was predominately responsible for the carbon dioxide production.

Examining the initial rates for the other five samples a trend can be seen assuming that the early rate is due either to aerobic respiration or the partial inhibition of it (see Graph VIII). If this is truly the cause, the greatest inhibition occurs at 10^{-3} and 10^{-4} and possibly 10^{-1} M treatments. The first two are supported at least in part by Ohwaki's

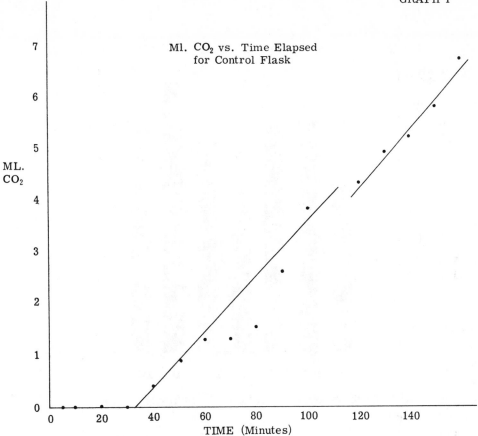

GRAPH I

Ml. CO_2 vs. Time Elapsed
for Control Flask

(Authors' Note: The above graph is included as a sample. Graphs II
through VII are not shown.)

study of *Oryza* coleoptiles (4) which states that concentrations of less than 10^{-4} of
malonic acid inhibit aerobic respiration and increase alcohol production.

An apparent stimulation of aerobic respiration is also noted in the same article,
where it says that 10^{-2} and 10^{-3} M malonate stimulate aerobic respiration in immature
plants while the same concentrations inhibit it in more mature plants.

The combined picture presented by several references did, however, present results
which the yeast in this experiment seemed to confirm allowing for minor differences in
various species and types of living organisms. Fawaz (2) reported that .03 M malonate
almost entirely inhibited the Citric Acid Cycle (aerobic respiration) in rat skeletal muscle.
Panteleev (5) reported that stimulation in onion respiration occurred with treatments of
.1 and .2 M malonic acid. Rybova (8) reported that 5×10^{-3} and 6×10^{-2} M malonate
stimulated aerobic respiration in brain tissue of guinea pigs. And Petrov-Spiridonov (6)
said that in soybean leaves only .0175 M malonic acid was required for stimulation of
aerobic respiration. Thus by combining these reports it would be expected that

GRAPH VIII

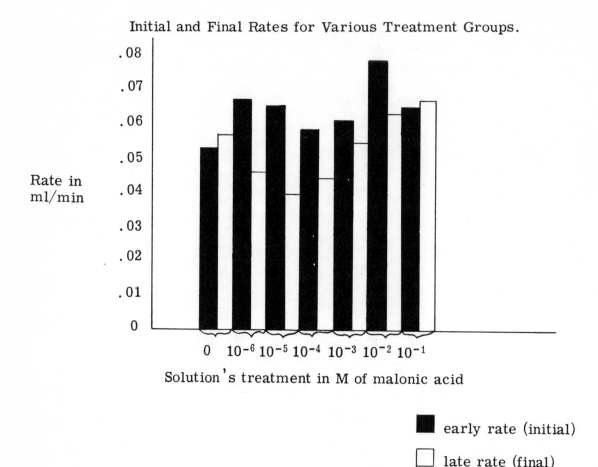

Initial and Final Rates for Various Treatment Groups.

Rate in ml/min

Solution's treatment in M of malonic acid

■ early rate (initial)

☐ late rate (final)

moderately high concentrations of malonic acid (in the range of 10^{-1} to 10^{-3} M) would stimulate aerobic respiration in the yeast plant.

The data obtained in this experiment does follow this general pattern with the possible exception of the 10^{-1} M system. All systems, however, fail to show any inhibitory reaction when compared with the control. The only explanation offered for the stimulation by malonic acid, was that at high concentrations the plant must convert it into a useable intermediate of the Citric Acid Cycle and thereby cancel any inhibitory effects on the succinic acid step by contributing itself to carbon dioxide production (5). This could occur only if the Citric Acid Cycle as presented in Figure 1 is not complete, but has several other possible links or bypasses. This solution was also suggested by Petrov-Spiridonov (6) and seems to be a reasonable solution although work in this area has provided no indication that such an alternate pathway involving malonic acid as an intermediate exists. (1).

The most baffling problem arising from this experiment was not, however, the stimulation of aerobic respiration but the fact that the data obtained looks as if there is an inhibition of the anaerobic respiration. If, as it was earlier hypothesized, the final rate for each treatment is dependent only on the anaerobic respiration, the amount of malonic acid added should have had no effect and the rates should have been approximately equal. As Table III and Graph VIII show, there does appear to be a dependency on the acid concentration. In all cases except the control and the 10^{-1} systems the anaerobic phase is less than the aerobic phase rate indicating a dominance of anaerobic phase in the final rates, but in no case is the reduction as great as would have been expected if there were no aerobic carbon dioxide being produced. Oxygen entering through a leak might be the answer and is supported by the irregularities in some of the ml-versus-time graphs, but it seems unlikely that any oxygen could have entered the system against the pressure gradient that must have existed after the 60 to 90 minutes of reaction, the time elapsed when the irregularities occurred.

It would be interesting to run this experiment in a quantitative way in which oxygen could be constantly supplied to the systems, thereby eliminating the spontaneous reversion to anaerobic respiration when the limited supply of oxygen present was consumed. Confusion between the two systems and whether or not lack of oxygen or presence of inhibitor caused the transfer from one to the other would be further simplified if the alcohol present were analyzed. More accurate control over the number of yeast plants present might also have proved valuable in obtaining accurate and reproducible data.

LITERATURE CITED

1. Bonner, J. 1950. Organic Acids of Plants. pp. 194-200. In: Plant Respiration. Academic Press Inc., New York, N.Y.
2. Fawaz, E.N. and Fawaz, G. 1962. Inhibition of Glycolysis in Rat Skeletal Muscle by Malonate. Biochem. J. Vol. 83. 438.
3. James, W.O. 1953. p. 240. In: Plant Respiration. Oxford Univ. Press, London.
4. Ohwaki, Y. 1962. The effect of malonate on the respiration and growth of Oryza coleoptiles. Sci. Repts Tokyo Univ. IV Ser. (Biol.) Vol. 28. 108. In: Biol. Abst. Vol. 42. 19372.
5. Panteleev, A.N. and Zhukov, L.B. 1963. Effect of malonic acid on respiration and conversion of organic acids in the onion. Vest Leningradsk univ. ser. biol. Vol. 18. 65. In: Biol. Abst. Vol. 45. 83853.
6. Petrov-Spiridonov, A.E. 1962. The action of malonic acid on the respiration of soybean leaves. Invest. Timiryazersk. Sel'skokhov. Akad. Vol. 2. 206. In: Biol. Abst, Vol. 45. 30125.
7. Quastel, J.H. 1962. Dehydrations produced by resting bacteria. IV. A theory of the mechanism of oxidation and reduction in vivo. Biochem. J. Vol. 20. 166.
8. Rybova, R. 1964. Inhibitory effect of malonate on glucose metabolism in brain cortex slices (guinea pig). R. Physiol Bohemoslov. Vol. 13. 28. In: Biol. Abst. Vol. 45. 77937.
9. White, A., Handler, P., and Smith, E.L. 1964. Respiration. In: Principals of Biochemistry. McGraw-Hill Book Co., New York, N.Y.

PROBLEMS AND PITFALLS IN
AUDIO-TUTORIAL METHODS

1.   Problems Associated with Structuring A-T

   A.   Lack of Specific Objectives—The clear specification of instruction objectives, as suggested by Mager,* is the most lacking element in unsuccessful A-T instruction. The design of optimal instructional sequences with an appropriate array of auditory, visual, printed, and actual object materials *requires* clearly stated objectives for student achievement. Since well-designed A-T lessons permit successful teaching of topics or concepts sometimes excluded from traditional lecture-laboratory courses, redefinition of objectives is necessary as A-T course design proceeds. Students must *know* what the instructional objectives are.

   B.   Lecture-on-tape—The simplest procedure for preparing audio-tapes is to use prior lecture notes. Unfortunately, lectures are rarely planned to incorporate simultaneous direct experience with study materials by students during didactic instruction; this is a principal advantage of A-T methods. Moreover, extended didactic presentation is often boring when live, and on audio-tape, the lecture can be narcotic.

   C.   Inappropriate Visuals—Together with appropriate audio guidance and study material, proper diagrammatic or model displays can direct learning efforts. Complex diagrams, unnecessarily long films or slide sequences, models or analogs of structures that confuse rather than clarify salient features, and irrelevant photographs detract from learning. The design of some Audio-Tutorial instruction when dominated by audio-visual departmental personnel can result in a detracting profusion of visual materials.

   D.   Inappropriate Study Material—Whenever practicable, actual materials being discussed or analyzed should be available to students unless adequate prior experience with the material can be assumed for all students. It is as wasteful of time and money to include unnecessary material for study as to exclude material essential for clarifying certain concepts or word meanings (see II-C below).

   E.   Auxiliary Experiences—In addition to instruction in carrel units, the effective A-T course provides students with a variety of important auxiliary experiences: planned field trips; independent study or experimentation; small-group discussion sessions (with or without supervision); demonstrations or experiments of mock-ups too costly or bulky to use in individual carrels; frequent quiz sessions or other evaluative feedback. All of the auxiliary experiences are highly desirable for most science classes. Discussion and evaluative feedback is essential so that students know the extent to which they are achieving the specified objectives of instruction.

   F.   Lack of Synchronization—When instructional objectives are clearly specified, it is possible to identify optimal sequences of audio, visual, or manipulatory experience.

*Mager, Robert F. *Preparing Objectives for Programmed Instruction.* San Francisco: Fearon Publishers, 1962.

This usually requires some empirical testing, for the exact timing of students' work (with a specimen, for example) seldom can be predicted accurately in advance. Audio guidance for loop films or slide sequences always requires some trial-and-error adjustment of timing.

Even more important is the design of sequential experiences involving perhaps some audio-guided study of specimens, observation of an experiment or exhibit in a central location, discussion with the laboratory instructor or colleagues—all these in some optimal order. Students are a valuable source of guidance for improving sequences of instruction when their counsel on this is sought or obtained in some systematic way.

2. Problems Associated with Psychological Issues.

A. Poor Overall Course Structure—B.F. Skinner, Robert Gagne, David Ausubel, Jerome Bruner, and other learning theorists all argue the critical importance that *structure* plays in instruction. Of the theorists, David Ausubel* has formulated the most comprehensive description to guide planning of A-T instruction. Contrary to widely held dogma in science education, planned instructional sequences do not necessarily lead to rote learning; when properly designed, structured lessons can lead to highly meaningful learning of concepts which show impressive longevity and usefulness for future learning and problem solving. The fad of "inquiry" or "discovery" dominated activity is not supported by the evidence from learning research nor by the total set of activities performed by scientists. "Discovery" or "inquiry" experience should be a part of A-T courses but only for those objectives which *require* this kind of activity; that is, to demonstrate problem-solving ability or to acquire *affective* objectives (see below).

According to Ausubel's theory, new meaningful learning proceeds to the extent that students have in cognitive structure the elemental concepts or "subsumers" for assimilating new information. When subsuming concepts are lacking, new material should be introduced with appropriate concrete experience with material and with "organizers." Preceding an instructional sequence with a more general statement or abstraction of the material to be learned in terms that have meaning for the student can serve as an "organizer" and facilitate subsequent learning. To design effective organizers for instructional sequences, as well as for larger segments of the course, requires a clear specification of instructional objectives (I-A above). Organizers should not be confused with statements of objectives or summary principles; a full discussion of the role of organizers in instructional design is beyond the scope of this section.

B. Pacing and Substructure—Since the cognitive structure of students varies, instruction must provide for varying rates of new knowledge assimilation. Students who have adequate subsuming concepts will assimilate new information *several times* more rapidly than students who must rote-learn all or some of the information. Providing "organizers" can reduce the amount of rote learning, but for some students, subsuming concepts will form in their cognitive structure only after a sufficient number of knowledge bits have been rotely acquired, together with perhaps necessary direct experience with materials. Unless adequate time is provided for this inefficient learning

*Ausubel, David P. *Educational Psychology: A Cognitive View.* New York: Holt Rinehart & Winston, 1968.

sequence in early instruction, *all* subsequent, related learning must be rote. Thus the student is perpetually victim of his cognitive structure limitations and large segments of a course may be meaningless to him, *albeit* he may reproduce sufficient rotely learned material on examinations to "pass" the course.

One of the reasons that no first generation A-T course can be optimally effective is that the principal source of information for proper pacing of instructional sequences derives from student feedback during initial instruction. It is common to find students reporting in large numbers that they had to repeat a certain portion of an A-T lesson. This is a highly tangible form of evidence that for this population of learners, necessary subsuming concepts were not available in their cognitive structures. The problem is corrected by providing "organizers" and/or modifying the pace of instruction, perhaps through adding more exemplars of the same concept. Conversely, some segments of the course may have unnecessary redundancy, and time as well as motivational gains can result by careful "pruning." The end result should be an A-T course with a psychological "substructure" not evident from the course outline or statements of objectives.

C. **Direct Experience Deficiencies**—The elementary school child is highly dependent on direct experience with materials if he is to learn meaningfully. High school and college students have had much experience with concept words such as heavy, cold, gas, etc., so concrete, empirical activity can be reduced and verbal or didactic instruction increased. However, in areas where new concept terms are to be introduced, as the idea of "metamorphic rock" or "molecular aggregate" (resulting from chelation), direct experience may be necessary to permit meaningful learning and concept differentiation. It is as wasteful of time and money to provide extensive direct experience with material when this is not needed as to omit such experience when needed, forcing students into rote-learning paradigms. The easily available feedback from students in A-T courses permits careful "optimizing" of direct experience levels.

D. **Feedback and Evaluative Deficiencies**—As indicated above, the design of optimal A-T courses requires continuous monitoring of student feedback. In addition to this role, evaluation can help students to clarify their concepts by showing them when they may lack facility in acquiring or interpreting information and in problem solving. One of the best methods for this feedback is to use small (6-10 students) discussion sessions, preferably with some structure and guidance provided by staff. However, when instructional objectives are made clear to students, peer interaction alone can provide highly valuable feedback to students.

On the other hand, it is possible to proliferate feedback and evaluation sessions to the point that instruction objectives are granulated into such small units that larger course objectives are lost. Since our objective is to produce learners with a hierarchical cognitive structure where smaller concepts are subsumed under larger, more inclusive concepts and thus gain stability and permanence, inordinate emphasis and small-step evaluation of learning can be deleterious. There are also motivational problems, for students have come to know that certain fuzzy concepts clear up as they acquire related (but not psychologically dependent) concepts.

E. **Affective Factors**—Students are not automata; they respond to hormonal and human drive factors as well as to information-processing determinants. It is easy to overestimate the value or liability conferred by affective factors, but this does not mean they should be ignored. *Cognitive drive,* the positive motivation resulting from the learner's awareness that he is learning meaningfully, is the most important affective factor in school learning over which we have control. Partly for this reason, good A-T instruction is "liked" by students. Nevertheless, other affective factors should be considered. Planning segments of A-T instruction or evaluation where groups of students can interact successfully capitalizes on social motivation. Providing opportunities for independent problem-solving conveys both the joy of discovery and the frustration of scientific search. Attractive room decor contributes to variety in sense experience and to the positive affective result from this. Where feasible, useful boy-girl associations may engage sex drive to catalyze learning though the results may be unpredictable.

3. Technical Deficiencies

A. Cost-Use Matching—The use of movie film to illustrate a concept shown equally well with a slide or drawing, an experiment with costly materials which provides experience already common to students, television images where audio-tape or printing is equal or better, and many similar abuses can be found in A-T courses. Even if course budgets were unlimited, the time required to design or maintain unnecessary equipment and materials used could be better spent for improving A-T course psychological structure. In fact, money is always limited with the result that every dollar or man-hour spent for unnecessarily complex equipment or experimentation must be subtracted from that available for course "structuring." It should be kept in mind throughout that the main objective is to improve students' cognitive growth, not to impress visitors..

B. Audio-Visual Quality—While it is common to see inordinately costly materials used in A-T instruction, it is also common to see inexcusably poor audio-visual or other materials incorporated. Some A-V aids made by course staff members are poor substitutes for commercially available materials which might be obtained at lower cost, especially when man-hours used are also considered. There is no "rule-of-thumb" for cost-quality decisions for equipment or materials. The course designer must search continuously for the best way to present concepts at lowest total cost. Some A-T courses subsidized by audio-visual departments have made poor allocations that later deprive course development, although good A-V personnel are valuable sources of information and better and/or cheaper A-V materials.

C. Space Distribution—Effective Audio-Tutorial courses involve more than study in a carrel unit. Whenever possible A-T carrels should be placed in an area where space for extensive exhibits or experimentation is also available. One or a few small conference rooms adjoining the carrel-demonstration area should be planned for new installations. A coffee-tea, bull session space can have affective as well as cognitive payoff. A reading and study area in or near the room would be desirable. Rarely are these space accommodations found in A-T courses.

D. Associated Systems—Audio-Tutorial instruction by virtue of its great flexibility permits the use of all kinds of learning resources. Accessible computer terminals can provide a valuable addition to an A-T course, especially for data processing, record keeping, and short evaluation sessions where the computer can be programmed to interrogate the student. When used for the latter purpose, computer printout can aid in psychological substructure development. Closed-circuit TV may be valuable for certain demonstrations or "current events" presentations, although abuses of closed-circuit TV are more common than augmentation. Live lectures and long movie films are more traditional but still useful adjuncts to A-T courses when selectively employed.

IDEALIZED LEARNING CENTER ARRANGEMENT

A more idealized learning center arrangement might consist of a complex of three or four rooms: the main study area and IQS room, a prep room, and a small greenhouse. The IQS room could be used for IQS quizzes, as a study room and reference library, and for seminars and coffee breaks. The prep room could serve for storage and preparation of materials, as a second room in which to give IQS quizzes, and as an area for students working on research problems. If a greenhouse is not available, growth shelves in the learning center or prep room can be used instead.

The above arrangement would be even more flexible if one large room were divided by easily moved, soundproof partitions. The pattern could then be varied as the need arose.

LEARNING CENTER

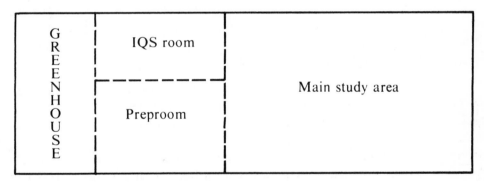

Idealized learning center for general botany.

SAMPLE ORIENTATION MATERIAL FOR MINICOURSES

BIOLOGY 109 (1970)   GENERAL INFORMATION SHEET

Code Used: GAS—General Assembly Session
               ISS—Independent Study Session
               IQS—Integrated Quiz Session
Room Numbers: GAS - 1-105; ISS - G-415, 416, 417 (Enter through G-416):
               IQS - G-424
               Dr. Hurst - G-305; Miss Heim - G-311
ISS Hours: 8:30 AM - 9:30 PM Monday - Friday
Texts: Biological Science by William Keeton
               Optional Readings: Scientific American Offprints
Materials: We recommend that you purchase a good pair of dissecting scissors, forceps, 15-centimeter ruler, and a probe or teasing needles. You may purchase a packaged dissecting kit if you wish, but it will be more expensive. Bring these items to the first 3 minicourses.

This information sheet may prove to be a most valuable guide if the time comes when you need a guide. Keep it handy and read it carefully.

Biology 108 and 109 are integrated companion courses. They are both taught on an "Audio-Tutorial" scheme which has been or will be explained to you in greater detail. The backbone of these two courses is a series of "minicourses" which are classified into four groups.

Group 1 minicourses are common to both courses and deal with fundamental concepts and principles which must be learned during a student's stay in 108-109. These minicourses start with the letter C.

Group 2 minicourses are those dealing primarily with the plants and they are prefixed by the letter P.

Group 3 minicourses deal primarily with animals and are prefixed by the letter A.

Group 4 minicourses are so-called "optional" minicourses, and within limits prescribed later on in this sheet, some student choice as to minicourses completed will be allowed. These courses have the prefix Op.

It is still possible to enter a 108-109 package either semester or to take only one of the two courses. If you are enrolled in 109 this semester, and you have not taken 108, the following will pertain:

Students will complete all of the common (C) minicourses, and all the animal (A) minicourses.

If you have completed 108 and are enrolled in 109 this semester the following will pertain:

Students will complete all the animal (A) minicourses. They will also complete 20 units of optional (Op) minicourses.

Weekly Oral and Written Quizzes

Each student will be scheduled for a one-hour IQS each week. The first half of this session will consist of an oral discussion of the minicourses schedule for that week (see "Units Offered" handout). Each student will be graded by his instructor as either a C or I for the minicourse(s) under discussion. He may also earn up to 2 A or B points for an exceptional performance during the oral quiz period. His instructor will award these points at the end of the session. The second half hour of the IQS may be spent taking a written quiz. The student should elect to take the written quiz at this time, but may take it at any time during the week between the hours of 8:00-4:30 Monday-Friday in Room G-424. You must complete both the oral and the written (approximately 80% of the questions right) to get credit for the minicourse.

If you do not complete either the written or oral quiz you must return to the Learning Center and demonstrate to an instructor there that you have taken steps to prepare yourself adequately to complete the quiz or quizzes on your second attempt. You may demonstrate your readiness by listening to the discussion or to parts of the discussion and following directions and/or by reading appropriate sections of the text or study guide. If any questions still remain after you check yourself out on the behavioral objectives, we suggest you talk with the instructor.

When you have assured yourself you are ready, you may present yourself to the instructor in the Learning Center who will administer an oral quiz and will give you a signed slip which indicates you have completed the oral (if you had not already done so) and now have permission to retake the written (if you received an I on that quiz the first time). Let's say it again and use examples so the system will be clear to you. If on minicourse A1 you receive an I on the oral and an I on the written, you will return to the Learning Center, prepare yourself and present yourself to the instructor. The instructor will administer an extensive oral quiz, and, if you are prepared, give you a signed slip which you will take to G-424 and present to the secretary there. She will now record a C for the oral quiz and allow you to take the written quiz. If you complete this quiz she will record a C and you will have completed the minicourse. If you do not complete the written quiz on this second attempt, the secretary will assign you to a special session with Dr. Hurst or Miss Heim where you will obtain help to prepare yourself for your final attempt (it might be smart to work a bit on your own before this session).If you are now prepared, they will give you a signed permission slip and you will return to G-424 and retake the written quiz for the final time. (2nd example) If on A1 you receive C on the oral and an I on the written, you will go through the procedure of preparation and oral quizzing to obtain the permission slip. When you report to G-424, you will already have had a C recorded for your oral quiz and you will be given the written quiz. Depending on your success or lack of the same, you will then follow the system outlined above. (3rd example) If on A 1 you receive an I on the oral and a C on the written, you will go through the same procedure of preparation and oral quizzing, receive your signed permission slip, take it to G-424, and the secretary will record a C for the oral and you have completed the minicourse.

A student will be allowed to retake a written quiz on any given minicourse a total of two times—each time obtaining a "permission slip." He must complete these attempts within a two-week period following the week of his first scheduled attempt. (Obviously, medical excuses will be taken into consideration whenever a time requirement is involved.)

We do not believe that any student who has adequately prepared himself will ever have to retake a minicourse quiz. We even more firmly believe that the "retake" policy we have adopted this semester will make it nearly impossible to do poorly on your first makeup, and impossible to do poorly on your second makeup. Be clever, use your list of behavioral objectives as a check-off of your preparedness. The only way you can do poorly on your retakes is to shortchange or cheat yourself on the effort you put in to prepare yourself for the makeup in the mistaken belief that you are shortchanging or cheating us. In the event you do not satisfy a minicourse after 3 attempts, you will receive an incomplete for the minicourse.

Students who miss their scheduled IQS will report to the secretary in G-424 who will assign them to one of the special sessions where they will try their oral for the first time. They may not complete their oral with the instructor in the Learning Center until they have tried in their scheduled IQS or in a special session. Students may miss their scheduled IQS only twice. After that, they must obtain permission from Dr. Hurst to continue in the course.

GAS

At this session you will meet with Dr. Hurst at 10:30 on Friday. This time will be used to clarify, integrate, and direct your study in the course. Announcements will also be given here. A schedule of what is to be covered in each General Assembly Session will be provided so that the student can determine for himself whether the session would be valuable to him. Although roll will not be taken, it is emphasized that there are times when the GAS is essential for the fullest understanding of the subject matter, and we are leaving it up to the student to determine this. When in doubt, it is best to attend! During the GAS of the 6th, 10th, and 14th weeks, exams will be given to those students attempting to earn an A or B.

IQS

You are signed up for one hour Integrated Quiz Session on Tuesday or Friday. When you meet your first scheduled IQS you will become oriented to the structuring of our course. The group will then be divided into smaller IQS groups of ten students each and an instructor will be assigned to each group. This session will be used for the weekly quizzes. Friday IQSs will be held during the week the minicourses are scheduled to be completed. Tuesday IQSs cover the minicourses scheduled the preceding week.

Bulletin Boards

It is each student's responsibility to check the bulletin boards in ISS each week for announcements.

ISS

According to your printed class schedule, you have been assigned a total of four hours per week to be arranged. These four hours are those you will spend in the ISS. The Learning Center will be open as indicated on the first page of this outline and you can arrange your ISS as you see fit. Some weeks will require perhaps more than four hours, some less than this. Some students will require more time in ISS than others. You may, of course, repeat any part or all of any minicourse until you feel confident you know the material. Most of your weekly study should take place in the ISS LEARNING CENTER (G-415, G-416, G-417). Each week you should pick up a copy of the OBJECTIVES in ISS. These should act as your guide for the week's ISS study and for the oral quiz. The Learning Center is a place where a student can exchange ideas with other students and the instructor, practice oral quiz, work study problems, read assignments, take a study break with a coke or a cup of coffee, etc. ISS hourly attendance will be posted each week so you can see when it is not crowded.

Your Responsibility

A good deal of money and thought has gone into making the LEARNING CENTER a pleasant, attractive place to study. We plan to help you as much as we're able. Help us . . . take care of the tapes, tape players, microscopes, movie projectors, lab equipment, booths, etc. We will NOT tolerate thoughtlessness!

Grading Procedure

Since all students must complete the oral quiz requirement and pass the written quiz "mastery level," which will be set for each minicourse individually according to the number and type of behavioral objectives, before getting credit for completing the minicourse, all students will earn a C grade when all minicourses are completed. Students who fail to complete all the minicourses by the end of the semester may do so the following semester or even the following year until they earn their C grade.

A and B grades will be earned by using points earned from optional reading, points earned by completing "quest" assignments or doing extra optional minicourses, points earned by exceptional performance during the oral quiz, and with points earned from A and B exams given the 6th, 10th, and 14th weeks during the GAS. The first of these exams will carry a point value of 40, the second and third a point value of 35 for a total of 110. These 110 plus the 50 points possible for optional readings, guests, etc., plus 26 points possible from the oral quiz, total 186 possible A-B points. A total of 85 points will earn you a B, and a total of 110 points will earn you an A.

A total of 50 A-B points may be earned as pointed out above by reading the optional Scientific American offprints, by doing quest assignments, by completing extra optional minicourses, and by doing bonus "operations" which will appear from time to time. The next few paragraphs will describe these assignments to you. You must keep track of the total points you have accumulated by completing these assignments since you cannot receive credit for a point total higher than 50.

Scientific American Articles

A-B points may be earned by those students who read certain articles assigned each week (see Assignment Sheet). A total of 2 points per article will be possible. No points will be given for reading parts of an article that may be assigned for a particular week. You will be asked to summarize the article; one point will be given if you convince your instructor that you read the article, and one point will be given if you seem to have clearly understood what you read. You must read the articles during the week they are scheduled (use our week guide for the correct week of the course).

Quest Assignments

Periodically you will find a quest assignment or two in the study guides for a given minicourse. Quests will typically cover topics which are either not too well understood, controversial, or not covered very well in your text. The number of points which can be earned by satisfactorily completing a quest assignment will vary with the topic (up to 4 points) and will be assigned to each quest suggestion. Students will be awarded points by the senior instructor from zero up to the total point value possible on that quest depending on the job they have done.

The following tells you what to do with a quest assignment:

Given a topic or a biological situation which has been found or might have been found to conflict in its treatment in various sources, prepare a brief paper (no more than two pages) using at least three reference works (your text could be one of these) which summarizes the topic or situation and presents the views of the sources, the view you accept, and the reasons for your acceptance.

Not all topics will be topics of conflict but may fall into the other two categories, but it behooves you to believe they are in conflict until you are fairly certain other things pertain. The burden of library research is on you. Quest assignments are due within two weeks after the minicourse was scheduled.

Extra Optional Minicourses

Hopefully this semester we will have available to you all the optional minicourses listed on this information sheet, plus others which will be made available as we go along. This will give you the opportunity to complete more than the 20 units you will need to complete 109 (if you have had 108 already). A-B points will be awarded on the total number of units you have completed beyond your required number on the basis of two points per unit.

Bonus "Operations"

From time to time opportunities will present themselves for you to complete some operation and check out your accomplishments with the instructor on duty in the Learning Center and earn up to a specified number of A-B points. These extra operations may take any avenue and will ask you to do something we don't have time to require of you, but something that may be of interest or value to you. The first week, for example, we have bonus "operations" (no pun intended I assure you) which are both dissections of specific organisms. At other times, specific laboratory or library experiences may be proffered you, and a possible point value assigned to them. Bonus operations must be completed during the week the minicourse is scheduled.

A-B Exams

As indicated above, these exams will be given during the GAS of the 6th, 10th, and 14th weeks. The first exam will have 40 points possible and the next two 35 points each. At least 25 questions on each of these exams will be taken from the minicourses you have completed (these will be synthesis-type questions however, not rote memorization items from these minicourses); the rest may be taken from the reading list below for each of the three exams. If you want to do your very best on these exams, I suggest you do the reading in addition to the minicourses you have of course completed.
Exam #1 over minicourses A1 through A8
Reading list: Chap. 22: pages 96-105; pages 432-438; pages 168-174; pages 176-198.
Exam #2 over minicourses A9 through A14
Reading list: pages 243-270; page 202; pages 209-220; pages 278-296; Chap. 10: pages 322-355.
Exam #3 over minicourses A15 through A19
Reading list: pages 439-450; pages 342-355; pages 508-518; pages 610-650.

Banking of Courses

Although you are enrolled in 108 or 109, you may take any minicourses in either course as long as you have completed the prerequisite minicourses as indicated on the "List of Minicourses" handout. You will satisfy the oral quiz requirement for that minicourse during the week it is scheduled in the other course by appearing at one of their quiz sessions and asking permission of the instructor to be quizzed on the minicourse. The written quiz can be taken in the quiz center Room G-424 and will be recorded on your master card. Bring your passport for identification and know the name of your IQS instructor to receive proper credit. All optional (Op) minicourses will be completed by passing a written quiz taken in the Quiz Center (Room G-424) anytime within a two-week period (which also includes the makeup period) after the minicourse is scheduled. Makeup procedures will be the same as those for animal or common minicourses.

General ISS Information

1. Procedure for entering lab:
   a) All students must enter (and leave) the Learning Center through Room G-416.
   b) Booths are numbered 1 through 34 in G-415, and 35 through 66 in G-417. On the "master board" each booth will be labeled with a tag as to the minicourse it

contains. Beside this "master board" is a "keyboard" indicating which mini-courses are offered each week.

c) There are three short steps required for signing into a booth:

    (1) When you locate the booth you want, place a plain white tag over the tag hanging on the numbered hook.

    (2) Proceed to the proper room (G-415 for BIO 108 students, G-417 for BIO 109 students) and locate your permanent sign-in card in the appropriate GAS box. Fill in the "Time In" space and place the card in the booth slot you are going to occupy (this may require carrying your card across G-416 to the opposite room if that is where the booth you signed into is located).

    (3) Go to your booth and soak up knowledge.

2. When you have completed your study:

a) Clean up your booth.

b) Turn off the tape player; there is no need to rewind the tape.

c) Indicate "Time Out" on your card and return it to the GAS box.

d) Return to G-416 and remove the plain white tag from the master board, indicating that your booth is free for the next person to study.

3. An instruction sheet on how to operate the tape players is posted in each booth. If you need any help, please ask the lab instructor. Anytime you think something is wrong with the tape or the tape player, call the instructor. An instructor will always be in the lab to answer any questions you may have about the week's material.

4. In keeping a lab open for long periods of time as we do, we must require certain things of the students:

a) Put any equipment that you use back where you got it.

b) Wash all the glassware you use before returning it.

c) Clean up your booth before you leave.

d) Stop the tape and flip the off-on button on your tape player to off whenever you leave the booth to look at a demonstration or leave the lab.

e) Do not touch the tape player, especially the reels, while you are listening to the tape.

f) Please help us keep the booths free from pen and pencil marks. If you must doodle, use a piece of scratch paper.

BIOLOGY 109

Bibliography Sheet for Scientific American Offprints

Bonus points may not be used to reach the required 80% mastery level needed to satis-factorily complete each minicourse.

Students may write the bonus for the following articles only during the week indicated.

Week	Offprint No.	Author and Title
2	47	Wald, G. 1954 (Aug) The Origin of Life
3	1064	McLean, F. 1955 (Feb) Bone
4	1132	Marples, M. 1969 (Jan) Life on the Human Skin
5	195 1010	Wecker, S. 1964 (Oct) Habitat Selection Carr, A. 1956 (May) The Navigation of the Green Turtle
6	1034 1108	Comroe, J. 1966 (Feb) The Lung Mykytowyez, R. 1968 (May) Territorial Marking by Rabbits
7	37 1126	Smith, H. 1953 (Jan) The Kidney Clarke, C. 1968 (Nov) The Prevention of "Rhesus" Babies
8	1154	Cavalli-Sforza, L. 1969 (Aug) "Genetic Drift" in an Italian Population
9	197 1135	MacNichol, E. Jr. 1964 (Dec) Three-Pigment Color Vision Clarke, J. 1969 (Mar) Thermal Pollution and Aquatic Life
10	182 1129	Allen, R. 1962 (Feb) Amoeboid Movement Tietze, C. and Lewit, S. 1969 (Jan) Abortion
11	192 1026	Wynne-Edwards, V. 1964 (Aug) Population Control in Animals Huxley, H. 1965 (Dec) The Mechanism of Muscle Contraction
12	155 157	Verzar, F. 1963 (Apr) The Aging of Collagen Wilson, E. 1963 (May) Pheromones
13	1022	Hokin, L. & Hokin, M. 1965 (Oct) The Chemistry of Cell Membranes
14	1100 1103	Taussig, H. 1962 (Aug) The Thalidomide Syndrome Hayflick, L. 1968 (Mar) Human Cells and Aging

8/25/70 MB

Minicourses Offered (BIO. 109) Suggested Sequence

No previous 108 Experience do common and animal
Previous 108 Experience do animal and 20 units of optional

WEEK	DATE	UNIT VALUE	COMMON	NO.	UNIT VALUE	ANIMAL	NO.	IQS OVER	UNIT VALUE	OPTIONAL	NO.
1	Sep 16-Sep 25	0.5	Diversity	1	1.0 / 2.0	Homeostasis: state – / Diversity of Animals: protostomes	1 / 2		1.0 / 0.5	Evolution / Origin of Life	1 / 10
2	Sep 28-Oct 2	0.5 / 2.0	Use of Microscope / Cell Structure	3 / 4	3.0	Diversity of Animals: Deuterostomes	3	A1, A2, C1	1.0 / 1.0 / 1.0	Evolution / Scientific Inquiry / Causal Res. in Biology	1 / 23 / 14
3	Oct 5-Oct 9	1.0 / 0.5	Phys. Phenomena/Cells / The Cell Membrane	5 / 6	1.0 / 2.0	Organizational Levels / Support Systems	4 / 5	A3, C3, 4	1.0 / 1.0 / 1.0	Scientific Inquiry / Causal Res. in Biology / Color of Man	23 / 14 / 19
4	Oct 12-Oct 16	0.5 / 1.0	Light / Pigments	7 / 8	2.0	Animal Nutrition	6	A4, 5-C5, 6	1.0 / 1.0 / 1.5	Scientific Inquiry / Evolution of Man / The Vertebrate Skeleton	23 / 20 / 12
5	Oct 19-Oct 23	1.5 / 1.0	Respiration / Synthesis & Degrad.	9 / 10	1.0 / 1.0	Digestion / Absorption & Utilization	7 / 8	A6, C7, C8	2.0 / 1.0 / 2.0	Behavior / Evolution of Man / Population Genetics	6 / 20 / 3
6	Oct 26-Oct 30	1.5	DNA Replication & Protein Synthesis	11	1.5 / 1.0	Transport / Gas Exchange	9 / 10	A7, 8-C9, 10	2.0 / 2.0 / 2.0	Behavior / Population Genetics / Human Genetics	6 / 3 / 8
7	Nov 2-Nov 6	1.5	Complementarity of Structure & Function	2	1.0 / 1.5	Excretion / Kidney Function	11 / 12	A9, 10 C11	1.0 / 1.0 / 2.0 / 1.0	Flower, Fruit & Seed / Regeneration / Human Genetics / Heart Dynamics	4 / 7 / 8 / 16
8	Nov 9-Nov 13	1.5	Mitosis	12	1.5	Coordination	13	A11, 12 C2	1.0 / 1.0 / 1.0 / 1.0	Flower, Fruit & Seed / Regeneration / Wood Anatomy / Heart Dynamics	4 / 7 / 9 / 16
9	Nov 16-Nov 20	0.5 / 0.5	Succession / Formations	13 / 14	1.5	Chemical Regulation	14	A13-C12	1.5 / 1.0	The Eye: Struc. & Function / Nerve Transmission	17 / 18
10	Nov 30-Dec 4				1.0	Locomotion	15	A14-C13, 14	2.0 / 2.0 / 1.5 / 1.0	Parasitism / Population / The Eye: Struc. & Function / Nerve Transmission	2 / 5 / 17 / 18
11	Dec 7-Dec 11	2.0	Photoperiodism	15	1.0	Muscle: Structure & Function	16	A15	1.0 / 2.0 / 1.5 / 1.0	Parasitism / Population / Antigens-Anti. & Immune / Ear: Struc. & Function	2 / 5 / 13 / 21
12	Dec 14-Dec 18	2.0	DNA-Passing to Off-spring	16	1.5	Adaptation	17	A16-C15	1.0 / 1.5 / 1.0	Birth Control / Antigens-Anti. & Immune / Cytological Techniques	11 / 13 / 15
13	Jan 4-Jan 8	4.0	Genetics	17	2.0	Gametogenesis & Reprod.	18	A17-C16	1.0 / 1.0 / 1.0 / 0.5	Birth Control / Cytological Techniques / Complementarity of Org. / BSCS Inquiry	11 / 15 / 22 / 24
14	Jan 11-Jan 15				2.0	Development	19	A18-C17	2.0 / 0.5	Complementarity of Org. / BSCS Inquiry	22 / 24

LIST OF MINICOURSES

Group 1   Series "C"

Mini-course No.	Units	Title	Pre-requisites
C 1	0.5	Diversity	
C 2	1.5	Complementarity of Structure & Function	
C 3	0.5	Use of the Microscope	
C 4	2.0	Cell Structure	C 3
C 5	1.0	Physical Phenomena of Cells	
C 6	0.5	The Cell Membrane	C 3
C 7	0.5	Light	
C 8	1.0	Pigments	C 7
C 9	1.5	Respiration	
C 10	1.0	Synthesis and Degradation	
C 11	1.5	DNA Replication & Protein Synthesis	C 4
C 12	1.5	Mitosis	C 11
C 13	0.5	Succession	
C 14	0.5	Formations	C 13
C 15	2.0	Photoperiodism	C 8
C 16	2.0	DNA-Passing to Offspring	C 11
C 17	4.0	Genetics	C 16

Group 2   Series "P"

Mini-course No.	Units	Title	Pre-requisites
P 1	2.0	Diversity of Plants	C 1
P 2	2.0	Germination	
P 3	1.0	Leaf	C3, C4
P 4	2.0	Transpiration	C5, P3
P 5	1.5	Photosynthesis	C7, C8
P 6	2.0	Mineral Nutrition	
P 7	0.5	Meristems	C 12
P 8	0.5	Twigs & Buds	P 7
P 9	2.0	Structure, Stem	P 7
P 10	1.0	Structure, Root	P 9
P 11	1.0	Plant Adaptation	
P 12	3.5	Growth & Development I	
P 13	2.0	Growth & Development II	
P 14	2.0	Reproduction	C 16
P 15	2.0	Asexual Reproduction	C 12, P 14
P 16	3.0	Life Cycles	P 15

Group 3   Series "A"

A 1	1.0	Homeostasis: the State of Changing Sameness
A 2	2.0	Diversity of Animals: the Protostomes
A 3	3.0	Diversity of Animals: the Deuterostomes
A 4	1.0	Organizational Levels
A 5	2.0	Support Systems
A 6	2.0	Animal Nutrition
A 7	1.0	Digestion
A 8	1.0	Absorption and Utilization
A 9	1.5	Transport
A 10	1.0	Gas Exchange
A 11	1.0	Excretion
A 12	1.5	Kidney Function
A 13	1.5	Coordination
A 14	1.5	Chemical Regulation
A 15	1.0	Locomotion
A 16	1.0	Muscle: Structure and Function
A 17	1.5	Adaptation
A 18	2.0	Gametogenesis and Reproduction
A 19	2.0	Development

Group 4   Series "Op"

			Pre-requisites
Op 1	1.0	Evolution	
Op 2	1.0	Parasitism	
Op 3	2.0	Population Genetics	C 17
Op 4	1.0	Flower, Fruit & Seed	
Op 5	2.0	Population	
Op 6	2.0	Behavior	
Op 7	1.0	Regeneration	
Op 8	2.0	Human Genetics	C 17
Op 9	1.0	Wood Anatomy	
Op 10	0.5	Origin of Life	
Op 11	1.0	Birth Control	A clean mind
Op 12	1.5	The Vertebrate Skeleton	A 5
Op 13	1.5	Antigen-Antibodies & the Immune Response	C 9-11
Op 14	1.0	Causal Research in Biology	
Op 15	1.0	Cytological Techniques	
Op 16	1.0	Heart Dynamics	A 9
Op 17	1.5	The Eye: Structure and Function	A 13
Op 18	1.0	Nerve Transmission	A 13

Op 19	0.5	Color of Man	Op 1 & C 17
Op 20	1.0	Evolution of Man	Op 1
Op 21	1.0	The Ear: Structure and Function	A 13
Op 22	2.0	Complementarity of Organism & Environment	
Op 23	1.0	Scientific Inquiry	
Op 24	0.5	BSCS Inquiry (Experimental) The Importance of the Nucleus	
Op 100	0.5 to 3.0	SPECIAL PROJECT	Op 23

SAMPLE BEHAVIORAL CHECKLIST

TASK SHEET

PROGRAM NO. 1   LEVEL I

PROGRAM REVISION DATE _____

STUDENT'S NAME _____ GROUP_____ TEST DATE_____

SCHOOL_____ EVALUATOR _____

	YES	NO
1. Pointed to button one.	____	____
2. Acknowledged shiny pans.	____	____
3. Responded "blocks."	____	____
4. Placed empty pan next to block pan.	____	____
5. Pointed to two like blocks.	____	____
6. Pointed to a different block.	____	____
7. Put one block into empty pan.	____	____
8. Put remaining like blocks into pan.	____	____
9. Picked up big and small block.	____	____
10. Put blocks back into pan.	____	____
11. Placed small blocks on table.	____	____
12. Placed big blocks on table.	____	____
13. Picked up big and small block.	____	____
14. Put heavier block on table.	____	____

	YES	NO
—2—		
15. Placed all blocks in one pan.	_____	_____
16. Pointed to leaves in picture.	_____	_____
17. Placed all plastic leaves on table.	_____	_____
18. Investigated plastic leaves.	_____	_____
19. Responded "yes" to separating leaves.	_____	_____
20. Repeated the word "separate."	_____	_____
21. Placed plastic leaves on shelf.	_____	_____
22. Acknowledged picture of flowers.	_____	_____
23. Responded "yes" to separating flowers.	_____	_____
24. Pointed to stop botton.	_____	_____
25. Pointed to button two.	_____	_____
26. Acknowledged little window on tape recorder.	_____	_____
27. Pointed to little wheels on tape recorder.	_____	_____
28. Pointed to stop button.	_____	_____
29. Stopped tape recorder.	_____	_____
30. Rewound tape recorder correctly.	_____	_____
31. Stopped tape recorder.	_____	_____

COMMENTS:_____

_____

_____

_____

_____

TASK SHEET

LEVEL ONE   LESSON 4

LESSON REVISION DATE_____ GROUP _____ TEST DATE _____

STUDENT'S NAME_____ EVALUATOR _____

SCHOOL_____

	YES	NO
1. Placed battery board in front of him.	____	____
2. Pointed to long red wire.	____	____
3. Pointed to black plug.	____	____
4. Took black plug out of holder.	____	____
5. Pointed to small light bulb.	____	____
6. Made correct contact to light bulb.	____	____
7. Repeated the words "light energy."	____	____
8. Lighted bulb again.	____	____
9. Placed black plug in holder.	____	____
10. Picked up one sheet of paper.	____	____
11. Pointed to pictures of lamps.	____	____
12. Took yellow crayon from dish.	____	____
13. Circled pictures of things in which electric energy changes to light energy.	____	____
14. Put yellow crayon back into dish.	____	____
15. Acknowledged lamp over science booth.	____	____
16. Felt air around light bulb.	____	____
17. Took red crayon from dish.	____	____

<u>LEVEL ONE</u>   —2—   <u>LESSON 4</u>

	YES	NO
18. Circled pictures of things in which electric energy changes to heat energy.	——	——
19. Put red crayon back into dish.	——	——
20. Placed battery board in front of him.	——	——
21. Placed finger on twisted wire.	——	——
22. Placed black plug into red circle.	——	——
23. Finger maintained on twisted wire.	——	——
24. Removed black plug from red circle.	——	——
25. Put black plug into holder.	——	——
26. Put his paper in front of him again.	——	——
27. Took red crayon from dish.	——	——
28. Circled pictures of things in which electric energy changes to heat energy.	——	——
29. Put red crayon back into dish.	——	——
30. Put battery board in front of him again.	——	——
31. Picked up black plug.	——	——
32. Made contact to start motor.	——	——
33. Put plug into holder.	——	——
34. Put his paper in front of him again.	——	——
35. Took blue crayon from dish.	——	——
36. Circled things in picture that moved when electric energy is being changed.	——	——
37. Put blue crayon back into dish.	——	——

		YES	NO
38.	Pointed to picture showing electric energy being changed to light energy.	____	____
39.	Pointed to booth lamp.	____	____
40.	Put name on paper.	____	____
41.	Put crayon back into dish.	____	____
42.	Stopped tape recorder.	____	____
43.	Rewound tape recorder correctly.	____	____
44.	Stopped tape recorder.	____	____